Greater Horseshoe Bat
(Rhinolophus
ferrumequinum) *in the*
winter roost. Free-hanging
between stalactites on the
roof of a cave, the animal is
wrapped almost completely in
its wing membranes.

The fascination of flight. Here a Greater Horseshoe Bat (Rhinolophus ferrumequinum) curves deftly through climbing ivy vines.

KLAUS RICHARZ
ALFRED LIMBRUNNER

THE WORLD OF
BATS

The flying goblins of the night.

Hunting in flight, a Common Long-eared Bat (Plecotus auritus) pursues a moth.

CONTENTS

Adaptations. The nocturnal fliers have exploited numerous dietary niches, ranging from drinking nectar to fishing. Shrew-like Long-tongued Bat (Glossophaga soricina, left) and Fisherman Bat (Noctilio leporinus, right).

The cries of bats

As you speed through the air at twilight, here, there, you cry loudly, but your cries are heard only by others of your kind. Treetops and bars, tumbledown church steeples throw back an echo, which you detect in flight and which tells you what sorts of obstacles rise up before you and where to find an open path. If your voice is silenced, you can no longer find your way; bumping into everything in your path and striking against walls, you fall dead to the ground. Without you, that which you otherwise devour proliferates and gains the upper hand: the insect.

Günter Kunert

The fascination of forms. Marianas Flying Fox (Pteropus mariannus) from Guam in the Mariana Islands (left), Grey Long-eared Bat (Plecotus austriacus, right).

The fascination of mass. Apart from the insects, some bat species in their roosts form the largest known gatherings of animals with counts of up to several million. Here thousands of young horseshoe bats (Rhinolophus rouxi) hang on the wall of a Sri Lankan cave in their "nursery compartment."

*The fascination of small size.
Bumblebee Bat (Craseonycteris
thonglongyai, top), the smallest bat
of all. The European "Tom Thumb,"
the Common Pipistrelle (Pipistrellus
pipistrellus, right).*

*The fascination of large size: Lyle's
Flying Fox (Pteropus lylei, bottom)*

*Serotine (*Eptesicus serotinus*) before taking flight.*

Mass flight. When the Mexican Free-tailed Bats (Tadarida brasiliensis) *leave their cave roost by the millions in the evening twilight, the sky seethes.*

Barbastelle (Barbastella barbastellus). This medium-sized, pug-faced bat hunts on long, narrow wings.

Flying mammals with a dark past

On three separate occasions, vertebrates (backboned animals) independently evolved active flight. In birds, the proportionately short wing skeleton is supplemented by long flight feathers. In contrast, the pterosaurs, long-extinct flying reptiles, possessed a flight membrane that stretched from a single, extremely elongated finger over the leg perhaps to the base of the tail. The bats (order Chiroptera) are true "hand fliers." They have a wing membrane (patagium) extending between the extremely elongated fingers and the hind leg and, in the majority of species, continuing to the tail.

The placement of bats in the zoological system has caused problems for a long time. "The bat is an animal intermediate between the bird and the mouse; thus it can rightly be called a flying mouse, though it can be classified neither among the birds nor the mice, because it possesses both forms within itself," wrote the Swiss naturalist Conrad Gesner in the 16th century in his *Historia Animalium*. In 1765, Carl von Linné, the "father of zoological systematics," classified them as relatives of the apes, the famous Swede considering the mammary glands located on the chest in both groups of animals to be the most important character.

The bats, after the rodents the most species-rich mammalian order, are divided today into 18 families by taxonomists. The diversity of bats is undoubtedly connected with their ability to fly and with their specializations. Their fluttering flight is without peer, and not only within the mammals! All other flying mammals, such as flying squirrels and marsupial gliding possums, are exclusively gliders. Using their lateral gliding membrane (plagiopatagium), stretching between the front and hind legs, they can travel modest distances in gliding flight but typically are unable to gain altitude. Bats, in addition to the lateral membrane, also have a wing membrane, the chiropatagium or dactylopatagium, between the greatly elongated second to fifth fingers. *(Chiro-* comes from the Latin for "hand," while *dactylo-* refers to the fingers.) Only their thumbs are short, clawed, and lack a wing membrane. In many bat species the tail is also incorporated almost completely into a flight membrane. The edge of this tail membrane (the uropatagium) is additionally supported and stiffened by a spur. Several genera (*Nyctalus*, for example) possess a stiff fold of skin, the epiblema, on the spur.

Through what intermediate steps the large wing-membrane surfaces of bats evolved still lies in the total darkness of their evolutionary past. Intermediate forms that could serve as a starting point for models of flight in bats are unknown to researchers, whether through fossil forms or the ontogenetic (embryonic) development of the species. Bats have mastered active flight and even echolocation for at least 50 million years. This is revealed by the well-preserved fossils from the famous Messel quarry near Darmstadt, Germany. These fossils, beautifully preserved in the oil shales, have allowed scientists to study the structure of the inner ear and larynx, proving that *Palaeochiropteryx*, *Cecilionycteris*, and *Archaeonycteris* already navigated by echolocation. These ancestors of present-day bats already required this ability. The likewise well-preserved stomach contents of the Messel bats show that they already hunted nocturnal flying insects in the Eocene epoch. Even the oldest known fossil bat, *Icaronycteris* from the early Eocene (about 55 million years ago) of North America, was

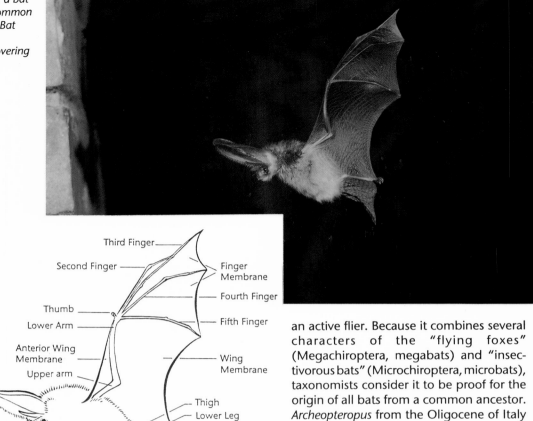

Anatomy of a bat (below). Common long-eared Bat (Plecotus auritus) hovering in profile.

Third Finger

Second Finger

Finger Membrane

Fourth Finger

Thumb

Lower Arm

Fifth Finger

Anterior Wing Membrane

Upper arm

Wing Membrane

Thigh

Lower Leg

Claws

Spurs

Ear

Tail Membrane

Eye

Tragus

Tail

an active flier. Because it combines several characters of the "flying foxes" (Megachiroptera, megabats) and "insectivorous bats" (Microchiroptera, microbats), taxonomists consider it to be proof for the origin of all bats from a common ancestor. *Archeopteropus* from the Oligocene of Italy (about 38 million years ago) also speaks on behalf of a single ancestor. This fossil find was originally classified as a flying fox. Now,

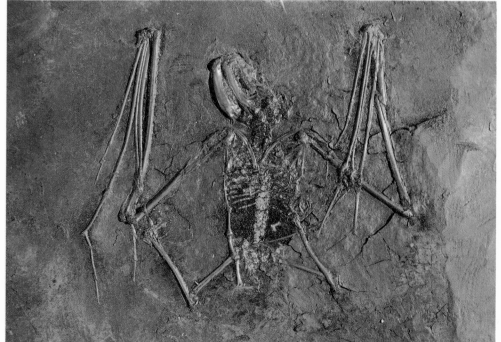

Fossil bat (Palaeochiropteryx tupaiodon) from the Messel oil-shale quarry near Darmstadt, Germany.

however, it is placed in the same basal group, the Eochiroptera, as the American ancestral bat. Besides the various structural characters, shared parasites—the highly specialized batflies—also argue in favor of the kinship of all bats.

On the other hand, some researchers, notably the Australian zoologist John Pettigrew, advocate a dual origin for bats. The flying foxes especially possess a number of characters they share with primates but not with the microbats. Among them are structural characters of the brain and central nervous system, the musculature, the skeleton, the circulatory and reproductive systems, and even the teeth. To those who subscribe to this view, the closest relatives of the flying foxes are not the insectivorous bats, but the lorises and pottos and other primitive primates.

The oldest described genus of true flying foxes at present is *Propotto* from Miocene East Africa (20 million years ago). The flying foxes apparently evolved in the tropics of the Old World (paleotropics) and spread from there as far as the western Pacific. Despite their ability to fly they have never reached the New World. Their ecological niche is filled there by microbats.

What the ancestor of bats may have looked like must remain hypothetical for the moment. Because the auditory region of the oldest discovered bat fossil, *Icaronycteris*, exhibits similarities with that of hedgehogs, primitive insectivores could be candidates for the ancestor of the bats. It is speculated today that bats evolved from such primitive arboreal (tree-dwelling) insectivores. First forms developed that, with the aid of membranes on the body and between elongated fingers, achieved gliding flight. Only when they had reached a certain wing size was the time ripe for the opening of a new "line" of flying mammals that was to be different from all others, namely that of the bats.

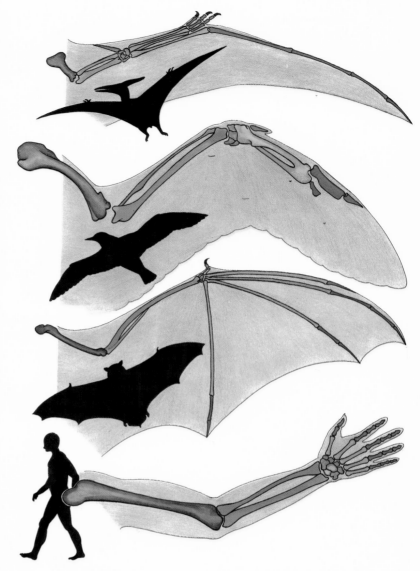

Pterodactyls span their wing membrane only between an elongated finger and the leg (top). The bird wing (top center) has feathers on a reduced hand skeleton. The bats remain true to the basic blueprint of mammals even in the structure of their wings. Only the proportions have changed (compare bat's wing, lower center, with human arm). Homologous bones are shown in the same color: upper arm blue, lower arm light blue, wrist violet, metacarpus orange, fingers red.

Form follows function (right). From "armor cracker" to "drinking straw"; the form of the skull and the set of teeth of New World leaf-nosed bats (Phyllostomidae) reveal what the species live on: A. Vampyrum (meat), B. Phyllostomus (meat and fruit), C. Tonatia (insects), D. Desmodus (blood), E. Artibeus (fruit), F. Anoura (nectar and pollen).

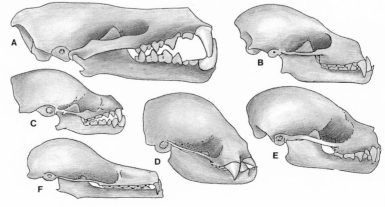

Sequence of wingbeats of a horseshoe bat in forward-directed rowing flight (after Nachtigall, 1986).

The flight of bats

Active flight requires more than just wings with the aerodynamic characteristics of airfoils. The development of a propulsive technique for moving forward in the air is also necessary, and the energy expenditure for the flier must be "economically" sustainable. How well the balance was struck by the bats is proved by their enduring virtually unchanged for 50 million years.

Despite all of the necessary "restructuring" needed for flight, they basically remain true to the mammalian blueprint. For reasons of stability, the greatly elongated forearm consists mainly of the sturdy radius, thereby limiting the range of movement of the wrist joint. The second and fifth metacarpals and the fingers articulated with them grow to enormous lengths. The thumb is the only remaining short finger and still has a claw; it is used for climbing and hanging. A claw on the second finger of many flying foxes is small and largely nonfunctional, while most microbats lack claws except on the thumb. The delicate-looking wings are double layers of skin with blood vessels, nerves, and small muscles that principally serve to brace the wings so they do not flutter in the airstream. Elastic fibers give the wing membranes great flexibility and strength. Injuries to the wing membranes heal amazingly fast; for example, holes with a diameter of 2 centimeters (almost an inch) in the wing membranes of flying foxes healed in 28 days.

During embryonic development the wing membrane develops from folds of skin on the sides of the body. Bats are born with

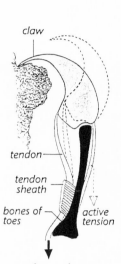

miniature wings that attain their final proportions during juvenile development.

Fast-flying bat species have long, narrow wings, while agile, slow-flying species have broad wings. The powerful wing musculature attaches to the robust sternum (breastbone) of the thoracic rib cage.

Though the parts of the wing close to the body generally serve as lifting surfaces, from high-speed filming it is known that the wing tips work like propellers and produce most of the forward propulsion. The tail membrane present in many species can increase the lifting surface and works in concert with the wing membranes; morever, it is useful as a "braking parachute" in the air.

As early as the 1930's, Martin Eisentraut was able to film the diverse flying techniques of bats. Besides being able to fly forward, some species are also able to hover. In hovering, forward thrust is canceled for several seconds. To accomplish this the animals assume an upright position and beat their wings back and forth with rotating wing tips. Takeoffs and landings are also just as variable as the flight style. Ground-hunting species take off from the ground with powerful wingbeats. Species that take off from an elevated perch begin with the first wingbeat before they let go of the substrate with the claws of their feet. Landings on branches, ceilings, and ledges are "artistic events" in many bats: the body rotates, the legs swing up, and the half-folded wings act as brakes.

However, the techniques that horseshoe bats, for example, have raised to an art can also be done more simply but less elegantly. Many flying foxes simply land with their bellies on the branches of their roost trees, then quickly grasp the branches with the claws of their feet and thumbs to switch over to the usual head-down position. This habit of hanging from branches or the like is possible because the hip joints are twisted upward and to the outside, with the feet pointing backward. Thanks to a tendon that prevents the toes from straightening, hanging head-down costs no energy and indeed can continue even after death.

claw

tendon

tendon sheath

bones of toes

active tension

passive tension

Seemingly the hardest of work, but in actuality requiring no expenditure of energy—a bat hanging at rest. In hanging, the bat uses its own body weight passively to stretch tendons without muscular exertion.

Landing maneuver of a Greater Horseshoe Bat (Rhinolophus ferrumequinum)— a work of art in itself. Before the landing the feet are already swung up to the "landing field" by the turning of the body (after Schober, 1983).

The Night as an Ecological Niche

Roof of a cave in Sri Lanka with thousands of horseshoe bats (Rhinolophus rouxi) and Sri Lankan Rousette Fruit Bats (Rousettus seminudus), of which only the eyes illuminated by the light are visible.

One day Walter Metzner, of the Zoological Institute of the University of Munich, asked us if we wanted to go with him to Sri Lanka to experience tropical bats "live." At the time, he was doing his doctoral research on the echolocation performance of bats as part of the research group of Gerhard Neuweiler. Naturally we wanted to go, so we accompanied the zoologists to "their" bat cave. The sight of many thousands of animals flying from the cave is described here by Walter Metzner:

"They had to come at any moment. We waited for the first of more than a quarter-million bats that had chosen the large cave on the edge of the Sri Lankan central mountain chain as their daily roost.

"There they were! The sun had barely set when the first of them flew from the dark hole in front of us into the still-darkening evening. They were horseshoe bats, and we had traveled all the way from disant Germany to study their habits. They now flew, totally silent, singly, and in rapid flight, just above the ground, following every change

in elevation. By the minute, thousands of horseshoe bats and other bat species poured from the opening to the cave. This display was accompanied only by an incessant bubbling sound that issued from the long, funnel-shaped cave shafts. Eddies produced by innumerable wingbeats broke against the walls of the cave, before being amplified many times and rising to this peculiar, muffled roar. The clicks of echolocating Sri Lankan Rousette Fruit Bats (*Rousettus seminudus*) were also just audible to the naked ear at times. But what a racket we heard when we switched on our bat detectors, small devices which made the ultrasonic echolocation calls audible! Suddenly we were surrounded by an almost indescribable squeaking and chattering. It seemed a minor miracle to us that the animals could find their way in this uproar. Nevertheless, they flew unswervingly and avoided all obstacles as they left the cave and disappeared into the night.

"In the meantime darkness had fallen and we had to turn on our flashlights. The reflective retinas in the large eyes of the *Rousettus,* a type of flying fox, gleamed an impressive reddish yellow in the beams of the flashlights. Driven by hunger, they flew rapidly to their feeding trees, where they would eat their fill of fruit.

"I suddenly felt a heavy blow on my temple and caught a glimpse of a rousette fruit bat disappearing into the valley. It was just as startled by the unexpected collision as I. A member of our group had been fascinated by the glowing, reddish eyes of this *Rousettus* and had so confused it with the light of the flashlight that the animal had lost its ability to hear and see. This incident demonstrated to me emphatically that the echolocation used by the flying foxes is not as good as that of some other bats. The fruit bats of the genus *Rousettus* are the only flying foxes that use clicking sounds produced by the tongue for orientation. They usually do this, however, only in their dark roost caves.

"They more than make up for the lack of echolocation, with their large eyes adapted for night vision. Because they live exclusively as fruit-eaters in the tropics, the eyes and the well-developed sense of smell are quite sufficient for this large group of bats. Flying foxes sit or, as the case may be, hang at the table that in the tropics is always laden with fruits—as long as a plantation owner does not take exception."

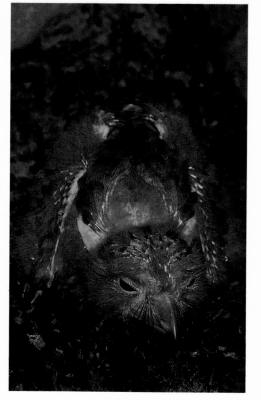

Sri Lankan Rousette Fruit Bats (Rousettus seminudus, *top*) navigate with clicks and sight as they leave the roosting cave at night.

(bottom): Young Oilbird (Steatornis caripensis, *left*) on its nest in a cave in Ecuador. Fed a diet of oily palm nuts by its parents, it becomes unbelievably fat.

23

Echolocation has been "Invented" Several Times

The "sound picture" (top) of a moth, received by a bat as an echo after emitting its echolocation call, could look something like this.

Left: Horseshoe bat hunting from a perch. Whereas the echo of its echolocation call reflected back by the dense vegetation scarcely differs from the transmitted signal, the wingbeats of an insect are audible in the echo in the form of periodic modulations in frequency and intensity.
Right: The horseshoe bat's sense of hearing is totally specialized for receiving its personal carrier frequency. In the inner ear is the narrow-band filter, which corresponds to and is overrepresented in the personal sending frequency (74-79 kHz in the Sri Lankan Horseshoe Bat).

Bats are not the only "inventors" of echolocation. Several highly developed vertebrates, including birds and mammals like Oilbirds, tenrecs, whales, and a few gliding marsupials and rodents also use this method of orientation. Echolocation must have developed totally independently several times. Notable feats of orientation with the aid of sonar pulses are accomplished by, for example, the toothed whales and seals. The Ganges Dolphin, a freshwater dolphin that occurs only in the Ganges and Indus Rivers, has become completely adapted to swimming in muddy water. Because the range of sight is limited to a few centimeters by suspended matter and optical orientation is thus inadequate, in the course of evolution the Ganges Dolphin has turned completely to acoustic spatial orientation and has lost its sense of sight.

Some birds also use echolocation. They include the Oilbird (*Steatornis*), related to the whippoorwills, in northern South America, and the cave swiftlets (*Collocalia*), swifts from Southeast Asia and Australia. In both genera of birds, as in the rousette fruit bats, echolocation is of no significance for food acquisition. In pitch-black caves, how-

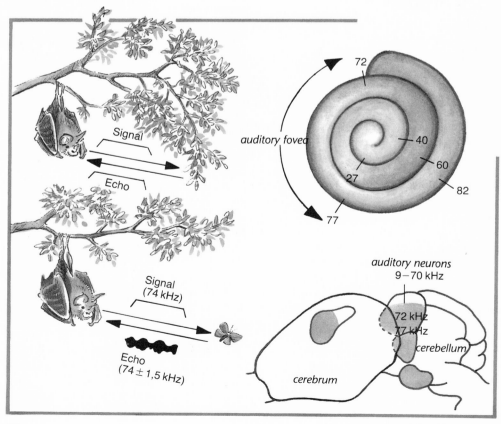

(after Neuweiler, 1990).

Normal flight, normal echolocation call (black: echolocation call, gray: echo); the common bat has located a prey animal—the number of ultrasonic clicks is increased greatly, but in return the duration of the clicks shrinks to one-fifth of what it was previously; the insect is captured; normal echolocation calls in continued

Comparison of echolocation techniques of common and horseshoe bats (greatly simplified). Top: Common bats (Vespertilionidae) usually send their short echolocation calls through the open mouth. From bottom to top:

flight. Bottom: In all species of horseshoe bats, the nasal process acts as a megaphone in the emission of the long echolocation calls through the nose. From bottom to top: Normal flight, normal echolocation call; the horseshoe bat has located a prey animal flying by and now sends out echolocation calls continuously.

ever, they can find their way with the aid of the echo of their clicking noises. Safe from many predators, Oilbirds and cave swiftlets nest in caves in large colonies. Only man can be a danger to them in these places. The Oilbirds of South America are called *guacharos*—screamers—because of the din they produce when people enter their dark realm. They are also called *pacharos del aceite*—oilbirds—in Spanish. Alexander von Humboldt was the first scientist to observe the Oilbird (*Steatornis caripensis*) in the rocky caves of Caripe in Venezuela. The up to 55-centimeter-long (22 inches) birds have coarse plumage and the broad mouth typical of whippoorwills, but the curved upper mandible resembles that of a raptor. In contrast to their relatives, the crepuscular (active at dawn and dusk) and nocturnal (active at night) Oilbirds and nocturnal oilbirds do not hunt insects, but rather feed on fruit. These are torn off in flight, the birds, like hummingbirds, being able to remain stationary in the air by means of whirring wingbeats and by raising and lowering the tail. They feed their nestlings with oily palm fruits. The youngsters become unbelievably

fat on this diet. After about ten months they easily weigh half again as much as their parents and are coveted sources of oil for the Indians. Rendered guacharo fat or oil serves as lamp and cooking oil.

The bowl-shaped saliva nests of cave swiftlets are marketed as an Asian delicacy. To get them, collectors risk their lives on swaying liana and bamboo scaffolds in tower-high caves. The trade is carefully regulated and licensed, and productive caves are handed down by law from generation to generation. In contrast to the "white gold" of the cave swiftlets, Oilbird nests are not suitable for human consumption. Their pyramidal nests, which are used year after year, consist of soil, regurgitated food pellets, and mostly droppings.

25

Echolocation—A Scientific "Who Done It"

*Greater Mouse-eared Bat (*Myotis myotis*). The largest German bat navigates while leaving its roost in typical common-bat manner with open mouth.*

Not exclusivity, but rather the persistent use of the system for orientation and to capture prey distinguishes the bats among all echolocators.

Up until the end of the 18th century, people were satisfied with a simple explanation for the feats of the nocturnal hunters in darkness: bats were possessed by the devil and thus had magical powers. Lazzaro Spallanzani (1729 -1799), mathematician, naturalist, logician, and Bishop of Padua, was not, however, satisfied with supersti-

tious explanations. This multitalented man began to experiment with nocturnal fliers. Though owls collided with objects when they flew in his absolutely dark studio, bats avoided even stretched threads under the same experimental conditions. Not until Spallanzani put opaque caps on the animals did they lose their skill. But their performance did not improve even with transparent caps. As Spallanzani experimented further and sealed their eyes or blinded them, to his surprise they retained their skill in flying. The logician then set up an experiment in the wild, for which he caught bats in a cave and then blinded several of them. All were marked and released. When the clever scientist recaptured the bats in the cave after a few days and examined their stomach contents, he discovered that the blind bats had been just as successful at catching insects as their sighted brethren.

Subsequently, Spallanzani wrote to his European scientific colleagues and reported that bats were not dependent on vision for orientation when hunting insect. The Genoese naturalist Louis Jurine read the report and experimented further. When he blocked the ears of bats with wax, they lost the ability to navigate. At the same, time Spallanzani performed an experiment in which he put small metal tubes, which could be plugged, in the ears of the bats. The animals with open tubes in their ears flew normally, but those with plugs lost their ability to navigate. In this way Jurine and Spallanzani concluded simultaneously that hearing had to be of significance for nocturnal orientation. "Is it possible to see with the ears?" wrote Spallanzani in his notes just before his death. They were to fall into obscurity for a long time after Georges Cuvier (1769-1832), the famous French naturalist, declared on the strength of his opinion alone that both scientists had doubtless been mistaken and that the orientation of bats was the result of a very fine sense of touch on their body surface and wings.

A purely technical achievement was to bring sound as a navigational aid under discussion again. After the tragic sinking of the *Titanic,* Hiram Maxim, inventor of the machine gun, invented a warning system based on sound in 1912. Maxim postulated that in a similar manner bats could also avoid obstacles in the dark, but missed the mark in believing that the animals produced low-frequency sounds through wing movements for this purpose. In 1920 the English neurophysiologist Hartridge discovered the old works of Spallanzani and Jurine and reasoned that the acoustic signal more likely was of high rather than low frequency. The final clarification of the 200-year-old scientific dispute was left to the young biologist Donald Griffin. When the Harvard student, carrying a cage full of bats, visited the physicist W. Priece, who analyzed high-pitched insect calls in his laboratory with the aid of a high-frequency detector, Griffin actually wanted to study the shrill, audible sounds of the bats. But when the bats were placed in front of the recording instrument, at first the bats and then the researchers were dumbfounded. When intense vocalizations of the seemingly silent animals came from the receiver, the key to the mysterious world of sound of the nocturnal hunters had finally been found. When the time is right for discoveries, they often hap-

Greater Horseshoe Bat (Rhinolophus ferrumequinum). Horseshoe bats are nasal echolocators. Their species-typical cutaneous nasal process acts as a megaphone.

pen twice and independently of each other: almost simultaneously with Griffin, Priece, and Galambos, who joined the Harvard research project, the Dutchman Dijkgraaf determined on the basis of his excellent hearing that bats emitted sounds for orientation and became disorientated when their sender (mouth) or receiver (ear) was disconnected.

ECHOLOCATION IS COMPLETELY INDIVIDUAL

With finer and finer and trickier meth-

Grey Long-eared Bat (Plecotus austriacus). With their extremely long ears, the two German long-eared bat species are unmistakable within the family of the common bats.

27

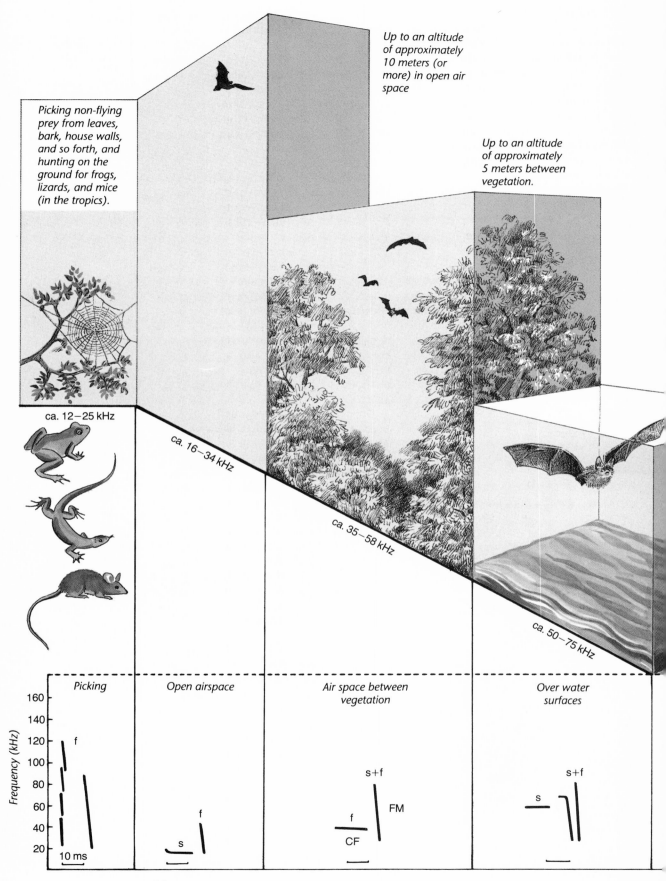

Up to an altitude of approximately 10 meters (or more) in open air space

Picking non-flying prey from leaves, bark, house walls, and so forth, and hunting on the ground for frogs, lizards, and mice (in the tropics).

Up to an altitude of approximately 5 meters between vegetation.

ca. 12–25 kHz

ca. 16–34 kHz

ca. 35–58 kHz

ca. 50–75 kHz

| Picking | Open airspace | Air space between vegetation | Over water surfaces |

Frequency (kHz)

160
140
120 f
100
80
60
40
20

10 ms

f

s   f

s+f

f   FM

CF

s+f

s

ods, scientists were hot on the trail of the echolocating bats. It was determined that the animals use many quite variable types of sounds, which differ in detail and which generally vary from species to species and often even include individual notes. Bats even seem to develop "dialects." For example, Common Pipistrelles in Scandinavia call differently than those in southern Germany or Greece. The echolocation calls, however, can be divided roughly into only a few groups of sounds.

Short direction-finding calls are given by many species; these very rapidly drop off in a wide range from high to low pitch. The frequencies change in the same way, and thus the direction-finding calls are strongly frequency modulated (FM). Their producers are therefore called FM bats. To this group belongs, for example, the Greater Mouse-eared Bat (*Myotis myotis*). A wide frequency range of this kind can also be covered in many small individual steps, which are always at uniform intervals to the keynote. Harmonic call types of this kind are

produced, for example, by the false vampire bats (Megadermatidae) and the New World leaf-nosed bats (Phyllostomidae). These very short calls (about a millisecond) with many overtones are called HF calls. In addition, other bats produce sounds that end more or less on a constant frequency. The European Common Pipistrelle of the genus *Pipistrellus* and the European Free-tailed Bat, *Tadarida teniotis,* send in this manner.

The horseshoe bats and leaf-nosed bats (Rhinolophidae, Hipposideridae) have developed a completely different form of sending. Their echolocation calls consist of a constant high-frequency component, bounded at the beginning and end of the call by frequency-modulated components. Accordingly, they are called CF/FM bats, where CF stands for constant frequency. Because a high percentage of the energy that must be expended for sound production flows only into a very limited frequency band, horseshoe bats can use direction-finding calls that in some cases are a hundered times longer than the calls of FM bats.

The majority of sounds produced by bats lie above our human threshold of hearing. We can, however, detect the low-frequency components of a few bat calls. Our hearing is able to detect, for example, the direction-finding calls of the European Free-tailed Bat. In the same way as human hearing is tuned to the frequency content of our speech, individual species of bats always receive best the frequencies they send. Like all mammals, bats produce their calls with the larynx. What so often makes bat faces look so grotesque to us are the expressions of the sound-conducting apparatus (noses) and the receiving organs (ears).

SENDING AND RECEIVING SYSTEMS

Though most bats emit their calls through the open mouth, the horseshoe bats and leaf-nosed bats, for example, use their nose as a sound-emitting organ. Their bizarre nasal appendages act as a megaphone. Nasal echolocation has clear advantages: other bats cannot send when they have prey in their mouth, but the nasal echolocaters can continue to navigate even while feeding. The sound receivers of bats are also highly variable in structure. Ear shape and size as well as the development and form of the tragus (the prominence in front of the external opening of the ear)

Types of echolocation calls, their relationship to hunting habits and hunting biotopes, as well as the most sensitive hearing ranges of different types of hunting bats. The schematic sonograms (bottom) show the types of echolocation calls, which are frequently used in the various biotopes during prey search (s) and prey capture (f). The time bars mark 10 milliseconds. FM = frequency modulated call or component of call, CF = constant frequency call or component of call (after Neuweiler, 1990).

Up to an altitude of approximately 2 meters above the water's surface.

Just above and on vegetation or while hunting from ambush.

On and in foliage

s+f

FM/CF/FM

ca. 70–155 kHz

often are so characteristic that they are used for species identification. There is still a long way to go before the function of the tragus can be fully explained. In the opinion of researchers, the tragus likely is used to discriminate direction in the vertical plane. Large ears are used to hear the sounds and calls of prey animals.

LIFE IN SNAPSHOTS

In contrast to optical orientation, an echolocater is presented only with a small extract of its environment, limited temporally by the duration of the echo. Whereas

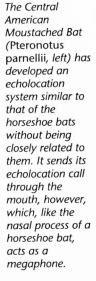

The Central American Moustached Bat (Pteronotus parnellii, left) has developed an echolocation system similar to that of the horseshoe bats without being closely related to them. It sends its echolocation call through the mouth, however, which, like the nasal process of a horseshoe bat, acts as a megaphone.

The Sri Lankan Leaf-nosed Bat (Hipposideros lancadiva, right) got its name from the nasal process it uses to navigate like the horseshoe bats.

we are presented with a continuous picture of our surroundings through our eyes, the bat receives, in a manner of speaking, "snapshots." By increasing the repetition rate of individual "pictures," an imaging system of this kind can also provide, much like the projection of a film, an almost continuous picture. Bats in fact always do just that whenever they need more precise information. When approaching a prey animal or obstacle, the repetition rate of their navigation calls increases, sometimes drastically. The problem is that a returning echo signal must be correlated with the appropriate echolocation call. In the final phase of the approach to an object, the bat is able to increase dramatically the calling rate only because the distance is so short. Because of the short distance the echo arrives soon after the echolocation call is sent and does not overlap with the call that will be sent out immediately thereafter.

TIME WINDOWS AND STOPWATCHES

Bats also have a kind of "time window" that is open only for a specific period after the echolocation call is sent. Everything that comes back later falls, in a manner of speaking, on deaf ears. In this way uninteresting or disruptive echoes from background objects can be cleverly filtered out. All information-processing systems must contend with this problem of suppressing and filtering out undesirable signals. For this purpose bats have found different solutions that in each case are optimal for their particular situation and that are amazingly similar to the technical solutions arrived at by humans.

Before we come to the solutions, however, we should first discuss another problem called damping. As a result of damping by the air, the very high frequency components of navigation calls, in particular, are already so greatly attenuated after a few dozen meters that they can no longer be detected in the echo. For that reason bats in open air use the lowest possible frequencies, which, although they tend to be absorbed by their prey, allow them to detect the prey over as wide a distance as possible. The time interval between sending and the detection of the echo is used as a measure of distance, and the call is the transport medium for the information. The bat brain functions here like a stopwatch; it begins running when the echolocation call is emitted and measures the time until the return of the echo signal. The nerve cells responsible for this, which measure precise time intervals in the range of thousandths of a second, were found in the American Moustached Bat, *Pteronotus parnellii,* and in horseshoe bats. These time intervals correspond to distances of about 30 centimeters to a few meters (a foot to a few yards). Because,

30

as is generally known, sound is transmitted at a velocity of about 331 meters per second (1088 feet per second) in air, a bat call that, for example, strikes a prey animal at a distance of 10 meters (33 feet) is reflected back to the bat's ear after only 60 milliseconds. But the bat's brain must be able to measure intervals of less than one millisecond. To do this, bats have for 50 million years possessed a biological clock that can be rivaled in precision only by our most modern quartz clocks. Interestingly, radar engineers, who routinely measure distances with sound, have calculated that the ideal

FLYING MATERIAL TESTERS

How do the nocturnal hunters know, however, whether something edible or merely an obstacle is in front of them? That structural differences can be detected with the aid of ultrasound is generally known to us principally from diagnostic medicine. There and in material testing the smallest possible wavelengths are used to resolve structures to a thousandth of a millimeter. Our flying material testers, on the other hand, must contend with limits at high frequencies set by the absorption of sound in air. How they find their food despite this

*The Particolored Bat (*Vespertilio murinus, *left) is the only one of three species of the genus* Vespertilio *that lives in Europe.*

*Leisler's Bat (*Nyctalus leisleri, *right). The external ear and the tragus of this medium-sized species have the same form as that of the Noctule.*

signal for this purpose should drop from high to low frequency rapidly at first and slowly toward the end, which corresponds exactly with the frequency distribution of many bat navigation calls.

But the bat not only must be able to measure as precisely as possible time as a measure of distance, but also simultaneously the direction of the sound (= the prey). The differences in running time are collected by the precision ears of the ultrasonic hunters. Thus, for example, an echo from the right first reaches the bat's right ear and in addition is louder than at the left ear. The difference in time depends alone on the distance between the ears and thereby on the head diameter. In bats this difference is in the range of 40 microseconds, thus 40 millionths of a second! For our ears the difference is a hundred times larger. Besides differences in time and loudness, direction-dependent changes in the frequency content of the echo also occur. The manner in which an object is heard, its "color" as it were, varies with the direction from which it is detected.

handicap is demonstrated by the method used by the horseshoe bats.

Their echolocation system functions like a shortwave radio, in that the transmitter (sender) and receiver are combined in one. The larynx as a radio transmitter produces a particular individual sending frequency, which is picked up by the ear as the radio receiver. Though we can select different senders (different receiving frequencies) with the radio, the horseshoe bat always hears the same sender. It thereby has the advantage that all information about its prey arrives clearly over its frequency, whereas less important information is expressed as background noise. Horseshoe bats (and leaf-nosed bats) as bush hunters thereby get around the problem of the "echo salad" in a muffled environment. The hunting method based on "sitting" on a frequency permits the "knights of the bushes" to concentrate exclusively on their prey.

A long-eared bat (Plecotus) with erect (top) and with half-folded ears (center). In hibernation the ears are squeezed completely under the wings; only the tragus is still erect and resembles an ear (bottom).

WINGBEATS—MUSIC TO A HORSESHOE BAT'S EARS

When the high-pitched echolocation signal of a horseshoe bat encounters a flying insect, the reflected echoes contain acoustic highlights in the rhythm of the wingbeats. These so-called "glints" are short modulations of the intensity and frequency of the echolocation call, produced by the movement of the insect's wings through the beam of sound. Ultimately they show just as little interest in their sending frequency as we do in the carrier frequency of the radio. Only the frequency modulations of the fluttering prey in the truest sense of the word are "music" to the bat's ear. To be able to hear the slight modulations well, the horseshoe bat has an audio filter in the inner ear. This filter is highly sensitive to the appropriate frequency band. Nevertheless, the tuned system still has a few snags. When the bat flies off, the transmitter and receiver move with the velocity of the bat, which produces a Doppler shift. Named for its discoverer, Christian Doppler, this phenomenon is well known to all of us: the noise of a moving source of sound, such as a motorcyle or train, always sounds more high pitched as it approaches and lower pitched as it recedes. Carried over to a hunting horseshoe bat, the echo from the prey would have to fall out of the range of the audio filter. The animals are able to compensate for the effect, however, in that they always cause the next echolocation call to sink by the amount that the previous echo signal was above the audio-filter frequency. In this way they couple their echolocation system with their own air speed, in the same way as is done with on-board radar devices.

DIRECTIONAL ANTENNAS AND AMPLIFIERS

The ground-hunters among the bats, however, often no longer detect and localize their prey at all with the use of echoes. With their typically huge external ears, which simultaneously function as directional antennas and amplifiers, they are tuned to the typical sounds of prey animals. In this way the Frog-eating Bat, *Trachops cirrhosus,* can distinguish edible from poisonous frogs by their calls. From experiments it is known that the Australian Giant False Vampire Bat, *Macroderma gigas,* even attacks tape recorders playing back bird calls. In the brain of several of these audio-hunters, noise-specific neurons were found that react with

unbelievable sensitivity. In the true vampire bats, which live on the blood of vertebrate animals and primarily stalk sleeping mammals and birds, the neurons react preferentially to persistent sounds, such as those produced by the quiet inhalation and exhalation during sleep. The experimental animals even reacted to the breathing of the experimenter.

EVEN DIFFERENT INSECT SPECIES ARE DISTINGUISHED

The fantastic capability of preformance of the echolocation system of bats is shown by recent studies of the Greater Horseshoe Bat. In training experiments, Gerhard von der Emde of the University of Tübingen was able to demonstrate that horseshoe bats distinguish different kinds of insects by the frequency of their wingbeats. The wingbeat frequency, which is reflected in the returning echo, gives them an indication of whether it would be worthwhile to chase the detected insect. The beat frequency depends principally on the insect's size. Horseshoe bat delicacies such as moths, large beetles, and craneflies all beat their wings 40 to 70 times a second.

Next von der Emde played back computer-simulated ultrasonic echoes to his bats: from one side that of a flying cranefly with 50 wingbeats per second, which the horseshoe bats had been exposed to in training, and from the other a digitally compiled echo such as would be produced by a cranefly with slower wing movements. The scientist allowed the two signals to become more and more similar until the two fictitious insects differed by only four wingbeats per second. Even so, the horseshoe bats were able to tell them apart readily.

Additional experiments suggest that the beat frequency of potential prey animals is not the only "call note" for bats. Every insect wing has, above and beyond the uniform staccato of powerful volume and frequency peaks in the beat rhythm, a unique "sound" in the ultrasonic echolocation beam. Surface structure and the beat path of the wings determine these less conspicuous modulations in the returning echo, which the horseshoe bats also know how to use.

THE SPATIAL MEMORY OF THE NEARSIGHTED

Yet what functions so perfectly at close range is unsuitable for long-range orientation. To compensate for the limited range of their echolocation calls, bats have a splendidly developed spatial memory. In the areas in which they customarily fly, this helps them to concentrate on the essential: catching prey. How strongly the flight routes are imprinted is demonstrated in that their customary hunting routes still pass around trees even after they have been cut down.

As they enter or leave their daytime roosts, they often depend totally on spatial memory. Bats have been known to collide with newly installed boards and glass panes where they had been used to having a clear path. The obstacles had yet to be entered into their spatial memory.

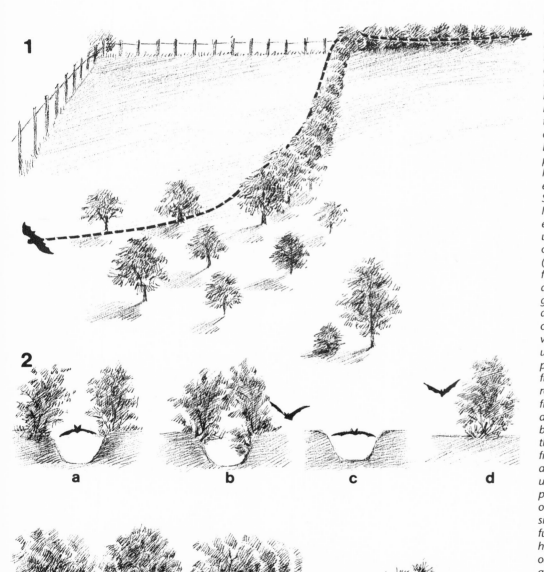

1. Flight paths of bats in an open agrarian landscape. Barbwire fences are not used as a flight path. The bats thus need more than a line to be able to orient themselves. Bats prefer particular linear landscape elements. 2. Several linear landscape elements and their use as flightpaths of bats: *a*: (optimal) gorge, frequently used as a flight path; *b*: gorge with too-dense vegetation; c: gorge without vegetation, rarely used as a flight path; *d*: dense, fully developed row of trees, frequently used as a flight path; the bats always fly on the side sheltered from the wind; *e*: alley, frequently used as a flight path; *f*: single row of trees, offering small gaps; *g*: fully developed hedge, only occasionally used as a flight path; *h*: sheared hedge, rarely used as a path (after illustrations by Helmer and Limpens).

Natterer's Bat (Myotis nattereri) has relatively long ears and broad wing membranes. Its slow flight and whirring wingbeats make possible maneuvers in the smallest space.

The insect hunters

Insects occur in diversity and abundance in almost all parts of the world. They also have high nutritional value and are therefore used by terrestrial and aquatic vertebrates as a source of food. An entire order of mammals is even named after its preferred food: the insectivores, including the families of the shrews, hedgehogs, moles, tenrecs, and golden moles. The army of nocturnal flying insects gave impetus to the development of the hunting bats and was the drive for the evolution of the insectivorous bats (Microchiroptera) in their present abundance of forms. A previously unused dietary potential virtually demanded the development of a flying nocturnal hunter with the appropriate orientation equipment.

Approximately 70 percent of today's bats live on insects and spiders. The palette of food animals includes practically the entire insect world. The nocturnal hunters most frequently feed on beetles (Coleoptera), butterflies and moths (Lepidoptera), and flies and mosquitoes (Diptera). To this are added cockroaches (Blattaria), termites (Isoptera), lacewings (Neuroptera), grasshoppers and crickets (Orthoptera), cicadas (Homoptera), true bugs (Hemiptera), and night-flying ants (Hymenoptera). The prey size ranges from tiny midges with wingspans of a few millimeters and a weight of a fifth of a milligram to moths weighing more than 200 milligrams with wingspans of 50 millimeters (2 inches) or more. It is estimated that a hunting bat consumes about a fourth to half its body weight in

insects a night. A 20-gram bat (there are 28 grams to an ounce) accordingly eats five to ten grams of insects nightly. The zoologist Erwin Kulzer collected and weighed in two consecutive years the droppings produced by a large colony of Mouse-eared Bats in Baden-Württemberg, Germany. The collected droppings weighed 93 kilograms (204.6 pounds) in 1987 and 90 kilograms (198 pounds) in 1988. Based on findings from laboratory experiments, in which mealworm larvae had been fed, in each year the Mouse-eared Bats must have consumed more than a ton of live insects.

Whereas bats in the temperate climatic zones must adapt to the seasonal insect supply and overcome the lack of food in winter, the insect supply in the warm regions of the earth is less seasonally dependent. Bat populations have developed there that up to a few decades ago numbered in the millions. A colony of the Mexican Free-tailed Bat (*Tadarida brasiliensis*) is presently estimated to number 50 million animals. With a weight of 20 grams per animal, in one season this colony will have consumed about 6700 tons (over 13 million pounds) of insects.

To understand the different habits of the individual bat species, it is important to know which insects the bats prefer to feed on. Because bats often are protected, the examination of the stomach contents of killed animals usually is out of the question.

Bat menus can be reconstructed by study-

The Greater
Horseshoe Bat
(Rhinolophus
ferrumequinum)
hunts adroitly
through the
branches in slow,
butterflylike flight.

The Serotine
(Eptesicus
serotinus) flies
slowly and hunts
in wide curves
around groups of
trees.

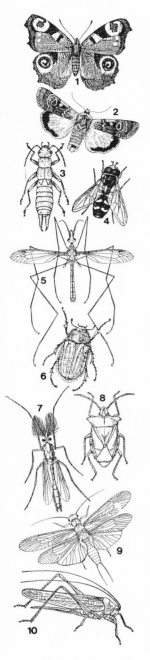

ing the food remains at the feeding site and by analyzing droppings, because unappetizing parts of larger insects are dropped to the ground and indigestible pieces of chitin are excreted with the droppings. Although this is real detective work, the method does have a long tradition. The naturalist Jäckel published bat prey lists as early as the last century. In food remains he found 71 insect species, among them 65 species of moths, as well as two species of large cranefly. Today, dietary analyses have become permanent components in studies of the habits and living-space requirements of bats, even though poking around in crumbs of droppings may seem to the layman to be comparable to reading coffee grounds.

A specialist in "crumb poking" is the Swiss zoologist Andres Beck, who carries out qualitative and quantitative dietary analyses of European bats. For this purpose he collects fresh droppings and the uneaten remains of prey from bat roosts. The individual balls of droppings are then laboriously softened in water, teased apart with forceps and dissecting needle at magnifications of 25X to 40X under the stereomicroscope, and examined for identifiable digested parts of food animals. Particularly valuable are recovered insect wings, the specific venation of which often permits precise classification in particular insect groups. After they are separated, the fragments are compared with mounted specimens. From the study of the droppings from two Swiss colonies of the Lesser Horseshoe Bat, Andres Beck discovered that, for example, the remains of flies (Diptera) were most abundant, even ahead of those of butterflies and moths (Lepidoptera) and lacewings (Neuroptera). The Lesser Horseshoe Bats preferentially preyed on larger flies (Tipulidae, Anisopodidae), but even the smallest prey animals like barklice (Psocoptera), aphids (Aphididae), and blackflies (Simuliidae) were part of the horseshoe bats' diet. The absence of the wings, legs, and head parts of large insects from the droppings suggested to the researcher that the Lesser Horseshoe Bat hunts from ambush. In this hunting method the bat returns with the prey to its perch and while feeding bites off inedible parts and lets them fall to the ground.

Andres Beck also studied the dietary habits of other bat species by analyzing droppings and food remains. His findings show that many bats seem to be able to detect and catch the smallest flying insects

in the air. Daubenton's Bat regularly feeds on aphids and mosquitoes. The Common Long-eared Bat also catches small flies and barklice, but it feeds mainly on moths. Furthermore, it also routinely gathers earwigs from a substrate, as is shown by the presence of completely folded wing covers in the droppings of the bats. Natterer's Bat also practices the art of harvesting prey animals from leaves, branches, and masonry. Diurnal (day-active) hoverflies, which they surprise in sleep, form part of their diet, as do the tiny flightless stages of aphids, which must be snapped up from among the vegetation. When the habits of these prey animals are analyzed, it can be presumed that many bat species concentrate in their search for food on wet regions as well as localities with lots of bushes and trees.

That bats also catch their prey on the ground was proved by the zoologist Anton Kolb from Bamberg, Germany, who found 14 species or genera of flightless groundbeetles in the droppings of Mouse-eared Bats. Kolb's thorough studies also showed that the Mouse-eared Bat's menu changed over the course of the summer. Groundbeetles represented a kind of "dietary staple" to which were added the particular insects that were in good supply in that season. When the other insects were abundant in the hunting range of his approximately 800-strong colony of Mouse-eared Bats, Kolb calculated that the bats captured about 55,000 of them a night.

More recent dietary analyses by the Swiss bat researchers Jürgen Gebhard and Hanspeter Stutz confirm that groundbeetles are typical prey for Mouse-eared Bats. High percentages of groundbeetle remains were found in various colonies. A number of these beetles are pure forest species and are hunted there by the bats. The diets of European long-eared bats *(Plecotus)* are easy to study because they preferentially hunt moths and usually consume them at favorite perches. With some practice and a good identification key, the discarded moth wings can be identified quite well even by beginners. From the collected prey fragments at the feeding sites alone, however, it is by no means possible to determine the complete menu of the long-eared bat, as is stressed by Wolfgang Heinicke and Andreas Krauss. Not all prey animals are eaten at the feeding place, usually only the remains of large and robust insects attract notice, and finally, even a slight breeze can scatter the wing fragments lying there like an open menu.

Food animals of northern bats: 1. tortoiseshell butterfly; 2. moth; 3. common earwig; 4. hoverfly; 5. cranefly; 6. June beetle; 7. midge; 8. stink bug; 9. stonefly; 10. grasshopper.

The Hunting Strategies of the Insect Hunters

Investigating the hunting behavior of the small, maneuverable nocturnal hunters is an art in itself. With persistence and the use of refined methods of observation, however, bat researchers have recently begun to understand the hunting behavior of a few species.

Different insectivorous bats have different strategies for food acquisition. By specializing in hunting in different parts of an area, several bat species can hunt nocturnal insects in the same hunting area at the same time without competing directly. Some bats hunt in the open air, which is divided into different zones of use by different species. Others harvest resting insects from leaves or masonry or hunt among vegetation. Depending on the species, bats either catch their prey in free and usually rapid flight, by searching surfaces in slow fluttering or hovering flight, or in "flycatcher style," in which they fly out from a perch only after they have detected a possible prey animal. Some species apparently also move about on the ground to reach their prey animals.

The adaptations of bats for food acquisition are displayed chiefly in physical characters. Variable wing shapes serve to optimize

Hunting territories and flight paths of several bat species: 1. Daubenton's Bat (Myotis daubentoni) makes its rounds over water. 2. Nathusius' Pipistrelle (Pipistrellus nathusii) flies along vegetative structures as a patrol hunter. 3. The Common Pipistrelle (Pipistrellus pipistrellus) follows its prey in rapid zigzag flight or hunts in the light of lamps. 4. The Noctule (Nyctalus noctula) hunts in fast flight in open sky.

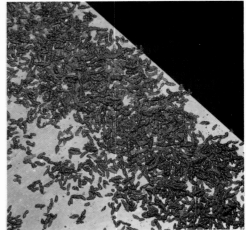

(top left):
Over the years large piles of droppings form under large Mouse-eared Bat colonies. Their size and location indicate the preferred hanging places of the colony in the rafters (top left).

(top right):
Droppings of the Common Pipistrelle on a window ledge. The Common Pipistrelle (Pipistrellus pipistrellus), as the smallest German species, produces very small pellets that trickle down from their hiding places in cracks (top right).

(bottom):
The remains of their diet of moths collect under the feeding places of long-eared bats (bottom).

different styles of flight. A particular structure of the ears can help to improve the detection of weak echoes. A specific dentition makes it possible for bats to crack even the hardest chitin armor of beetles. Finally, the echolocation system must also be appropriate. The Swiss zoologists Hanspeter Stutz and Marianne Haffner described how Noctules, Common Pipistrelles, and Nathusius' Pipistrelles hunt.

THE NOCTULE—A FAST HUNTER IN THE OPEN AIR

With a wingspan of about 40 centimeters (16 inches), the Noctule (*Nyctalus noctula*) is one of the largest European bats. The very narrow wings are well adapted for swallowlike, fast, and impressive flight. Noctules leave their diurnal roost, often a tree hole, soon after sundown and often fly directly to the nearest river course. Distances of several kilometers are traversed effortlessly. Noctules often fly more than 100 meters (110 yards) above the ground and can easily be confused with swifts

against the still-bright evening sky.

As soon as it reaches its hunting grounds, the Noctule flies down to an altitude of 5 to 20 meters (5.5 to 22 yards) and starts its hunting flight. Now the Noctule is easy to distinguish from the swifts, which in any case now soon return to their nests. The Noctule attacks its insect prey in steep dives. After a flight maneuver has been completed it usually regains the altitude it lost in the dive. A landscape with a wide river (usually more than 50 meters—55 yards—wide) and an adjoining strip of meadow, enclosed by a line of trees, a forest edge, or a row of houses, represents a typical hunting ground for Noctules.

Insects determine the hunting area

If there is no wind the Noctule likes to fly over open water surfaces and strips of meadow at a medium altitude of 10 meters (11 yards). Sometimes many individuals hunt together as a group. Each bat usually follows for minutes the same, often elliptical, up to 100-meter-long (110 yards) flight path.

In windy weather the insects retreat to the wind shadows of vegetation along rivers or rows of houses, which forces the Noctule to hunt along the surface structures. Its dives then often bring it down as low as head height. At these times it often hunts away from rivers as well. Even on the flight to the hunting grounds the bat snaps at anything edible that crosses its flight path. Sometimes it stays for a few minutes in a particularly favorable locality, such as above the maze of houses of a town, for this is where crepuscular insects start to swarm in the rising air that was heated during the day. Large parks lit by powerful mercury-vapor lamps are artificial, but very popular, hunting grounds. The heat radiating from the large park surfaces and the ultraviolet component of the artificial light attract insects—and the Noctule knows how to take advantage.

Snacks and sleep to digest the meal

The Noctule does not hunt continuously through the night. The evening hunt typically lasts about 90 to 120 minutes, then the sated insect-hunters return to their roosts to digest the food thoroughly. Just before daybreak, as long as the temperature is above 8° C (46°F), Noctules appear again for a one-hour "breakfast hunt." Fritz Kronwitter, in his studies of the Noctule in the region of the Ebersberger Forest near Munich, Germany, confirmed many of the Swiss zoologists' observations. Using an observation technique refined with the aid of a small radio transmitter, he demonstrated the existence of another nocturnal hunting flight for the Noctule. While all of the bats usually participated in the first and third periods of activity simultaneously, usually they did not take part in the "midnight hunt." In this hunting period only a few insect-hunters were on the wing at any one time, which kept intraspecific competition to a minimum. Fritz Kronwitter attributes the extremely high (250 to 500 meters, 275 to 550 yards) or long (up to 26 kilometers, 15.6 miles) flights of the Noctule in the period from mid-August to mid-September to the hunt for migrating insects. The Noctules also hunted briefly over a garbage dump in the Ebersberger Forest. Flights of as many as 60 animals mainly hunted crickets.

THE COMMON PIPISTRELLE—SMALL AND AGILE

With a wingspan of 20 centimeters (8 inches), the Common Pipistrelle (*Pipistrellus pipistrellus*) is Europe's smallest native species. It sometimes leaves its daytime roost when the sun is still shining or shortly after sundown. It likes to hunt along the edges of bodies of water with extensive vegetation at an altitude of 2 to 6 meters (2.2 to 6.6 yards). Neck-breaking flight maneuvers are very typical. The Common Pipistrelle often flies back and forth in the same spot with dozens of turns and loops in the smallest space. In fast and agile flight, the smallest flight spaces under overhanging riparian (near water) vegetation and bridges are

used in this way. Anyone who wants to observe hunting Common Pipistrelles should stand beneath the spreading limbs of riparian trees while pointing a powerful flashlight held at head height parallel to the bank. Soon a Common Pipistrelle will be seen fluttering around our head, because we are standing in its customary flight path. If we also wave our arms about, we will be critically "observed" (or, better said, besounded!) from all sides by the Common Pipistrelle. Furthermore, the bat often will scold us loudly and unmistakably, as if saying, "Beat it!"

The distribution of insects depends greatly on the local wind conditions. For this reason structures that produce wind shadows are of great significance to hunting Common Pipistrelles. They typically hunt around bushes and treetops, as well as along forest edges and in the open spaces above roads near woods. In populated areas they often hunt insects that gather in the glare of street lamps. In untiring whirring flight, circling around the lamp again and again, they clear away the bountiful buffet. In southern European countries, the Common Pipistrelle and the closely related Kuhl's Pipistrelle (*Pipistrellus kuhli*) are the typical bats seen hunting in cities and towns. Small groups of Common Pipistrelles, often adhering to a rigid spatial and temporal pattern, visit a variety of hunting grounds in the course of a night. On these hunting trips the animals often travel up to 5 kilometers (3 miles) from their roosts.

NATHUSIUS' PIPISTRELLE—DELIBERATE PATROLLING HUNTER

Nathusius' Pipistrelle (*Pipistrellus nathusii*) leaves its daytime roost only after the onset

(Nyctalus noctula) demonstrates emphatically that it can bite hard with its insectivore-like teeth and can crack even strong chitinous armor.

The insects are caught directly with the mouth; with larger prey the forward-directed tail membrane serves as a pouch. The wings, however, are also skilfully used as catchers. Finally, a morsel can even be flipped in the direction of the mouth (after Schober, 1983).

of twilight. It is broader-winged and larger than the Common Pipistrelle. The differences are too slight, however, to be used to distinguish the two species in flight. The broader wings nevertheless have a decisive influence on the hunting behavior—they allow Nathusius' Pipistrelle to fly slowly and quietly.

Because it leaves the roost late, usually is found only in small numbers on its hunting grounds, and also flies silently and follows the surface structure, Nathusius' Pipistrelle is much harder to observe than the Noctule and Common Pipistrelle.

In contrast to the closely related Common Pipistrelle, Nathusius' Pipistrelle does not hunt in confined spaces, but rather along vegetative structures such as hedges, lines of trees, and woodland margins. It usually flies at an altitude of 3 to 7 meters (3.3-7.7 yards) above the ground, close to the vegetation, silently and in a straight line. A hunting territory of this kind is several dozen to several hundred meters long. Accordingly, Nathusius' Pipistrelle can be described as a patrolling hunter.

It now becomes clear why many individuals never appear simultaneously in a locality. Often each animal hunts for itself alone. If we wait patiently along a woodland edge or a hedge and shine a flashlight along the vegetation, a hunting Nathusius' Pipistrelle will suddenly turn up, fly over the observer, and disappear again. But if we turn around and wait, the same animal will soon return and again disappear in the other direction. Although this species hunts almost exclusively in flight, short flights to the vegetation suggest that it also harvests its prey from leaves.

DAUBENTON'S BAT—LOW FLIER OVER STILL WATERS

By using a night-vision device Elisabeth Kalko, on the Altrhein near Illingen, Germany, observed the hunting behavior of Daubenton's Bat (*Myotis daubentoni*). With the aid of a cleverly designed multiple flash unit, she preserved their hunting flights in a photographic series. The medium-sized, broad-winged Daubenton's Bat leaves its daytime roost only after total darkness and navigates along fixed flight paths, oriented to structures, to its hunting grounds. It prefers to hunt above standing or slow-flowing bodies of water. Daubenton's Bat patrols a hunting route directly above the water's surface for a certain period of time, turning to and fro to search it thoroughly. The flight paths often run parallel to the banks; wider points on the water's surface are used for turning. Where several animals hunted simultaneously over larger areas, Elisabeth Kalko also observed evasive maneuvers and mutual chasing. The main constituents of the diet of Daubenton's Bat are crepuscular and nocturnal insects that are dependent on water and occur in high density: mayflies, caddisflies, and various midges.

In low-level flight, Daubenton's Bat catches its insect prey exclusively with its tail membrane. In this method of prey capture, the bat first approaches the insect, catches it in the lowered tail membrane, and then rolls up to eat the prey. Finally it returns to hunting.

After detecting a flying insect at higher altitude, Daubenton's Bat flies up to it either on a steep or a more curving path. After it reaches the insect it is either captured as in low-level flight with the tail membrane alone or with the assistance of a wing. If the prey is captured with a wing, it is apparently then moved to the tail membrane. The bat finally eats the insect, as in the low-level capture, by tucking its head down and moving its tail forward. Elisabeth Kalko has calculated that a normal prey capture, from the time the tail is lowered until the bat stretches out again from the tuck position, is only 150 to 200 milliseconds. Daubenton's Bat does not waste any time on feeding either. It immediately consumes the insects in flight.

How closely Daubenton's Bat is bound to the medium of water in hunting is shown by measurements of the flight and capture altitudes. In undisturbed searching flight, Daubenton's Bat flies about 15 centimeters (6 inches) above the water, and in low-level captures it drops to only 3 centimeters (1 inch). High-altitude captures are accomplished between 40 centimeters and one meter (16-39 inches) above the wet element.

(top): In the capture of prey at altitude, Daubenton's Bat (Myotis daubentoni) locates an insect flying higher, catches it with the tail membrane, rolls it up until it is taken in the mouth, and then flies in search of the next tidbit (after Kalko, 1987).

(bottom): Hunting sequence of a Daubenton's Bat (Myotis daubentoni) in low-altitude flight (after Kalko, 1987).

HORSESHOE BATS—HUNTING SUCCESS FROM AMBUSH

Several species of horseshoe bat appear to hunt from ambush. Although it is only suspected that this hunting strategy is practiced by the Lesser Horseshoe Bat (*Rhinolophus hipposideros*), it has been confirmed for the Greater Horseshoe Bat (*Rhinolophus ferrumequinum*) and for an Asiatic species (*Rhinolophus rouxi*) on Sri Lanka. The animals do not actually "perch," of course, but rather hang from small branches, usually under overhanging vegetation. While hanging, the body and head are turned to locate insects flying by. Because, like flycatchers, they usually return to the same branch after a successful capture, the term "flycatcher style" has been adopted for the hunting method used by horseshoe bats.

and hunted a few minutes without interruption in the observed region before then flying to hunting grounds located further from the roost. The briefly hunted, easily surveyed areas were called "intermediate hunting grounds." A maximum of three animals hunted simultaneously in an intermediate hunting ground, where the average hunting time was one to five minutes.

Directly in, as well as on, the foliage, Geoffroy's Bats caught flying insects, but they mainly hunted arthropods, such as flies, lacewings, and spiders resting on the leaves, needles, and branches. The hunting altitude depended on the height of the vegetation; the animals hunted only the top half of the foliage. Resting prey animals were captured using "gleaning" behavior. In this hunting strategy the Geoffroy's Bats constantly flew to leaves and branches from short distances (a few centimeters to one meter) or flew along the vegetation, before then hovering in the air and "picking off" the prey. These aerial acrobats also flew into the foliage, and even the "flycatcher style" characteristic of horseshoe bats is not unknown to them.

*An "ambush hunter," the Greater Horseshoe Bat (*Rhinolophus ferrumequinum, top): Hanging from a small branch or rocky outcropping under a tunnel of vegetation, it locates prey flying by.*

GEOFFROY'S BAT—STUNT FLIER IN SHRUBBERY AND COWSHED

How flexibly a single species of bat can use the available food supply is shown by studies of one of the few confirmed colonies of the Geoffroy's Bat (*Myotis emarginatus*) in Germany. Only eight colonies of this warmth-loving species are known in Germany at present; six of them are located in the climatically favorable Chiemgau in Upper Bavaria. The nursery colony of about 100 animals in Dettendorf in Upper Bavaria was the first colony to be rediscovered in Bavaria. Twenty-four years earlier, the first nursery colony of Geoffroy's Bat to be discovered in Germany, in the attic of Schloss Herrenchiemsee, had abandoned its roost after the rafters were treated with a fire-retardant material. They had been discovered by the researchers Brigitte and Willi Issel.

Dorothea Krull and Alfred Schumm have made detailed studies of the hunting behavior of the Geoffroy's Bats of Dettendorf.

Up to two hours after the Geoffroy's Bats had left their roost, the researchers were able to observe them in a radius of about 500 meters (550 yards) around their roost, a church in the village. The animals approached from the direction of the church

*As a "patrol hunter," Nathusius' Pipistrelle (*Pipistrellus nathusii, right) likes to fly along lines of trees, forest edges, and hedges.*

Over an open courtyard, in the middle of which a shallow compost heap was located, the Geoffroy's Bats hunted flying insects in a circling flight path of 3 to 5 meters (3.3 to 5.5 yards) radius and one to 4 (1.1-4.4 yards) meters above the ground. The courtyard and compost heap is an example of an open, obstacle-free hunting ground, and the stereotypical hunting behavior is characteristic of such an ecological situation. In the vicinity of the village cemetery as well as over streets and meadows, the Geoffroy's Bats hunted in the same manner, though the flight paths were determined by the hunting grounds and were not always circular.

Hunting over cattle

Our working group was most amazed while observing Geoffroy's Bats hunting for prey both in flight and resting on the ceiling of a low, angled cowshed, divided by columns, rafters, and cattle stalls. Besides spiders, mainly flies rested in large numbers on the rough ceiling of the shed. Alfred Schumm counted up to 40 larger flies and 400 fruitflies per square meter of shed ceiling. Even after

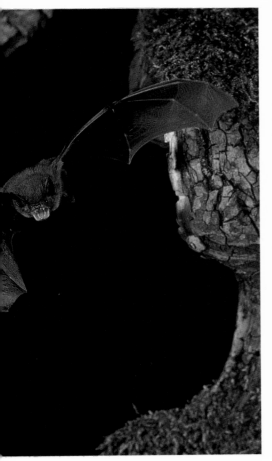

Barn Swallows had stopped hawking for insects in the stall and had returned to their nests to sleep, there was no rest for the fly population. At twilight the flies moved to the shed's ceiling to copulate; their presence was revealed by a clear buzzing. Not until total darkness did they rest motionless and lethargically on the ceiling and rafters. The first Geoffroy's Bats appeared in the stall at dusk. The nocturnal hunters flew to the roof or the rafters again and again in pendular flights, "plucked" resting flies and spiders from their resting places, and immediately flew away. Only rarely did they hang on briefly or stop flying for longer periods. A second strategy used by the bats in the stall was to hunt for flying prey on a circular flight path. During the actual capture the bats moved out of their uniform path, which had a radius of about 1.5 to 3 meters (1.7 to 3.3 yards) and which tended to be just below the ceiling. Some bats exhibited both hunting strategies, while others used exclusively one behavior. The Geoffroy's Bats hunted more often by far in pendular flights. On only one occasion was a bat observed hovering before a column.

Alternative roosting sites and hunting strategies

The more distant hunting grounds of our Geoffroy's Bats are located in forested regions, which are intersected by numerous streams and are above all distinguished by vegetative edges. Nursing females often

When hunting from a perch, the Greater Horseshoe Bat follows its prey by turning its body or head. When the echo of its echolocation call signals that something edible is nearby, time has almost always run out for the moth.

43

Geoffroy's Bat (Myotis emarginatus). After flying from the roost, it flies to trees and bushes (1). It hunts its prey by flying close to (3) or in the vegetation (5). Undulating flight (4), as in the barn, can be observed, as can hovering flight near foliage (6). An additional hunting strategy is hunting from ambush (2) in the style of horseshoe bats (after Schumm, 1988).

Geoffroy's Bat catches its prey animals while circling one to 3 meters above the compost heap. At other times it hunts along the wall of the barn.

flew back to the colony after a short time, but some animals also used hollow trees and buildings as alternative roosting sites on the hunting grounds. The temporary residence in the alternative roost sites located 2.5 to 10.5 kilometers (1.5 to 6.3 miles) from the colony must have helped the bats to save energy.

Noteworthy are the two completely different hunting strategies of a single bat species. In the first, the Geoffroy's Bat searches for a prey animal resting on a structured, in part restless (for example, through the movement of leaves), background. The flight is slow and the distance covered is short. In the other method it hunts flying insects in comparatively fast and long search flights. In this case the prey is differentiated clearly from the background.

As the studies of Alfred Schumm show, the echolocation system of Geoffroy's Bat is adapted to the diverse ecological circumstances. The information content of the echo, the capture of the prey, and the energy expenditure required to do so can be optimized.

PARTITION OF THE AIR SPACE AVOIDS COMPETITION

In southern India, Jörg Habersetzer studied the ecological niches of nine bat species. There the Egyptian Free-tailed Bat (*Tadarida aegyptiaca*) and two tomb bat species (*Taphozous kachhensis* and *Taphozous melanopogon*) occur in open air space high above the treetops, where they often cover long stretches in fast hunting flights. A mouse-tailed bat species (*Rhinopoma hardwickei*) also hunts high up, but usually at a somewhat lower altitude. The hunting grounds of the two Indian pipistrelle species, *Pipistrellus dormeri* and *Pipistrellus mimus*, are located considerably lower. The leaf-nosed bat species *Hipposideros speoris* and *Hipposideros bicolor*, on the other hand, are almost always located in the vicinity of dense vegetation or close to other objects like walls and houses. Furthermore, the smaller of the two (*Hipposideros bicolor*) also hunts among shrubbery and even takes prey from the ground. Finally, the Indian False Vampire Bat (*Megaderma lyra*) is a true ground-hunter. Its range of prey, besides large insects and birds, includes small fishes, mice, and rats.

In the same way as Habersetzer has studied Indian bats living in one region, Dorothea Krull has developed a scheme for European insectivorous bats that reflects the possible division of different hunting grounds in combination with the hunting strategies. It includes seven of the total of 13 species that occur in our study area in Rosenheim, Germany. Three groups can be differentiated. The Noctule (*Nyctalus noctula*) hunts above or just below the treetops and in open air space. It seldom leaves this hunting area at high altitude, and then only briefly. Daubenton's Bat (*Myotis daubentoni*) can also be considered a hunter of open air space on its hunting grounds. It usually hunts over open water surfaces, but at very low altitude. Common Pipistrelles (*Pipistrellus pipistrellus*) hunt outside vegetation, but orient themselves strongly to peripheral structures and also circle street lamps. As a true generalist, whether in forest, at forest edges, or over water, the Whiskered Bat (*Myotis mystacinus*) is found everywhere. It flies at almost all altitudes and is often attracted to peripheral structures, where it hunts in a set way. Though all of the species mentioned above catch their prey exclusively in flight, the hunting strategy of the Greater Mouse-eared Bat (*Myotis myotis*) is still unclear. Until recently it was widely believed that the Greater Mouse-eared Bat primarily hunts groundbeetles from the ground in the forest as an "ambush hunter." The analysis of droppings seems to argue in favor of this view. The telemetric results of our colleague Doris Audet, however, point to a different hunting behavior. To be sure, Greater Mouse-eared Bats primarily hunted in forested regions, but during the hunting phase they flew constantly, which argues against the "hunter waiting in ambush" theory.

The third group of bats hunts very close to and in vegetation (gleaning). Because Geoffroy's Bat (*Myotis emarginatus*) must be reckoned among the gleaners, it must compete with the Common Long-eared Bat (*Plecotus auritus*) and Natterer's Bat (*Myotis nattereri*), which occur in the same region and which also pluck insects from surfaces. Geoffroy's Bats avoid this competition by hunting only at particular altitudes, preferred by them alone. In addition, they take a different range of prey (above all flies, spiders, and lacewings, in contrast to the butterflies and moths taken by Long- eared Bats and the beetles and flies preyed on by Natterer's Bat) and they have the ability to hunt opportunistically in open air space.

In the cow shed, Geoffroy's Bat in oscillating flight plucks the resting horseflies and fruitflies from the ceiling (front) or catches the flying prey animals in the air (rear) while circling the ceiling of the shed.

Hunting grounds of a nursery colony of Geoffroy's Bats *(Myotis emarginatus)* in Upper Bavaria. The fields with scattered fruit trees, trees in courtyards, and the agricultural landscape (with compost heaps and barns) are used as intermediate hunting grounds. The main hunting grounds are forests south of the freeway. To reach these the Geoffroy's bats do not simply cross the freeway. They make detours, flying along the green structures and crossing under the freeway at an underpass.

47

Tricks used by prey animals to avoid predation

Specialized hearing organs (tympanal organs) of certain moths (here Vivienna moma*) and lacewings are tuned to the ultrasonic echolocation calls of their hunters. Deliberately dropping and "diving" into the vegetation prolongs the life of many a moth.*

The location and morphological structure of the tympanal organ of Vivienna moma, *a moth (from Hill & Smith, 1984).*

Insects do not allow themselves to be eaten by bats without putting up some resistance. While the insect hunters refined their hunting strategies more and more in the course of their evolution, the prey animals also evolved a diversity of methods to protect themselves from predation. Some flies and a number of moths, for example, can detect the ultrasonic calls of bats with the aid of specialized organs of hearing. If a predator is within hearing range, these insects try to take evasive action to escape or allow themselves to fall to the ground with closed wings. But even here they can be outfoxed by their hunters: Some bat species use higher echolocation frequencies than the insects can detect.

Other moths, such as the foul-tasting wooly bear species, signal to their pursuers through clicking noises that they are inedible. The acoustic warning signal has the same meaning as the warning colors of certain diurnal insects that are addressed to birds as predators. Ultimately it does little good to a wooly bear if it is captured by the bat, bitten to death, and only then spit out. Other moths act as jamming stations. They produce their own ultrasonic signals to confuse the echolocating insect hunters. But here too bats have a few of their own tricks up their sleeve. In the same way as the Indian False Vampire Bat (*Megaderma lyra*) apparently can localize and catch its prey using the prey's own vocalizations alone, the most long-eared representatives of a number of bat families probably are also able to hear and learn the communication signals of their prey animals.

Some leaf katydids in Panama have learned to react to this "eavesdropping" by predators. The males dispense with their revealing courtship song and instead make themselves noticeable by vibrating their bodies. These vibrations travel through the plants to the females without being detectable to hunting bats.

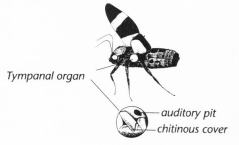

Tympanal organ

— *auditory pit*
— *chitinous cover*

D'Orbigny's Round-eared Bat (Tonatia sylvicola) with a captured katydid. It lives in the Panamanian rainforest and detects its prey animals by "eavesdropping" on their courtship songs.

Hunters of meat and fish

Less than one percent of all bats hunt small terrestrial vertebrates. Two species of the false vampire bat family (Megadermatidae), *Megaderma lyra* (India and Southeast Asia) and the Australian Giant False Vampire Bat, *Macroderma gigas,* regularly hunt and prey on small rodents, birds, frogs, lizards, and even other small bats. From the family of New World leaf-nosed bats (Phyllostomidae), *Phyllostomus hastatus, Vampyrum spectrum, Trachops cirrhosus,* and *Chrotopterus auritus* are known to be carnivorous. In the same way as the false vampire bats, these four species feed on small vertebrates, but to a varying degree also take insects and fruits. All vertebrate hunters are conspicuously large and have to be reckoned among the "giants" of the bat world. The Spectral Vampire (*Vampyrum spectrum*), native to South America and with a wingspan of almost one meter, is the largest bat in the New World.

The Australian Giant False Vampire Bat (*Macroderma gigas*) is the largest (or one of the largest) bat of the Old World microbats. It lives in semi-arid regions, chiefly in north-

The Australian Giant False Vampire (Macroderma gigas) uses its highly sensitive hearing to detect the quietest sounds of its vertebrate prey (small mammals, including bats, and birds).

49

eastern Australia, where it combs its hunting grounds by echolocation and doubtless also with the aid of its large eyes. In the zoological institute of the University of Tübingen, the bat researcher Erwin Kulzer has kept two of these interesting animals for more than 17 years. Each is fed a mouse almost daily. In the time they have been in Tübingen, the two *Macroderma* used have accordingly consumed more than 10,000 laboratory mice. Australian Giant False Vampire Bats employ a kind of "hunting from ambush" strategy. They fly only when a potential prey animal is within "hearing distance."

Erwin Kulzer (1988) gave a riveting account of one of these mouse hunts: "Even faint noises caused by a mouse on the ground arouse the greatest alertness with these bats. Then they turn the huge external ears toward the source of the sound. If the intended prey is still too far away, the bat first flies to a better starting point, often only a meter from the victim. From here the prey is 'listened to' again. Now the echolocation sounds, directed precisely at the prey animal, also become audible. They know their prey very well and are never fooled by dummies. The bats become especially active and excited when they hear the distress calls of young mice somewhere. These are in the ultrasonic range and are normally inaudible to our ears. To determine the exact location of a prey animal, *Macroderma* also flies in the immediate vicinity. In so doing it hovers for seconds only 20 to 30 centimeters above the prey. When it then makes its approach it will have a certain catch, which is played out in fractions of a second. The bat dives with its wings raised like a bell over the prey and lands on it. The contact between the wings and the prey is essential, for only after that does the well-aimed death bite on the nape or throat follow. Occasionally, however, the prey is also grabbed by the nape and carried away in flight. In this case it is killed by several head bites immediately after landing. At the landing place the prey is devoured with skin and hair. The molars and jaws of these bats must have the power of garden shears to be able to cut the prey apart piece by piece. When the bats feed the bursting of the bones is clearly audible. The digestive power of the gastric juices must be enormous as well, for except the mouse's claws and teeth and a few robust vertebrae, no bones appear in the droppings. These re-

mains are densely packed with the likewise indigestible hair."

As is the case with the insectivorous bats, the leavings at the feeding places provide information about the dietary habits of these secretive hunters. Whether flying foxes also occasionally become carnivores is not yet clear. The fruit-eating Hammer-headed Fruit Bat (*Hypsignathus monstrosus*) from western and central Africa has been documented as feeding on discarded dead birds and is also supposed to kill chicks occasionally.

The New Zealand Short-tailed Bat (*Mystacina tuberculata*) is in many respects unusual and has also been observed feeding on dead birds. Apparently carrion is a supplemental source of food in winter for this species.

What fascinating relationships can evolve between predator and prey is shown by the American bat researcher and protector Merlin D. Tuttle with the Frog-eating Bat, *Trachops cirrhosus*. These bats from tropical Central and South America hunt frogs, which they recognize by their songs during the breeding season. To attract females, the male frogs must give their courtship songs. Being detected by the courtship song and possibly even eaten before the mating act is, however, a high price to pay in the name of love. All seemingly simple solutions, such as changing songs, irregular calling, or courting only from a safe refuge, have a decisive disadvantage: to be sure, the courter is not eaten as often, but he is found rarely or not at all by the female. However, there is another, but considerably trickier, method. Bats can readily distinguish the edible frogs from the poisonous ones that occur in the same living space by their calls. For this reason some edible frogs mimic the calls of the poisonous frogs and thereby remain unmolested. Yet another tactic is to abruptly fall silent when a bat appears. How the frogs detect the approaching bats is still unknown. Despite all these tricks, *Trachops cirrhosus* need have no fear of starving. In the end there are always enough unwary "lovers."

THE FISHING BATS

A few bat species prey on fishes. The two most familiar fish-eaters live in the tropics and subtropics of the New World. Though the Fisherman Bat (*Noctilio leporinus*) hunts mostly freshwater fishes, the Fishing Bat, *Pizonyx vivesi*, a close relative of the common *Myotis,* hunts saltwater fishes in still lagoons of the Gulf of California. A *Myotis* species in the Far East has also specialized in catching fishes.

Although it had been suspected for almost a century that the Fisherman Bat caught fishes, for a long time there was a difference of opinion among zoologists as to how the bat finds and catches its prey. Not until the studies by Prentice Bloedel in the 1950's in Panama with film and photographic documentation was light shed on the controversy. The bats, which fly just above the water's surface, detect the fishes only indirectly in that they echolocate the tiny ripples or irregularities of the water's surface. When a fish is detected in this manner, the bats submerge their two large-clawed feet in the water like two grappling irons and grab their unsuspecting prey. The wing and tail membranes do not impede this maneuver. The membrane of the narrow wings only reaches the knee, and with the aid of thick spurs on the legs the tail membrane is pressed tightly to the lower legs when the feet are submerged in the water. As a result the legs suddenly appear to be completely separated from each other. The legs immediately carry the prey to the mouth, and the prey, at least when it is relatively small, is devoured in flight. Thirty to 40 small fishes can be the take from a single night's hunting. Larger fishes are carried by the bats to feeding places where they are consumed. The Fisherman Bat roosts in caves or hollow trees. As a result of the tell-tale fishy smell, the roosts often are easy to find. Because *Pizonyx* catches marine fishes and must occasionally also take in salt water, this fishing bat requires special physiological adaptations of the renal system.

But how did bats take up fishing? It is possible that their ancestors frequently harvested insects from the water's surface and in so doing occasionally also snapped up a little fish. Maybe the Daubenton's Bat (*Myotis daubentoni*) is such a living example of an early fish-hunter. In any case, fish scales and the remains of gill arches of small fishes have been found in the droppings of wild Daubenton's Bats. Daubenton's Bat also has large feet equipped with long toes, which could possibly be used for fishing. In her studies of the hunting behavior of Daubenton's Bat, the zoologist Elisabeth Kalko from Tübingen, Germany, noted that the animals principally take up insects with

The South American Trachops cirrhosus *has specialized in hunting frogs. It distinguishes between poisonous and edible frogs by their calls.*

the tail membrane, sometimes also from the water's surface. To the researcher it appeared that the mass of Daubenton's Bat is too low and the feet of the animal too weak for lifting fishes. Above all, however, the tail membrane would probably get in the way. It cannot be folded away as elegantly as that of the Fisherman Bat and presumably would act as a brake when the feet are deeply submerged, which could make the bat lose its balance.

The plant visitors

Gambian Epauleted Fruit Bat (Epomophorus gambianus, right) "picks" a ripe fig.

A Nile Rousette Fruit Bat (Rousettus aegyptiacus, below) feeding on fruit. They eat only overripe fruits and thus engage in—besides their contribution to the dispersal of food plants—a cost-free harvest in gardens.

Approximately 29 percent of all bats are partially or completely dependent on plants for their food. The flying vegetarians live with these plants in a system of mutual benefit. Whereas they obtain food in the form of nectar, pollen, or fruit, the bats with their mobility contribute to the dispersal of the plants by pollinating them and scattering their seeds.

With few exceptions the bat—plant relationships are limited to tropical and subtropical regions. All members of the Megachiroptera, which includes only one family, the flying foxes (Pteropodidae), and numerous species in the Old World from Africa to Australia, are almost exclusively vegetarian. They likely eat a few insects by accident that are resting on the fruits or flowers. On the other hand, the numerous

plant visitors among the South American leaf-nosed bats (Phyllostomidae) appear to have evolved from insectivorous species. Because many insects readily feed on ripe fruits and their larvae often live in fruits, it is possible that leaf-nosed bats could have developed a taste for fruit while catching insects. It is certain that this type of dietary specialization in bats must have evolved independently on two separate occasions. At the same time, the fruit-eaters have developed many similar (convergent) characters. Both flying foxes and fruit-eating leaf-nosed bats have teeth with broad chewing surfaces and heavily grooved palates for squeezing out fruit juice. Common to all fruit-eaters is a good sense of smell; on the other hand, other methods of orientation point to the variable ancestry. While the

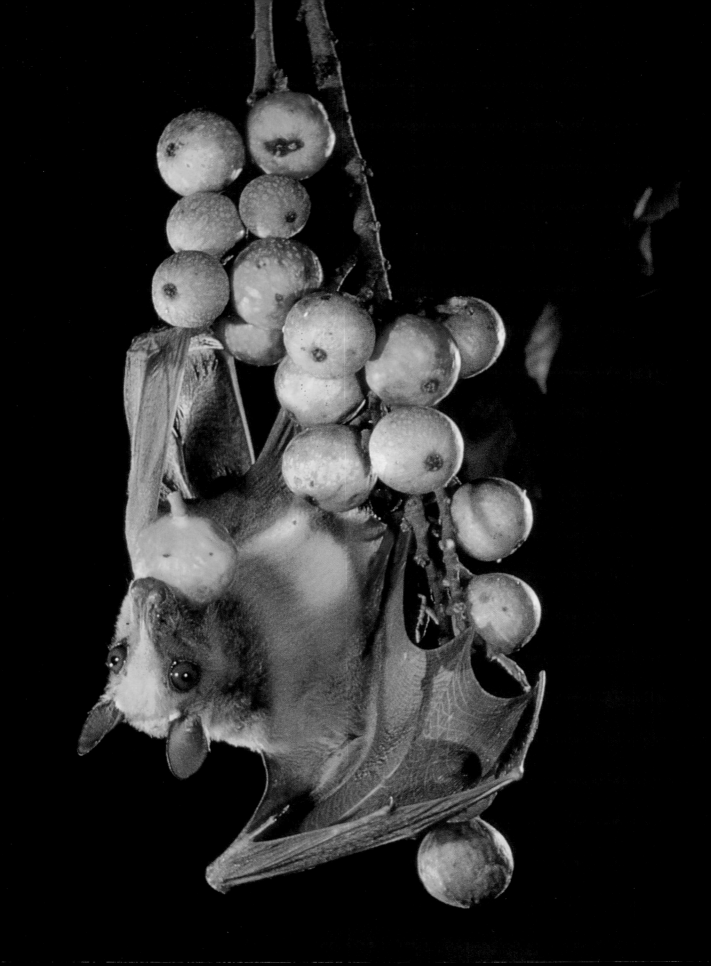

The Mexican Fruit Bat (Artibeus jamaicensis), a member of the South American family of leaf-nosed bats (Phyllostomidae), has seized a ripe fig before carrying it off to consume. Owing to this transport technique, the fig seeds are excreted somewhere else and are thus dispersed.

flying foxes find their food trees with night vision and a good sense of direction, the long-range orientation of the leaf-nosed bats, as is typical of bats, is acoustical with the aid of ultrasound.

The fruit-eaters use the entire supply of tropical fruits, from mangoes, cactus, papayas, guavas, bananas, dates, and citrus fruits to fruits of the fig and pandanus trees. Depending on size, the fruits are either eaten on the spot or carried off. Farmers of all countries are ill-disposed toward the vegetarian bats, because they visit their plantations and devour the fruit. As is so often the case, when man and animal are interested in the same food, the latter is soon branded as a pest.

The reality, however, is much more complex. Merlin D. Tuttle demonstrated with his studies of African epauleted fruit bats that they even do the farmers an important service. In a kind of selective harvesting, the bats seek out only overripe fruits, which otherwise would serve as food for the larvae of the dreaded fruitflies. In the tropical rainforest of Panama in a forested area of 25 hectars, D. W. Morrison recorded all fruiting fig trees and studied their yield. The Neotropical fruit bats, *Artibeus jamaicensis,* that

lived there on ripe figs were equipped with small radio transmitters that were used to determine where the bats consumed their figs. The plant visitors performed thorough gardening work, in that they carried off at least seven percent of the 200,000 figs, corresponding to about 650 kilograms (1430 pounds) that grew in the study area annually. Thus, their digestive systems contributed substantially to the dissemination of the figs.

FLOWER-FEEDING BATS—BAT-POLLINATED FLOWERS

Until the 18th century it was still believed that at least the color and odor of flowers were created by God solely for the edification of mankind. Beyond the symbolic content of their forms, colors, and scents, much of the biological function of flowers as "pollinating entities" remains unknown even today. Because in the flowering plants the male reproductive cells (pollen) cannot actively reach the egg cells to fertilize them, plants use wind, water, or animals as a transport medium.

Most frequently, and probably most successfully, flowers are pollinated by animals. It is necessary, though, that the individual flowering plants must in each case engage the best-suited animal as the pollinator. While wind- and water-pollinated plants do not have to attract anything and their flowers therefore remain small and inconspicuous, the animal-pollinated plants are conspicuous in color, form, and smell. They have evolved a range of attractants. They often lure pollinators visually through conspicuous flowers or inflorescences and chemically through aromatic substances.

Often the attracted pollinator receives a reward in the form of food in the flowers. This can be surplus pollen or nectar produced by the plants. In some species these rewards are freely accessible to any interested party, but in others only certain visitors, such as insects with long proboscises or long-billed birds (hummingbirds, sunbirds) can partake of them. Specialized food hairs are produced by some orchids that are "grazed" by the visitor. Some plants even lure their pollinators with sex. Many ragweed species disperse sex pheromones and mimic female insects with their flowers to lure males of specific insect species from long distances.

The drive for the evolution of flower—pollinator relationships was the competi-

The South American Blossum Fruit Bat (Artibeus lituratus, *above*) simultaneously pollinates its host plant while feeding on pollen.

African Wahlberg's Epauleted Fruit Bat (Epomophorus wahlbergi, *left*) flying to a bat flower.

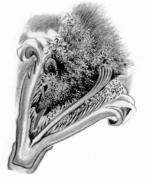

Bat flowers. Cobaea (Cobaea scandens, top). Long-nosed bats pollinate the flowers of columnar cacti (Leptonycteris curasoae, center, and Leptonycteris sanborni, bottom) (after Tuttle).

tion between flowers for potential pollinators as well as the pollinators' competition for flowers. In the course of a long evolution this interaction led to great diversity and a system of mutual adaptation. This process is called co-evolution, and the adaptations that develop in the course of it are called co-adaptations.

To ensure the efficient transfer of pollen, the attracted vistor must as far as possible continue only to visit flowers of the same species. For this reason, flowers have evolved special traits that make them recognizable to the visitors, as well as mechanisms that limit the possible range of visitors.

Whereas it has long been known that plants use insects and birds as pollinators, the pollinating activities of bats remained "in the dark" for a long time. Yet associations between mammals and flowers are comparatively widespread and their ecology is particularly interesting. Five percent of all bats have specialized in visiting flowers and thereby play an important role in pollination. To the flower visitors and nectar drinkers belong the long-tongued fruit bats *(Macroglossus)* as well as various species of the New World leaf-nosed bats. In the opinion of researchers, the evolution of this mode of feeding must have occurred independently on at least two occasions. In both cases in the course of evolution a true symbiosis, a system of mutual benefit between plant and animal, was achieved. The

botanist Klaus Dobat along with Therese Peikert-Holle in 1985 collected and evaluated in one book for the first time all of the scattered research reports about flower-visiting bats.

The first clear indication that bats visit flowers came from a traveler in the year 1772 who observed numerous flying foxes on palms on Réunion Island. Not until the 1950's did scientists begin to study this phenomenon intensively.

The plants pollinated by bats are most commonly trees, shrubs, or columnar cacti. Many lianas and tree-dwelling epiphytes are pollinated by bats as well, whereas small perennials and herbs, the flowers of which do not rise much above the ground, are rarely visited. Apparently the main point is to make it easier for the bats to fly to the flower. To this end some plants have evolved standing or hanging pedicels that can be several meters long. Other flowers grow directly from the stalk and so attract the attention of the visitor to themselves. The flowers are predominantly bell- and cone-shaped. Bats, however, also visit entire inflorescences. Typical of bat flowers are tough perianths (corolla and sepals) that can withstand the claws of the perching visitor. Because bats visit in twilight or at night and are probably colorblind anyway, flower coloration seems less important. Decisive, on the other hand, are nocturnal opening times and scent. The description of the palette of scents ranges from "cabbage smell" to "rancid," "winey," or simply "foul." Interestingly, comparable smells are also found in the fruits of many plants whose seeds are dispersed by fruit-eating bats. In some cases the flower scent resembles that of the animal itself, which apparently has an especially appealing effect on the visitors.

Bat-pollinated flowers often wilt surprisingly fast. The short blooming period is balanced out in that many flowers on one plant bloom on consecutive nights and produce abundant amounts of pollen.

As a reward for visiting a flower, bats usually obtain nectar or a sugary attractive food ("food body"). Plants have also evolved a variety of strategies for "powdering" the visitors' fur in very specific places and thereby ensuring the transfer of pollen.

Mutual evolution has also led to numerous adaptations on the part of the flower-visiting bats. In them the teeth, jaws, and chewing muscles have degenerated, while the facial area of the skull is pointed well forward. The flower specialists also have a long, tapered, and highly mobile tongue with which it is particularly easy to take up nectar. "Brushy tongues," which result from numerous long papillae on the surface, simplify the uptake of fluids.

Though the small flower-visiting flying foxes of Africa and Southeast Asia and the less specialized leaf-nosed bats of America (Phyllostominae, Carolliinae, Stenodermatinae) always land on the flower when feeding and lap up nectar and pollen while perching or hanging, the long-tongued bats (glossophagines), the "hummingbirds of the night," hover before the throat of flower and reach the nectar like a flash with their long tongue. With twelve licking movements per second, *Glossophaga soricina*, the Shrewish Long-tongued Bat, is able to suck out about a milliliter (0.2 teaspoon) of nectar in hovering flight. The researchers Otto and Dagmar von Helversen from Erlangen, Germany, have studied in detail the hovering flight of this species in the wild and in laboratory experiments and also have calculated the necessary energy budget of the bat.

What at first glance looks so effortless to the human observer turns out to be hard work upon closer examination. By supplying only very small portions of nectar, the flowers have ensured that the bats must visit often. Completely in their own "evolutionary interest," this increases the likelihood of pollination, particularly when many individuals compete for the nectar in the flowers. The flower-visiting bat thus absolutely does not fly through a "land of milk and honey," although the highly concentrated flower nectar can satisfy the animal's energy requirement better than any other food.

If we consider the total area in which bat-pollinated flowers occur, two main areas of distribution can be distinguished. The larger area encompasses predominantly the moist, warm, and forested zones of Africa, Asia, and Australia, and largely coincides with the occurrence of the flying foxes. The smaller extends across the tropics and subtropics of North, Central, and South America, where representatives of the microbats occupy suitable ecological niches. Decisive for the occurrence of bat pollination are not, as is often assumed, tropical climatic conditions, but rather the absence of a limiting vegetative phase, such as winter. Therefore, both main areas of occurrence are located between the latitudes of 30 degrees north and

In the Old World, flying foxes occupy the position of flower feeders. A Long-tongued Fruit Bat (Macroglossus sobrinus, top) has landed on an inflorescence of Oroxylum indicum to feast from an open blossom (after a photograph by v. Helversen). The Indian Short-faced Fruit Bat (Cynopterus sphinx, center) takes its flower meal on a wild banana (after a photograph by Tuttle).

An example of the typical flight path of a flower-visiting flying fox in Malaysia (right). After making the rounds of open Oroxylum blossoms, the animal dives a story lower to the inflorescence of a wild banana (after Dobat, 1985).

57

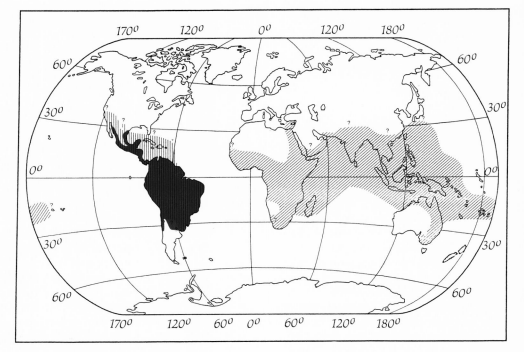

Flowers and blood. Distribution of blood-feeding in bats and the true vampires (Desmodontinae). Vertical lines = area of bat pollination (New World); diagonal lines = area of flying fox pollination (Old World); the exception makes the rule: on New Zealand Mystacina tuberculata *is the only insectivorous bat of the Old World that feeds on pollen; red areas = occurrence of true vampires (after Dobat, 1985, supplemented after Yalden & Morris, 1975).*

30 degrees south and also include the subtropics.

A continuous food supply is ensured in that the flowering periods of the bat-pollinated flowers overlap. In addition, for some flower-visiting bats there is also the possiblity of changing over to a mixed feeding strategy or temporarily switching to fruits or insects. Species that have not adopted this strategy can also fly to the flowers in seasonal migrations.

The flower diet in the Old World is otherwise exploited only by the flying foxes, and the New Zealand Short-tailed Bat, *Mystacina tuberculata,* is the only insectivorous bat of the Old World that is also a pollen-feeder, as has been shown by examination of the stomach contents. The zoologist Daniel subsequently also found pollen on the head and breast fur of these animals and was even able to observe nectar and pollen uptake in captivity. These findings argue for at least occasional feeding on flower products. Whether this is a question of a long-standing plant association that was retained on the isolated island of New Zealand, or whether we are experiencing a new symbiosis in its early stages, will possibly remain a secret of the New Zealand bats forever. One species of the two in the genus has already disappeared because of changes due to colonization, and the second *(M. tuberculata)* is severely threatened or perhaps already extinct.

Generally speaking, because of the continued destruction of the tropical rainforests, many open questions about the symbiosis of flowers and bats will never be answered.

Real draculas

Only three species from the great diversity of the bats do what many people first call to mind about bats: suck blood. The sucking of the essential fluids of others has doubtless always stirred mankind's imagination. A thing that elicits disgust also has the power to instill fear. Thus it was suspected at first that the Asiatic flying fox named *Vespertilio vampyrus* by Linnaeus and the Spectral Vampire (*Vampyrum spectrum*), the largest bat in South America, were blood suckers. But as is so often the case, reality turns out to be completely different. The true vampires are neither especially large, nor are they terrifying, and they are native only to Central and South America. Moreover, they are particularly affectionate among themselves. Members of the large New World leaf-nosed bat family Phyllostomidae, today the three blood-sucking species are classified in a separate subfamily, Desmodontinae. They are the only warm-blooded animals that feed exclusively on blood, and they have thereby attained the most extreme dietary specialization of all the bats and are the only true parasites.

The Hairy-legged Vampire (*Diphylla ecaudata*) feeds almost exclusively on bird blood, and the quite rare White-winged Vampire (*Diaemus youngi*) is also supposed to prefer the blood of birds. On the other hand, the most common and familiar species of this subfamily, the Common Vampire Bat (*Desmodus rotundus*), lives almost exclusively on mammal blood. The Common Vampire Bats have certainly profited from cattle ranching in Central and South America. Whereas originally they were able to feed only on the blood of wild animals, in the enormous herds of cattle in Latin America they found an inexhaustible blood bank. Not the loss of blood, but rather the communication of rabies and other diseases seriously threatened the cattle herds. Therefore, in the 1960's the FAO, a worldwide health organization, sent a goup of experts to develop effective control measures against vampire bats. In addition to the work of American zoologist Greenhall, who has dedicated decades of his life to the vampire problem, we have learned a great deal about the fascinating lives of vampires above all through the field and laboratory studies of the zoologist Uwe Schmidt from Bonn, Germany.

The Common Vampire Bat roosts in fairly small colonies. The animals hang close together in mixed groups of males and females. They spend a lot of time grooming, in which the social component plays a large role. The animals recognize one another individually. Studies of the feeding behavior in the laboratory reveal the existence of a hierarchy. Fights during food intake or while roosting are, however, always resolved without bloodshed. Although they occasionally raise quite a ruckus with shrill cries and beating wings, the vampires never use their sharp teeth on one another. On the contrary, they raise their heads and turn their open mouths away from their rival in close combat. They merely clinch and beat with the folded wings like boxers. Not until the onset of darkness do the shy animals leave their roosts. Often two to six animals travel together. In contrast to many insectivorous bats, vampires fly just above the ground. The extreme dietary specialization requires specialized sensory performance. By smell, by appearance, or with the aid of echolocation, and even by the radiated body heat and breathing sounds, the vampire bats recognize and locate their hosts, which often lie hidden under shrubbery or houses. Without disturbing their victims,

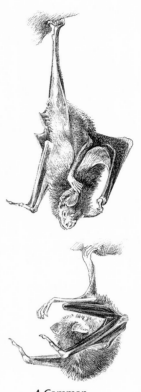

A Common Vampire (*Desmodus rotundus*) *in the act of grooming: "combing" with the foot (above) and licking (below).*

A Common Vampire (*Desmodus rotundus*) *taking a blood meal from a chicken's leg.*

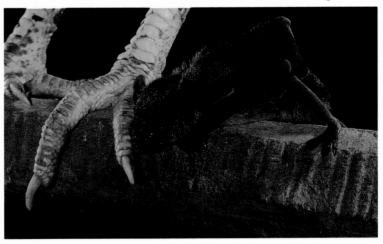

The adaptation becomes clear in portrait: the Common Vampire (Desmodus rotundus) has a flat face so as to be able to use the pointed, razor-sharp upper incisors on the host animal. The blood meal is drunk in pipette fashion between the tongue and the lower groove in the mouth.

the bats must find a suitable place to bite. Vampires do not fall upon their blood donors, but rather approach them "on tiptoes." The vampire bat either lands directly on the chosen animal or just alongside it on the ground. Jumping in all directions, they can avoid the movements of the host and almost seem to stalk around their victim as if performing a dance. Several minutes go by before the first drops of blood flow.

Uwe Schmidt has observed the process closely and described it impressively. First the vampire carefully licks an area of its victim's skin about a square centimeter (half an inch) in size and slobbers heavily on the surface. Then it presses its open mouth to the skin and closes it while continuing to lick. In this way finally a tiny fold of skin ends up between the pointed and razor-sharp upper incisors and the tiny lower incisors. Now the bat leans forward abruptly, closes its jaws, and bites off the fold of skin. The victim scarcely notices the painless bite. At this moment the bat jumps back, spits out the skin, and prepares to take up the freshly flowing blood. In so doing the vampire does not suck up the blood, but rather places its lower lip at the edge of the wound and moves its tongue back and forth about two to three millimeters (less than an eight of an inch). The blood forms a small bridge between the wound and the lower lip and then flows into the mouth. It then reaches the gullet through a groove in the middle of the tongue. To drink its fill a vampire must stay at the wound for eight to ten minutes. Often several animals can share a bite, because it takes a while for it to close because of the anticoagulants that enter the wound in the bats' saliva. It has also been observed that a bat visited the same victim

60

on several consecutive nights and always reopened the old wound.

Blood-sucking is in other respects a very "weighty" proposition. A vampire bat ingests up to 40 milliliters (8 teaspoons) of blood a night, which corresponds to about 132 percent of its body weight. The high water content in blood is a great burden on the bat's body. The bats first excrete a portion of the fluid during food intake through the urine; furthermore, the blood is rapidly concentrated in the stomach and intestinal tract. Even so, a large volume of fluid remains. It is stored in a 15-centimeter-long (6 inches) gastric blind sac that fills up almost the entire abdominal cavity. Filled up in this way, the vampire must still carry a heavy weight on the flight back to the roost. Calculations have shown that a net gain in energy through the intake of blood is possible only in the tropics. In the temperate zones, because of the lower ambient air temperature, more energy is expended to maintain bodily functions. Therefore, a vampire could meet this increased energy demand only through the increased intake of food and would have to take as much as twice as much blood as in the tropics. This would be impossible for even the most industrious vampire.

It is now known why vampires in South America feed on Swiss cows more frequently than Zebu cattle, as well as why they prefer calves and cows in heat. The zoologist Dennis C. Turner discovered that these preferences are not questions of taste, but rather can be explained by the behavior of the animals. Vampires choose their victims based on how exposed and accessible they are. Thus the Swiss cattle were always found at the perimeter of the herd. Calves slept longer than their mothers, and cows in heat likewise maintained an exposed position on the edge of the herd. Though Turner found

most bites on the neck and shoulder areas of the cattle, from the middle of the rainy season on he observed more wounds on unusual parts of the body. Turner's explanation is that young vampire bats now were present and had to learn where best to bite.

The highly specialized food intake demands correspondingly complex adaptations. After a long gestation period of a full seven months, female vampires generally give birth to one youngster. The juvenile development of the vampire bat also takes place very slowly in comparison with the majority of other bat species. The young continue to be suckled up to an age of nine months. The change from a milk to a blood diet seems to be very difficult, first requiring a change in the physiology of digestion. The transfer of specific strains of bacteria through the intake of droppings probably plays an essential role here. Relatively early on, the youngsters will lick small amounts of blood from the mouths of returning adults.

Motherless youngsters are not doomed to starve, but are adopted by other females. In the event that the female is not producing milk at that time, the orphaned youngster activates the mammary glands by sucking on them.

Starting at about the fourth to fifth month of life, the young accompany the mother while foraging and initially drink from the same wound. A characteristic appeasement behavior protects the youngster from aggressive altercations with conspecifics on the host animal. In addition, it lifts its folded wings away from the side of the body when it approaches, and in this way signals unequivocally: "I am still small and inexperienced." Who would have expected vampires to have such social tendencies?

Dance of the vampires—not around the Golden Calf, but rather to satisfy hunger. Vampire bats can approach their blood donors stealthily "on all fours" and avoid them in implike fashion by hopping in any direction (after Schober, 1983).

61

Hunter and Hunted— the Rivals

Above:
In Europe the Pine Marten finds its bat prey by "groping" in tree holes.

Right:
An Indian Brown Hawk-Owl (Ninox scutulata, right) has caught a Yellow House Bat (Scotophilus heathi).

page 63 (top):
The African Harrier-Hawk (left) probes deftly with its long legs downward (for chicks) and upward (for bats).

page 63 (bottom):
Rare, but possible—a rainbow trout seizes a bat that is hunting just above the water's surface.

page 63 (center):
A Southeastern Myotis (Myotis austroriparius, below) in the jaws of a Corn Snake, Elaphe guttata.

Sometimes the nocturnal hunters themselves become the hunted. For example, an African and Asian raptor, the Bat Hawk, *Macheiramphus alcinus*, has successfully specialized on bats, which it catches and eats as they enter and leave their roosts. Other birds of prey in these regions also profit from hunting near tropical caves with bat roosts. The African Harrier-Hawk (*Polyboroides typus*) employs a specialized hunting technique. With its unusually long, very nimble legs it checks tree cavities for prey. This specialist preys on birds, probably mainly nestlings, as well as bats. The Eurasian Tree Marten employs similar techniques. From prey lists and direct observations we know that several European owls, the Northern Goshawk, Peregrine, Eurasian Hobby, and Eurasian Kestrel occasionally kill bats, with Common Pipistrelles (*Pipistrellus pipistrellus*) and Noctules (*Nyctalus noctula*) caught most frequently. Probably the most successful bat hunter is the Common Barn Owl, followed by the Tawny Owl. As "roostmates," individual Common Barn Owls can almost specialize in preying on bats. Posted at the narrow exit of a Mouse-eared Bat roost, tasty *Myotis myotis* literally fall into their laps.

Raccoons (*Procyon lotor*), skunks (*Conepatus* and *Mephitis*), and a few snakes are occasional bat-hunters. The Asiatic rat snakes (*Ptyas* and *Elaphe*), like birds of prey, sometimes wait outside bat caves for bats leaving the roost. Pythons have also been observed "clearing" flying foxes from their roosts. The list of successful bat-hunters can be extended. The American Bobcat (*Lynx rufus*) occasionally captures young bats when they fall from the roof of their cave. The potto (*Perodicticus potto*), an African representative of the primates, has been

observed eating a Straw-colored Fruit Bat (*Eidolon helvum*). It has been reported that the American Greater Roadrunner (*Geococcyx velox*) catches Red Bats (*Lasiurus borealis*). American and Asiatic crows have also been observed with bat prey. And even bullfrogs (*Rana catesbeiana*) and rainbow trout number among the "bat catchers." Domestic cats can also become bat-hunters when they find a roost in their territory and can station themselves at the roost's exit. Where bats fly by regularly, they can also be caught in flight. Finally, in tropical regions bats have enemies even within their own ranks. The large carnivorous species, such as *Phyllostomus hastatus* and *Vampyrum spectrum* in South America, and the African Slit-faced Bat (*Nycteris grandis*) as well as the Asiatic and Australian false vampire bats (Megadermatidae), successfully hunt their smaller relatives. The South American Peters's Woolly False Vampire (*Chrotopterus auritus australis*), which hunts from ambush, is most successful with young, unwary vampires (*Desmodus*) that carelessly approach its hanging and perching places. This bat envelops them like a flash with its wings in Count Dracula fashion and kills them with a bite without leaving its perch.

Finally, a bat's life can even end in a spider web. One Papua New Guinea Com-

mon Pipistrelle would have met its end as a spider cocktail in the web of the Silk Spider, *Nephila maculata*, had it not been discovered in time and released after its wings were cleaned successfully.

Small Pests—the Parasites

Besides fleas, bat flies, bugs, and mites, ticks also number among the parasites of bats. Here a tick takes its blood meal above the eye of a Natterer's Bat (Myotis nattereri).

Like any other mammal, probably no bat is totally free of parasites. Some live as internal parasites (endoparasites) inside the host animal's body. The external parasites (ectoparasites) profit from the gregarious and sedentary social life of their bat hosts as well as the favorable environment in the roost. Though among the bats there are only three true blood-drinkers, a whole army of small pests feeds on the essential fluids of bats. Many highly specialized mite species and a few ticks suck blood from their hosts. While ticks attach firmly to one spot, the smaller mites are extremely mobile parasites in the pelt and on the wing membranes, which they can even perforate. More

by swimming than running, the spiderlike, flightless bat flies (Nycteribiidae), of which there are more than 250 species worldwide, flit around in bat pelts. European bats alone are host to 11 different flea species of the family Ischnopsyllidae.

Other typical bat parasites include the true bugs (Cimicidae). Among bug researchers it is speculated that the Bedbug (*Cimex lectularius*) made the transfer to our beds when people in remote antiquity settled in caves with bat colonies. The bugs stay on their host only to feed. At other times they remain at the roost. Because of the roost-faithful habits of the inhabitants, they can even stay at the summer roost when the bats withdraw to their winter roost. The following spring the involuntary blood donors are of course sure to return! A few bugs, however, occasionally make the trip with the hosts. It has been determined that fertilized female bugs go along on flights and in this way successfully disperse their offspring to new roosts.

Even the occurrence and distribution of bat species can be determined from the distribution of highly specialized bat parasites. As Dieter Kock determined in his studies, in Europe the most northeasterly reports and documentation of the bat fly *Phthiridium biarticulatum*, which lives exclusively on horseshoe bats, all date from the last century. For the bat researcher this is proof that the decline of horseshoe bats in central Europe had already begun in the 19th century. Today the populations of the hosts no longer appear to be dense enough to support the reproductive cycle of the parasites.

Love and Death—a Bat's Life

The reproductive behavior of bats can be just as variable as their habits. Depending on the living space, the food supply, and the availability of roosts, different species have developed different reproductive strategies, starting with mate selection and courtship behavior and ending with the rearing of the young.

LARGE AND SMALL DIFFERENCES

Among European species, the sexes can be distinguished only with difficulty. As is true of most bats of the temperate climatic zones, their secondary sex characters are minimally expressed or even absent. Their primary sex characters are usually well hidden in the pelt or, as in the common bats, additionally covered in the resting state by the tail membrane folded onto the belly. Here the "small difference" can be a dependable aid to identification with difficult to distinguish species. For example, the end of the penis is clearly thickened in full-grown males of Brandt's Bat (*Myotis brandti*), but males of the Whiskered Bat (*Myotis mystacinus*) have a thin penis without thickening at the end. Males of the Grey and Common Long-eared Bats (*Plecotus austriacus*, *Plecotus auritus*) can also be distinguished in this way. The testes and epididymis are located side by side in the lower part of the abdominal cavity and protrude only during mating season.

Larger sex differences are found only in a few tropical bat species. Body size, fur color, specific olfactory glands, and even the dentition can be conspicuous secondary sex characters. Males of the flying fox genera *Pteropus* and *Epomophorus*, for example, are considerably larger than the females. The opposite is true with a few slit-faced bats (Nycteridae), false vampire bats (Megadermatidae), and New World leaf-nosed bats (Phyllostomidae). Finally, the sexes of the Hammer-headed Fruit Bat (*Hypsignathus monstrosus*), with the virtually rectangular and hammer-shaped head

of the male, are unmistakable. The richer pelt color of the male can also be used as a distinguishing character.

In a few species the males exhibit conspicuous hair growths. When the courting males of the African free-tailed bats *Tadarida chapini*, *T. pumila*, and *T. nigeriae* erect the tuft of long hair on the head, in profile they seem to sport a "Mohawk" hairdo. Male little collared fruit bats (*Myonycteris*) and the males of various tomb bats (*Taphozous*) have a beardlike tuft of hair in the throat region. The shoulder fur of *Epomophorus* males gave these bats their common name "epauleted fruit bats." Specialized skin glands in various places on the body characterize the males of many bat species. Because of a brushlike haired glandular field in the middle of the forehead of their males, a species of leaf-nosed bat is named for the one-eyed Greek giants: *Hipposideros cyclops*.

BAT LOVE—MATING BEHAVIOR OF BATS

"Bats copulate like most animals of the order of the primates (!) from the front, whereby they embrace each other with the front legs," wrote the German bat researcher Koch in 1865. This observation by the old master of bat science, however, seems to be just as erroneous as reports asserting that the American Red Bat, *Lasiurus borealis*, mates in flight. The mating position of bats is much more commonplace than that: it takes place while hanging and—as is usual for the majority of mammals—from behind (with respect to the female's back). But the particulars are often very unusual.

The mating season of European bats begins when the nursery roosts break up. In many species it can extend throughout the stay in the winter roost and on into the spring. The sperm of the males develop in late summer and, as the zoologists Racey and Kulzer have described, can be stored the entire winter in the mature state in the

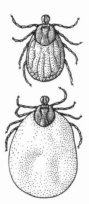

Bat parasites. From top to bottom. Tick; engorged tick; bat fly (Nycteribia biarticulata).

65

This storage of sperm has clear advantages: The male sperm can mature at a time when the bats are in peak condition after a food-rich summer. On the other hand, it is beneficial to delay germinal development so that embryonic development and the birth of the young take place at a time when the females can take in sufficient food, so that they can store up the necessary energy for reproductive performance.

In Europe only Schreiber's Bat (*Miniopterus schreibersi*) attains the same goal by a different method. During the winter there are no longer any sperm in the epididymis of the males of this species and winter copulations do not occur. Schreiber's Bat uses another, among mammals more common, method to bridge over the winter season. Immediately after mating in the fall, the ovum is fertilized, but embryonic development is then interrupted at an early stage of development and is not started again until the spring. Reproductive strategies similar to those of the bats of the temperate climatic zones have also been found in a few tropical leaf-nosed bats (Emballonuridae). In this way they can ensure that their young will be born at the start of the food-rich rainy season.

LIVELY GOINGS ON IN THE WINTER ROOST

That European bats do not sleep away the winter, but rather also mate in the winter roost, was a surprising research finding. Matings in winter have been observed in the Pond Bat (*Myotis dasycneme*), the Whiskered Bat (*Myotis mystacinus*), Natterer's Bat (*Myotis nattereri*), the Barbastelle (*Barbastella barbastellus*), the Common Long-eared Bat (*Plecotus auritus*), and particularly frequently in Daubenton's Bat (*Myotis daubentoni*). Roer and Egsbaek made in-depth studies of the mating behavior of Daubenton's Bats in the chalk mines of Jutland. In addition, the bat experts Grimmberger and Hackethal together with their Polish colleague Urbanczyk observed and photographed the activities in what is probably the largest European winter roost in Nietoperek in western Poland.

The most frequent mating activites of Daubenton's Bat were confirmed for the months of October to November by all observers. The animals mated in the warmer parts of the winter roost (temperature between 7.5 and 9.2° C, 46 and 49°F), whereas they hibernated in other areas with lower

Greater Mouse-eared Bats (Myotis myotis, top) mate in so-called "honeymoon suites." Local knowledge and possibly also pheromone glands of the "groom" attract successive females.

A pair of Indian Leaf-nosed Bats (Hipposideros bicolor, bottom) just before mating.

epididymis. On the other hand, the ovaries and vagina of the females are in a pre-estral condition from the start of the mating season and through the winter. Only in conjunction with the winter sleep do the female oocytes mature, and only then can they be fertilized. Bats have achieved the delay between copulation and fertilization with the "trick" of sperm storage: the sperm remain in a resting state in the female genital tract. Only after ovulation in the spring do the until then immobile sperm reactivate and fertilize the female's egg.

temperatures. The actively breeding male Daubenton's Bats fly around in the winter roost and land repeatedly on the walls in their search for females, before crawling around for a short distance.

Trial and error play a large role in the search for mates in Daubenton's Bat. Everything that can happen before successful mating is achieved was observed by Grimmberger, Hackethal, and Urbanczyk. An active male Daubenton's Bat searched for a female in a cluster consisting of Daubenton's Bats (*Myotis daubentoni*), the Greater Mouse-eared Bat (*Myotis myotis*), and the Common Long-eared Bat (*Plecotus auritus*). "In so doing it crawled between and over the sleeping animals, even across their nape fur and ears, forced its head under the animal it was examining at the moment and inspected the genital region; in short pauses inbetween it licked its own genitals. In this way in a short time all of the animals in the cluster, regardless of the species they belonged to, had been disturbed from their winter sleep. They emitted the typical prolonged, shrill vocalizations of bats disturbed in hibernation, but soon fell silent again when the male turned its attention to another potential mate. When the male has found a female, it assumes the mating posture. In so doing it as a rule embraces with its lower arms those of the female, and its trunk rests on the female's back, with its head reaching the female's nape region. Both sexes hold their ears spread to the side, not erect as is usual in the active, undisturbed state. Both the female and the male cling fast to the substrate with their hind legs. At first the male beats against

Like the horseshoe bats, the leaf-nosed bats also live in mixed-sex groups. Here the father shows interest in his offspring, which is holding onto the belly fur of the mother and also sucks tightly to a sturdy false teat (Hipposideros bicolor, above).

The male Grey Long-eared Bat (Plecotus austriacus, left) has mounted its mate to copulate.

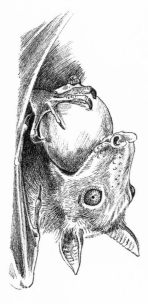

Hammer-headed Fruit Bat (Hypsignatus monstrosus). Above a male, below a female with a fig (from a photograph by Tuttle).

the sleeping female with his forearms, kicks her with his hind legs, rubs her head on his nape region, or bites her in the nape fur or on the ears. Apparently only when the female starts to become active does the intromission (insertion) of the penis follow under the uropatagium (tail membrane) of the female. Because the Vespertilionidae fold the uropatagium onto the belly at rest, the female must first spread this slightly before the penis can be inserted. There then follow phases in which the male carries out frequent pelvic movements for a few seconds, while simultaneously biting the nape fur and the ears of the female, while the female scolds loudly with wide-open mouth and raised head."

The difference in degrees of wakefulness during mating in the winter roost is probably unique for mammals. While the ready-to-mate males are fully active, the females have just awakened during mating and during this waking phase still find themselves in a semilethargic state. Thus they have no chance to select their mate or even to avoid copulation. The male Daubenton's Bat can practically dispense with courtship behavior. For mating success it is sufficient merely to find and awaken a female. Further stimulation of the female seems superfluous. The sperm is merely deposited in the uterus; months will still go by before actual fertilization.

Though it is not yet known whether the

vocalizations of the female Daubenton's Bat during mating have a stimulating effect on other males, such a transfer of mood plays a large role with the Indian Giant Flying Fox.

CRIES OF PROTEST LEAD TO MASS COPULATION

The zoologist Gerhard Neuweiler was able to observe from a high perch for a period of 14 months life in a colony of about a thousand Indian Giant Flying Foxes (*Pteropus giganteus*) that roosted in four free-standing banyan trees in a garden in the middle of Madras. With these animals, which were always observed from a distance, the first problem for males was to overcome the individual distance of the females. Neuweiler observed that in the breeding season no true pairs formed, but rather the sexually mature males copulated with any female that alighted next to them. The researcher writes:

"Copulation is always initiated by the male; even during the height of the mating season in July/August the females behave passively and even brusquely. Males sniff as they approach the females and try to lick them in the genital region. This licking makes the females less unfriendly and more accommodating. Then the male tries to hang behind the female. It grabs the female by the nape with the teeth, shoves the long, erect penis between the female's legs forward to the vulva, and begins to copulate. The females always react with shrill defensive cries against copulation. Very rarely does the first copulation lead to fertilization; usually the male does not ejaculate until the third, immediately successive copulation. Successful copulation is recognizable by white drops of fluid on the female's vulva and by the male's quiet behavior. After unsuccessful copulations or when the female succeeds in warding off the male, the male reacts with persistent, very loud cries of protest, which is thought to intimidate the female and make her more receptive to renewed attempts at copulation. This shrill cry of protest also sounds when the female tries to leave its roosting place.

"The cries of protest, however, also have a stimulating effect on the whole colony. At the height of the breeding season the cries of protest of a single male stimulate other males to make their own attempts at copulation. Within a few minutes such a colony of flying foxes, which until then had been quiet, is transformed into a deafening screeching and copulating mass."

Neuweiler determined that during the height of the breeding season these synchronous mass copulations, triggered by the cries of protest of a single male, can last up to an hour.

ATTRACTION AND COURTSHIP

Intimidation tactics and simultaneous copulations with hibernating females are not the only ways male bats approach their mates. Some species are also—in human terms—much more charming in their search for mates.

Male tree bats, such as Noctules and Nathusius' Pipistrelles, exhibit a fairly well-developed mating behavior. In the breeding season they occupy their courtship roosts, such as tree cavities or bat boxes, in which they stay for several weeks. In his studies of a population of Noctules in the Ebersberger Forest east of Munich, Germany, Fritz Kronwitter found that the roosting behavior of males changed during mating season. At other times several animals usually shared a tree cavity and frequently changed roosts, but now individual male Noctules occupied a tree cavity for a fairly long period of time and defended it against others of their sex. With monotonous calls given inside their roosts they attempted to attract females. Jürgen Gebhard, a bat researcher from Basel, Switzerland, was able to observe this behavior in his bat station with his tame male noctule, "Apus," at close range. When Apus, who was kept at liberty, developed into a territorial male (that is, he occupied and defended a territory) in the fall, he positioned himself at the entrance of Gebhard's bat station and began to "sing." In this way he attracted 26 new arrivals in September, 1986.

The bat researcher Heise observed the mating behavior of Nathusius' Pipistrelle in the Uckermark. The males occupied bat boxes hung up as courtship roosts. Then they defended these roosts and the surrounding territories against other males. Through courtship calls given from the box or in flight in the breeding territory, the male Nathusius's Pipistrelles attract females and also pursue them in flight. Then, together with the females of their harem, they occupy their courtship roost. But while a breeding territory is often occupied by the same male for years, the females are much more fickle and enter several harems in

succession. The smallest European species, the Common Pipistrelle, displays a similar breeding behavior.

Particolored Bats (*Vespertilio murinus*) also occupy courtship territories during their migrations. This species, which probably inhabited crevices originally, seems to readily accept and occupy as a courtship territory tall, clifflike buildings during courtship. Particolored Bats apppear to settle in these territories during the migrations they undertake. According to observations by von Helversen, the cathedral in Freiburg, Germany, which projects like an isolated, jagged

Mating of Daubenton's Bat (Myotis daubentoni) in the winter roost. Though the mounting male is wide awake, the female is in a lethargic state. The slowly awakening female often scolds loudly in the direction of the "suitor" with open mouth and raised head.

peak, seems to have a special attraction for Particolored Bats. He writes on this subject, "Every year on nights in late fall, calling animals (presumably courting males) can be detected on the Freiburg cathedral. The courtship-flying animals (usually one, occasionally two animals) fly in relatively slow, direct flight in large loops above the cathedral courtyard and adjoining streets, and pass by the cathedral towers at intervals of several minutes. The loud call, a high, rapid, steady 'zit/zit/zit/zit . . .,' is clearly audible to young people. The highest courtship intensity occurs in November, with the animals preferring warmer, often misty nights." We were able to observe something similar around the towers of the Church of Our Lady in Munich.

"LADIES' CHOICE" IN THE "HONEYMOON SUITE"

Male Mouse-eared Bats seem to behave more passively. During the summer they live separately from their females and oc-

cupy individual roosts near the nursery roost, which they defend against other males. After the nursery roost breaks up, the lone males are visited by females. In this way the male roosts become "honeymoon suites," as Brigitte and Willi Issel have so aptly named them. Our observations at Mouse-eared Bat colonies in the Au show that the males sometimes make their individual roosts under the same roof as the females. Nevertheless, even then the males do not pursue females. Territorial male Mouse-eared Bats do not appear to need active courtship. The pheromones released by their large facial glands and the glandular secretion smeared at the hanging place are apparently completely sufficient to lure as if by magic ready-to-mate females.

"LADIES' CHOICE" AT THE SINGING LESSON

When bats live in colonies, finding mates does not seem to be much of a problem. But how do lone bats find each other in the riot of plants in tropical forests? Such a problem is presented to us by the Hammer-headed Fruit Bat (*Hypsignathus monstrosus*). In 1977 the American zoologist J. W. Bradbury described possibly the most interesting mating behavior of any bat. Courtship sites (leks) where males gather to display during breeding season are used by birds, including several grouse and pheasant species as well as bowerbirds. Among mammals only the Uganda Kob, a species of African antelope, and the aforementioned Hammer-headed Fruit Bat exhibit a pronounced "arena or lek courtship." Whereas the male birds court for the females with conspicuous plumage, the male Uganda Kobs use the advantage of the open savanna to be visually conspicuous in their small breeding territories. The Hammer-heads, as nocturnal animals, have arrived at an acoustic solution to attract the attention of females.

The huge male Hammer-heads fly to special, traditional hanging sites, where they land close together in the trees and begin their peculiar singing session. The grotesque appearance of the males, with their greatly distended snout, the lobelike enlarged sucking lips, and the huge larynx, is all due to modifications in the name of courtship. Scarcely have the first singers landed when there begins a loud, metallic squawking, "honk . . . honk . . . honk . . .," which is repeated in a regular rhythm 50 to 120 times a minute. More and more males

Aroused by a female hanging above it in the roost tree, the Indian Giant Flying Fox (Pteropus giganteus, above) from Sri Lanka licks its erect penis.

A male Particolored Bat (Vespertilio murinus, right) launches itself from a cliff on its courtship flight.

In slow, relatively direct flights, crags or, by way of substitute, buildings are circled by the male Particolored Bat (Vespertilio murinus) while emitting high-pitched, rapid courtship calls to attract females.

gather, until the honking chorus resembles an overflowing frog pond. If another male gets too close to a "singer," he is driven off with hissing, wheezing, and beating of the wings. After nightfall the much more delicate females appear and fly silently toward the parade of singers. Brought to a state of excitement, the up to 100-member chorus of males now intensifies its concert. When a female takes a liking to a particular male, she flutters back and forth in front of him. The chosen one now intensifies his courting through more rapid wing beating and increased staccato squawking, which now sounds something like "honkhonkhonk." The females are choosy and often repeatedly fly up to and away from the males. Finally, a female lands next to the singer of her choice. The male stops squawking during the 30- to 60-second copulation, but renews the concert after his "bride of the moment" has flown away. Though the meetings of singers in the rainy season occur briefly and sporadically, the lek courtship of the Hammer-headed Fruit Bat in calling territories reaches its height in the dry season from June to August and December to February.

Lesser Horseshoe Bat with youngster on belly fur (Rhinolophus hipposideros). Besides the lactating milk teats, female horseshoe bats also have a pair of false teats in the loin region.

The youngster sucks tightly on a false teat and thereby gains a stronger hold.

71

MOTHER AND CHILD

Because the time between mating and fertilization or between fertilization and embryonic development is elastic due to sperm storage and suspended germination (delayed implantation), no precise gestation periods can be given for many bat species. In addition, the length of the gestation period also depends on how often the females have to lower their body temperature because of external conditions. Each reduction of the maternal temperature ultimately leads to the retarded development of the embryos. Among European species the gestation period lasts between 45 and 70 days, with the Common Pipistrelle holding the record for the shortest period. Schreiber's Bat can exhibit a much longer period of embryonic development because of delayed implantation. The gestation period of this cosmopolitan species, however, shortens in the warmer regions of the Earth to as low as four months.

The longest gestation period for bats, at almost eight months, was recorded for the highly specialized Common Vampire Bat (*Desmodus rotundus*). In the flying foxes, embryonic development takes 115 to 125 days in the Short-nosed Fruit Bat (*Cynopterus sphinx*) and up to five to six months with the larger flying fox species (*Pteropus*). In the Straw-colored Fruit Bat (*Eidolon helvum*) in Africa the gestation period, because of delayed embryonic development, can last up to nine months, though actual embryonic

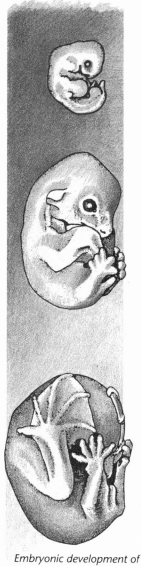

Embryonic development of Rousettus amplexicaudatus (Pteropodidae). That the embryo will develop eventually into a flier is shown by the developing elastic membranes between the bones of the arm and fingers. In the almost ready to be born fetus (right), the legs and claws of the toes for holding on are already fully developed. The small wing membranes would still be much too short and weak for flying. They require further growth during juvenile development (after Hill & Smith, 1984).

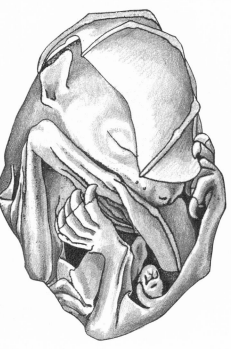

development may occur during only four of these months.

Felix Heidinger from our working group demonstrated through his measurements and observations of a Mouse-eared Bat colony how the pregnant females can actively influence embryonic development. To bring their young into the world at the smallest cost, they use all available energy-saving tricks. When the pregnant females find sufficient food and their energy requirement is adequately met, they maintain their body temperature as high as possible even during the lowest ambient temperatures. They achieve the advantage of rapid embryonic development through social thermoregulation, pressing as close together as possible at mass hanging sites. If there is a shortage of food, however, this trick for saving energy is not sufficient. Now the only thing that will help is to move apart and to lower the body temperature, so as to reduce the expenditure of energy—though at the expense of a rapid birth.

BIRTH—A TRAPEZE ACT?

"How do bats give birth to their young?" is a question often asked by bat enthusiasts. Many find it difficult to imagine a birth upside down in trapeze-artist fashion without a net. But even in this essential process bats remain more-or-less true to their upside-down world. Without the security of the nest used by many small mammals, the young are born and reared totally in "bat fashion" in a hanging posture. Many baby bats, however, do not actually have to make do without a "safety net" when they come into the world. Females often turn 180 degrees during birth, so that the youngster, after it has emerged from the birth canal, can glide gently into the tail membrane as if in a pocket. In addition, the strong umbilical cord functions as a "safety line" to prevent mishaps. The mothers seem to prefer horizontal birthing positions over the normal hanging posture. Bats predominantly give birth during their daytime rest period. The young are usually born tail-first, but occasionally emerge head-first.

Günter Heise was able to observe in his Nathusius' Pipistrelles that the newborns, when they crawl up in the direction of the teats, make swaying searching movements with the head and are diligently licked by the mother immediately after birth. During this time they give continuous "tsett-tsett-tsett" calls. By means of these "contact calls" the young bats maintain contact with their mother during all their juvenile development.

Two female Noctules we kept also gave birth in the upright position and let the newborns glide into the tail membrane. Here too, contact calls by the young and zealous licking by the mother were essential behaviors for forming a close mother-baby bond.

In our Mouse-eared Bat colony in the Au, Susanne Vogel was able to observe a number of births under natural conditions. All of them took place in the morning hours. Each expectant female had separated somewhat from the colony and usually hung alone from a diagonal beam in the attic roost. There she clung tightly to the beam with all four limbs, with the head oriented upward or at least horizontally. The hind legs were spread slightly and the tail membrane folded up toward the belly. The female often lowered her head into the pocket formed in this fashion; because it was positioned with the belly toward the wood, it was impossible to tell what happened there. Finally, movements in the tail membrane pocket were observed—birth had occurred. The mother bent her head down to the newborn and licked the youngster intensely for several minutes. Because no placenta was ever found under the hanging site, it can be assumed that it was eaten by the mother. About ten minutes after the beginning of the first observation, the newborn, with the aid of the mother, had attached itself to a teat and the female again hung upside-down in the colony.

Erwin Kulzer and Gerhard Neuweiler have observed and described births in flying foxes. The female Nile Flying Fox kept by Kulzer gave birth in the normal resting position. The newborn were licked dry and gave their contact calls. How important such sounds can be is described by Gerhard Neuweiler in his observations in the wild of Indian Giant Flying Foxes: "The pregnant females gather in the top branches of roost trees in late January, and the young are born in March. The newborn fall head-first into the bend of the mother's elbow, where they immediately start peeping and searching for the teat. If this peeping call of the newborn is not given (in stillbirths or premature births), the mother's licking of the youngster gradually turns to biting and chewing and the newborn is eaten."

Transporting and "parking"

Female flying foxes carry their young along on the evening feeding flights to the food trees. The young hold tightly to the teats with the teeth and to the mother's belly fur with the claws of the feet. In the larger flying foxes and a few tropical leaf-nosed bats the young are then "parked" on a branch by the mothers for the duration of feeding. For hunting bats, carrying the young would be too much of a burden. From the start they leave their young behind in the roost during their nocturnal hunting flights. There the babies often press together in dense clusters, and each youngster waits patiently for the return of its individual "source of milk." We have observed that our nursing female Mouse-eared Bats seem to be in a hurry to return to the roost. Though females without young often spent the whole night outside the roost, the mothers, especially during the youngsters' first two weeks of life, often returned within an hour to the roost to nurse. An hour later they usually resumed their interrupted hunting flight. For their first meal before nursing, the female Mouse-eared Bats usually sought out the closest possible hunting grounds.

In the roost the contact between mother and youngster is usually very intimate. Even when they are not hungry, the little ones like to hang on their mothers' teats. Often only a lump under its wing reveals that a female has offspring.

Milk and false teats

The mammary glands are located in the shoulder region in all bats. The females of some bat families (mouse-tailed bats, slit-faced bats, false vampire bats, Old World leaf-nosed bats, and a few species of common bats) also have additional "false teats" in the belly region that do not produce milk. The young suck firmly on them when they do not happen to be thirsty. When hunger calls they simply change their sucking position on the mother's belly.

Whereas the young of European common bats have well-developed milk teeth with very sharp small cusps, also called "clamping teeth," the first teeth of horseshoe bats have already degenerated before birth. It is possible that the false teats of the mother in these species have developed, in a manner of speaking, as a "tooth substitute" for the young, to enable the initially toothless young to take a firm hold.

The change in proportion between the body and wing size in an approximately two-day-old Common Pipistrelle and a fully grown animal.

73

Juvenile
development
using the example
of the Noctule
(Nyctalus
noctula). Left:
The one-day-old,
naked and blind
young hang onto
the belly fur of the
mother with their
strong hind feet.
Center: The young
Noctules are five
days old. When
the mother bats
make their

Several species of free-tailed bats, which roost in narrow crevices, carry their young in piggyback style on the back.

A well cared for "only child"

The intensive care given bat young did not come about by accident. The birth rate of generally only one youngster per year for a small mammal is not exactly high. Proper maternal care is essential if as many young as possible are to survive. With some species, however, litter sizes are somewhat larger. Among the European bats, Noctules as well as the species of the genus *Pipistrellus* usually give birth to two young. The

ultimate size at birth, the forearm is only 30 to 40 percent of its later size. The thumbs and hind legs, which are oversized in proportion to the baby bat's body, are essential for clinging. If the mother is present, the young can hold tightly to the mother's fur and can also suck firmly on the milk and false teats. On the other hand, during their mother's hunting flights they are totally dependent on their own feet. A firm foothold at the hanging place is therefore essential for the survival of the young. It is often claimed that youngsters that have fallen from their roost are hopelessly lost, but the mother-child bond can still function. Fallen

nocturnal hunting
flights, the
youngsters stay
behind in the
roost and cling
close together at
the hanging place
(here a tree hole).
Right: Young
noctules, ten days
old. While one
animal nurses, the
second licks its
wings. The first
attempts at
grooming begin
very early in bats.

Particolored Bat (*Vespertilio murinus*), in which a female can have three young, has to be considered almost prolific. The mother is specially equipped for this increased litter size in that it is the only European bat species with two pairs of nipples. It is suspected that females of this species should be able to rear four young, the same number as the American *Lasiurus* species. In the flying foxes, the birth of twins is known only for the species *Epomops dobsoni* and *Pteropus rufus*.

When young bats are fed well they grow very fast. In species with one youngster, the newborn weighs about a fifth to a third of the mother's weight. In Europe, the Common Pipistrelle gives birth to the smallest young, with birth weights of 1.3 to 1.4 grams (there are 28 grams in an ounce). At first usually naked and blind, baby bats already have enormously enlarged extremities. Though the hind legs and the thumbs have already attained 80 percent of their

young in our Mouse-eared Bat colony that still peeped loudly when we put them on a slanting beam were flown to a short time later and retrieved by the mother.

Susanne Vogel even observed how a female Mouse-eared Bat in our roost in the Au landed on a youngster that had died from feebleness during a period of bad weather and had fallen to the floor. The female crouched closely over the dead youngster. Her position with head bent down slightly and partially spread wings resembled the posture of females that pick up a youngster.

Besides the contact calls, the sense of smell also plays an important role in finding the mother's own youngster. The mother Mouse-eared Bats we marked, upon their return from hunting flights, usually landed directly in the area of the rafter in which they had left their young hanging. The group of youngsters reacted to the landing of the adult with peeping sounds, and the mother crept back and forth between the young while sniffing. Once the mother had finally found her offspring, the mother sniffed and licked it especially in the muzzle region and placed her wings over the youngster.

As Susanne Vogel's studies showed, in the first days of life the task of finding the right youngster is left totally to the mother, but after only four to five days the youngsters, even though their eyes were still closed, were already able to climb up to the mother and clambered under the wings to reach the teats. In our observations of the behavior of Mouse-eared Bats we were never able to confirm that the mothers also cared for

Among European species, the eyes of the young open between the third and tenth day of life. The pinkish newborns have sparse, virtually unpigmented hair. Within the first week of life the true fur starts to grow. After a few days the youngsters can run and clamber about quite quickly. The permanent teeth of the young bats start to erupt by about the tenth day. At an age of only three to four weeks the little Nathusius' and Common Pipistrelles can fly. Young Mouse-eared Bats and Noctules need about a week longer to reach this stage. The weaning of the young begins at four to six weeks of age. The young of the New World

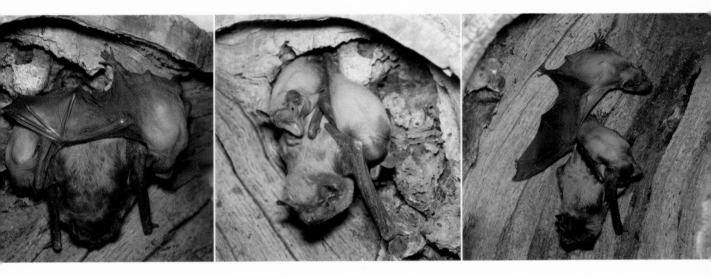

strange youngsters. Such "babysitting behavior" has been described for several bat species. In the two Mouse-eared Bat species *Myotis thysanodes* and *Myotis lucifugus*, a few females always stayed behind with the young while the other mothers hunted. Even in the enormous colonies of the Mexican Free-tailed Bats (*Tadarida brasiliensis mexicana*) the mothers can find their offspring among millions of young. With both that bat species and Schreiber's Bat (*Miniopterus schreibersi*), the mutual care of the young also includes mutual nursing. "Child welfare" is most developed in the Common Vampire Bat (*Desmodus rotundus*). Here orphaned youngsters are even adopted by females. In virtally all species the care of the young is purely a maternal affair. An exception is the Spear-nosed Bat (*Phyllostomus discolor*), which lives in harems. The males in the harem often carry small, naked, sleeping youngsters on their backs.

leaf-nosed bat *Carollia perspicillata* come into the world considerably more developed. Already almost fully furred, with open eyes and ears, they are the equivalent of precocial birds among the bats. But even this advanced development requires maternal care.

The young of the larger species of flying foxes, such as *Pteropus giganteus*, remain with the mother for up to eight months and are still nursed at an age of five months.

In the roost almost all young bats are fed exclusively with mother's milk. The carnivorous false vampire bats (megadermatids), however, also carry captured prey back to the roost to feed to their young. Vampire bats introduce their young to the taste of blood from mouth to mouth. With our young Mouse-eared Bats we were never able to observe actual feeding, but the youngsters did lick the mouth of their mother vigorously. Jürgen Gebhard found the same behavior with the Noctule. Whether it is a

Left: The youngsters are 12 days old. One youngster stretches the free wing while nursing. Center: Feeding is hard work. While one youngster still nurses, the satiated sibling yawns widely (age: three weeks). Right: The young Noctules are five weeks old. More and more frequently the wings are tested by stretching them in the cramped tree hole.

question here of the transfer of antibodies, taste or food samples, enzymes or fluids, or simply of the strengthening of the mother-offspring bond requires further explanation.

Flying and navigating appear to be learned

Young bats start their flying lessons early. At first they simply open their wings alternately; as yet they are still incapable of supporting them in flight. The "first lesson" can even be practiced hanging from the mother's belly fur. In the confined space of tree holes and crevices, young bats can carry out only these wing-stretching exercises until they fly from the roost for the first time. On the other hand, young bats in more spacious roosts have an advantage. There they begin true flight lessons early in the safety of the roost. Susanne Vogel observed such Mouse-eared Bat flight lessons starting with the 23rd day of life. They occurred even during the day in an attic. The youngsters climbed down a vertical post and took a long time orienting themselves particularly thoroughly, in the course of which they moved the head horizontally back and forth several times.

Finally they flew in a more-or-less downward curve to the opposite post. They landed head-up with the wings spread. If something got in their way, such as the observer or the measuring instruments, they could not avoid it, but rather landed on the obstacle. If the flight was successful, the youngsters moved back into the takeoff position and continued with their practice flights.

Echolocation is also learned! The first calls of the bats are relatively low and undifferentiated. They serve only as contact calls with the mother. Measurements have shown, for example, that the calls of young Mouse-eared Bats up to an age of 18 days have a frequency of 20 to 30 kilohertz and only then begin climbing slowly to 50 to 70 kilohertz. Species that take their maiden flight with their mothers fly behind the mother in a kind of "sound trail." Bodo Stratmann described how a female Noctule (*Nyctalus noctula*) taught a youngster to orient itself and find its way home, calling to the youngster to lure the young bat from the roost and follow her. Young horseshoe bats and common bats have been observed following their mothers on hunting flights. Young Two-lined Bats (*Saccopteryx leptura*) were observed flying behind their mothers and imitating all the movements the mothers made while hunting insects.

The behavior of our Mouse-eared Bats stands in contrast to the mother-offspring relations described above. By marking mother-offspring pairs we were able to show that mother and youngster do not fly out simultaneously, and thus the youngster cannot learn anything from the mother. On its maiden flight from the roost the young mouse-eared bat must already fend for itself. It learns to fly and echolocate beforehand through self-training in the roost. It must also teach itself how to hunt successfully. Therefore, the still unsure youngsters find the rich hunting grounds in the immediate vicinity of the roost of utmost importance. Observations by Susanne Vogel, however, have shown that with the first flight from the roost, which can take place starting on the 35th day of life, the separation of the youngsters from their mothers is far from being complete. Vogel saw 61- and 64-day-old youngsters still nursing with their mothers. This observation also explained why "juvenile droppings," a mixture of milk droppings and the remains of solid food, were still found in the roosts in late August. The long nursing period of Mouse-eared Bats must favor the survival of the young. Even when there is little success in hunting, a source of milk at least awaits the young students!

Life and death

Despite the best of care, the mortality among young bats is quite high. It is estimated that a total of only 30 to 40 percent of youngsters reach the second year of life and thereby can contribute to the survival of the species through reproduction. Ivan Horacek gives a juvenile mortality of five to ten percent under normal conditions for the Mouse-eared Bat colonies he studied. In cold, wet summers, when the females can find little food during prolonged periods of bad weather, the mortality rate of the young rises drastically. For Mouse-eared Bat colonies, losses of young at this critical time of over 50 percent have been confirmed.

That the female Mouse-eared Bats provide less care for their young when it is cold, and even leave them alone for days in the roost during periods of bad weather, at first sight looks like anything but proper maternal care. Nevertheless, under certain circumstances this is a life-saving strategy for the young, as Felix Heidinger was able to determine. This is because the youngsters' energy reserves last considerably longer when the body temperature sinks and they fall into a state of suspended animation. During times of food shortage the youngsters do not grow at all. To the same degree as energy consumption is reduced during torpor, the growth of the young at low temperatures also decreases. If, on the other hand, the females cared for their young at low ambient temperatures and raised their body temperature, the little ones would pay for the brief growth phase with their lives, for their energy reserves would be used up. With the metabolism of the mother in a delicate balance in periods of cold, the growth of the young must be completely secondary to survival at a low level of bodily function. Female Mouse-eared Bats that do not tend to their young during periods of bad weather are therefore anything but "cruel mothers"!

Accidents that befall small youngsters are particularly dramatic in large colonies. In a colony of thousands of horseshoe bats (*Rhinolophus rouxi*) in a cave in Sri Lanka, we saw a gruesome sight. The mountain of bat droppings was strewn with the decomposing bodies of baby bats. We were able to observe youngsters falling time and again. They had been unable to find a secure enough hold on the brittle rock of the roof of the cave. Their way back to the safety of the nursery could be followed like an ant trail. The young horseshoe bats apparently sought to find—in what seems to be a typical behavior of flightless young bats on the ground—the vertical walls of the cave by moving backward. As was shown by the trail of little dead bodies, many did not reach the distant goal. To see life and death in such close proximity disturbed us. Yet as long as man does not intervene detrimentally, even the death of youngsters is a

Reproductive cycle of European bats. The seasonal variation in the food supply determines the rhythm in which European bat species typically visit their roosts, migrate, and reproduce. Because of sperm storage, copulation and fertilization can take place independently of each other in time. (The illustration shows a variety of species.)

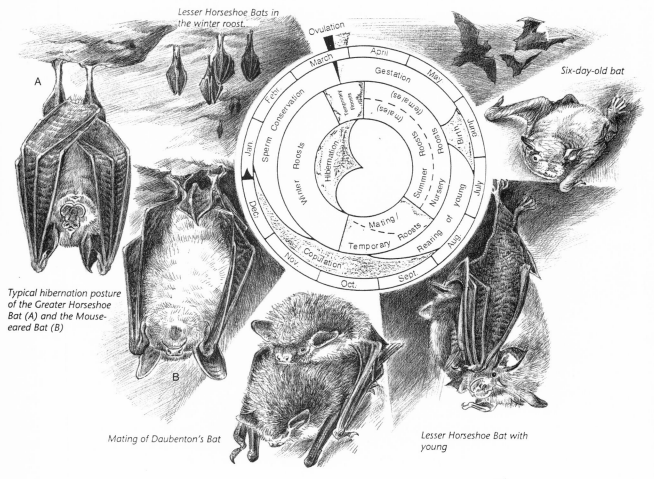

Lesser Horseshoe Bats in the winter roost.

Six-day-old bat

Typical hibernation posture of the Greater Horseshoe Bat (A) and the Mouse-eared Bat (B)

Mating of Daubenton's Bat

Lesser Horseshoe Bat with young

Among the throng of youngsters in the nursery colony of the Sri Lankan Horseshoe Bat (Rhinolophus rouxi, right), a few females always stay behind as if "baby sitting."

Under the hanging place of the youngsters, small bodies of baby Sri Lankan Horseshoe Bats (Rhinolophus rouxi, below) pile up. They fell from the brittle ceiling of the cave and could not make their way back.

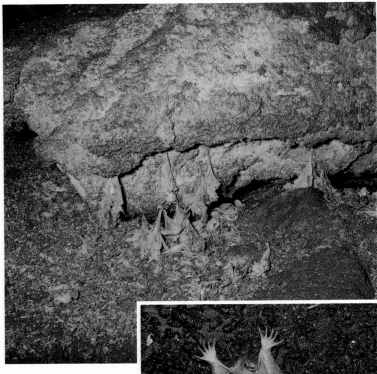

Dead baby Greater Mouse-eared Bat (Myotis myotis, right) beneath the nursery colony. During periods of bad weather the loss of young is particularly high in the early phases of rearing.

natural, calculated process in the circle of life. The critical phase of young bats is the time after they are weaned from their mothers. They are in particular danger in bad weather, because they have minimal fat reserves and are also relatively inexperienced.

LITTLE METHUSELAHS

For small mammals, bats live to virtually Biblical ages. The maximum recorded age of the Lesser Horseshoe Bat (*Rhinolophus hipposideros*) is 21 years, and that of the Greater Horseshoe Bat is an amazing 30 years. The flying foxes also appear to live to a ripe old age. The Straw-colored Fruit Bat (*Eidolon helvum*) lives to an age of 21.8 years, and the record age of the Indian Giant Flying Fox (*Pteropus giganteus*), at 17.2 years, is nothing to scoff at.

The North American Little Brown Bat (*Myotis lucifugus*), which has attained an age of 30 years, can hold its own with the Greater Horseshoe Bat.

The Noctule and Nathusius' Pipistrelle, with documented maximum ages of about seven years, lag considerably behind the record ages of the genera *Myotis* and *Rhinolophus*. They are forest-dwelling, long-distance wanderers and, in contrast to the species that overwinter in caves, regularly give birth to two young. They appear to balance out the higher risk associated with migration with a higher reproductive rate. Nevertheless, only a few individuals ever live to old age.

From population studies it is known that

losses are highest in the time from birth to weaning. Accidents and scarcity of food are the most frequent causes of death. The first hibernation and the preparations necessary for it also cost many bats their lives. The juvenile bat that has successfully steered clear of this rocky shore can count on reaching an age of seven to eight years, which some 40 to 80 percent of all adult animals achieve. At an age of six to seven years the death rate rises dramatically again. Except for the few surviving "Methuselahs," a population will have renewed itself totally every six to seven years. Whether bats can let their biological program run according to the natural cycle of birth and death, however, ultimately depends more and more on man.

On warm days the animals of a Greater Mouse-eared Bat (Myotis myotis) nursery colony disperse throughout the entire ridge.

Here a colony of Noctules (Nyctalus noctula) has accepted a nest box as a "substitute tree hole."

Colonizers and Groups –
the Social Relationships

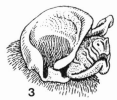

Bats that live in more or less large colonies: 1. Choeronycteris mexicana, a leaf-nosed bat; 2. Lonchorhina aurita, another leaf-nosed bat; 3. Tadarida megalotis, a free-tailed bat; 4. Pteropus vampyrus, the Malayan kalong; 5. Megaderma lyra, the Indian false vampire bat; and 6. Pteropus capistratus, one of the largest flying foxes.

Besides species that live a solitary existence except to mate, five basic forms of social units can be distinguished in mammals: the pair (1 male, 1 female), the harem (1, 2+), the female unit (0, 2+), the male unit (2+ , 0), and the mixed group (2+, 2 +). A social unit is a long-term attachment of at least two adult animals that exists independently of the mating season and that is kept separate from other social units. As they approach sexual maturity, growing juveniles are usually forced out of such a unit. The American bat researcher J. W. Bradbury in 1977 divided the social structures of bats as follows: 1) solitary species; 2) groups that exist the whole year (seasonally invariable) with the three organizational forms of the harem, mixed groups, and monogamous species with stable pair bonding; and 3) seasonally variable groups. To the solitary bats appear to belong the African Banana Bat (*Pipistrellus nanus*), the White Bat (*Diclidurus albus*), and several *Lasiurus* species. Smaller species of flying foxes, such as long-tongued fruit bats of the genera *Macroglossus* and *Megaloglossus* as well as the species *Myonycteris torquata* and *Micropteropus pusillus*, have also been found to lead solitary lives. Stable pairs with their offspring have been found, for example, among the African slit-faced bats *Nycteris hispida*, *N. nana*, and *N. arge*; the Woolly Horseshoe Bat (*Rhinolophus luctus*), the African Yellow-winged Bat (*Lavia frons*), and the Spectral Vampire (*Vampyrum spectrum*).

A few tropical bats live in harems all year. On Trinidad, the South American White-lined Bat (*Saccopteryx bilineata*) forms harems of an adult male and up to eight females. The harem groups make their roosts in suitable trunks of large trees. The male harem owner defends this roost territory through vocalizations and drives off male intruders. Any female in his harem that tries to test his strength is thrashed with the wings. On the other hand, the harem owner uses visual, olfactory, and auditory signals to bring females into the harem. The females of the harem are not immune to the seductions of other harem owners and probably change harems occasionally. The young born at the beginning of the rainy season spend the day in the harem group and are carried by their mothers on the nightly search for food. The larger offspring are left behind in a nearby tree. When the male White-lined Bats return toward morning, territorial fights take place that are accompanied by vocalizations and visual displays. Finally, each male gathers or enlarges his harem again for the daily rest period. The Two-lined Bat (*Saccopteryx leptura*), in contrast, lives in mixed groups.

Though single male White-lined Bats (*Saccopteryx bilineata*) live alone and often in close proximity to a harem, single males of the Asian *Thylonycteris* species form bachelor groups. With the spear-nosed bat *Phyllostomus hastatus*, the harems can include up to 100 females. They live in cavities, in which single males also live in groups. The single males often move from one roost to another. The males of this species of leaf-nosed bat make no attempt to attract females. The females of their harem often remain faithful to them for more than a year. The male spear-nose defends his harem through territorial behavior. This keeps the harem owner so busy that he scarcely finds the time to feed. When the females go in search of food, they leave the roost for only a short time. The demands of harem ownership are such that the males spend most of their time in the roost.

An example of long-term mixed groups is given by the Indian Giant Flying Fox,

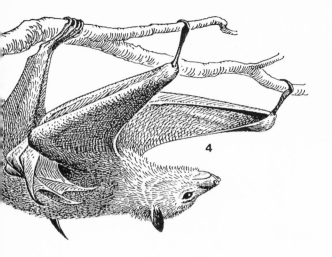

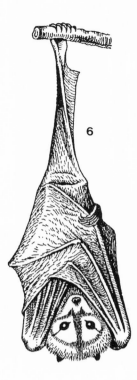

Pteropus giganteus, from India and Sri Lanka. The hierarchy of the colony-dwellers in their roost trees can be inferred from their hanging places. The dominant males demonstrate their preeminent position by taking possession of the highest hanging sites in the tree. Subordinate males and juveniles must take their place on the lower "rungs of the ladder": they hang on the lower and outer branches. The males make an effort to keep their permanent hanging places. In contrast, the females often change their places in the roost tree from day to day.

For the very large groups of Australian flying foxes, which gather in roosts of 50,000 to 100,000 in particular rainforest regions or in mangrove zones, the term "daytime camp" has come into use with Australian zoologists. Within their groups the bats maintain variable distances. In many species the colony-dwellers clump close together in the roost, but others maintain particular individual distances.

The changing season in the temperate climatic zones also affects the social relations of the bat species that live there. To a greater or lesser degree, three phases can be distinguished in the annual cycle. In the first phase, the sexes hibernate together. The second phase begins with the birth of the young and ends with their independence. The sexes live separately—the females in colonies, the males singly or in bachelor groups. In the fall, mating groups often form. A good model for this social structure is provided by the Common Pipistrelle (*Pipistrellus pipistrellus*), the cycle of which was described by Grimmberger: a) Winter roost without separation of the sexes with up to more than 1000 individuals in the time from November to March. b)

Beginning in late May colonies containing 20 to 250 females. At this time the males live solitarily or in small groups. The colonies break up from about late July to mid-August. At this time the invasion groups (of up to more than 100 individuals) form, consisting predominantly of juveniles. c) After the colonies break up, mating groups (harems) form, as with Nathusius' Pipistrelle (*Pipistrellus nathusii*) and the Noctule (*Nyctalus noctula*). Günter Heise and Axel Schmidt independently studied the social organization and ecology of the Common Long-eared Bat (*Plecotus auritus*). They determined that the females live in closed groups, with the majority of the female offspring staying with the group after they reach maturity. The groups of females thus build up from close relatives. The young males also usually return to their birth community in their first spring, but then wander off and thus provide for gene exchange with other communities.

Only rarely is mutual grooming observed in the European bat species. That is certainly not the case with the Common Vampire Bat (*Desmodus rotundus*). Here, based on observations by Uwe Schmidt, mates spend a lot of time engaged in social grooming. They lick each other on the mouth, head, belly, and behind the wings. Often, for minutes at a time, all of the members of the group lick one another and embrace each other with their wings. Vampires have the strongest social behavior among bats.

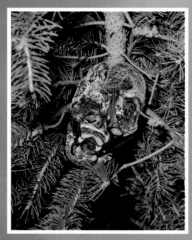

The North American Hoary Bat (Lasiurus cinereus, left) is one of the few foilage-dwelling bats of the temperate zones. Here a female with its two already quite large young is free-hanging in the branches.

The hanging places in the traditional roost trees of the Indian Giant Flying Fox (Pteropus giganteus, large photograph) are soon defoliated by the claws of the users.

From Leaves to the Bungalow

Roosts play an important role in the life of a bat. Bats spend more than half their lives in the roost. There they sleep during the day, mate, rear their young, and, depending on the species, hibernate in winter. Roosts promote social relations and digestion and offer protection from the vagaries of weather and enemies.

Suitable daytime roosts are as important in a bat's life as sufficient food. Only where there is an adequate supply of potential roosts can bats colonize. Because—with certain exceptions—they do not build their own housing, bats are dependent on existing suitable hiding places. Although they are not master builders, bats are at least masterful when it comes to finding hiding places. Besides innumerable natural roosts, bats also allow others to build for them. As later tenants or subtenants, numerous bats occupy the structures of other animals as well as human buildings. In some regions bat species are even dependent on this "tenancy" in human buildings.

INHABITANTS OF PLANT ROOSTS

Bat species that select roosts on or in trees, bushes, and other plants are called "phytophilic" (plant-loving). Particularly in the tropics, many bats still live in a natural style. In the tropics, plants offer the animals potential roosts in inexhaustible profusion. The majority of flying foxes simply hang freely from branches and spend the day in this way in large or small groups. Often such trees hold nothing but flying foxes. As a result of the mass of animals, traditional flying fox roost trees are not only defoliated, but also are debarked because of the thousands of bats that hang from and climb around with their claws. When the flying foxes doze there during the day wrapped in their wings, from a distance it appears as if the tree bears fruit. On the other hand, the smaller species of flying foxes and various representatives of the American leaf-nosed bats often can be found in their roosts only with difficulty. Hanging motionless in dense foliage, and sometimes additionally provided with striped markings, the animals almost disappear in the play of light and shadow.

All foliage-dwellers can lay claim to their roost only temporarily. When the leaves die or fall off, the plants no longer offer suitable housing. Foliage roosts therefore promote a nomadic life with frequent changes of roosts and offer little protection against changes in temperature and humidity. Most foliage-dwelling bats live solitarily or in small groups.

Only the largest species of flying fox form groups of many individuals in trees. The few leaf-dwelling bats of the temperate zones must adapt to the autumnal leaf fall. Thus the *Lasiurus* species, which hang in the deciduous forests of North America, abandon their usual locales in the fall. Populations living in the southern United States have an easier time of it. When the apricot

South American Yellow-eared Bats (Ectophylla alba). Hanging under the leaf gable, they become virtually "invisible" in the light shining through.

Short-faced flying foxes (Cynopterus brachyotis) have found their preferred sleeping place under a palm leaf in Thailand.

83

trees lose their leaves, they move to the evergreen orange trees. Spanish moss and vines also provide hiding places for *Lasiurus; Lasiurus cinereus,* with its silvery gray fur, is well-camouflaged visually from predators in Spanish moss.

The crowns of tall palms provide particularly good hiding places for bats. One palm species, which occurs in Cuba and Central American countries, almost appears to have been created expressly as a roosting place for bats. Its tuftlike foliage consists in its lower half only of dry fronds, which are closely spaced and hang downward, thus offering an excellent refuge for tenants. Up to 3000 bats roost in a single tree of this kind and betray their presence by the thick layer of droppings at the base of the trunk. They were even responsible for the naming of this species of palm: it was christened *Copernicia vespertilionum* (bat palm) by botanists.

That banana leaves offer ideal protection from sun and rain is soon recognized by bats. Under the central rib of the large, drooping leaves, several species of bat can be found alongside one another. Even in regions where bananas were introduced by man, these are now in the hands (or rather, feet) of bats. Before they unfurl, young banana leaves form cones. Two African common bat species, *Myotis bocagei* and the Banana Bat (*Pipistrellus nanus*), as well as the Madagascan *Myzopoda aurita,* have developed a special liking for these leaf cones, although the time of occupancy is extremely limited. Usually after only a few days the leaf unfurls and makes a change of residence necessary. In the same way as *Myzopoda,* two species of American disk-winged bats (Thyropteridae) have evolved specialized suction discs on the wrist and ankle with which they can attach themselves firmly in the rolled-up leaves. In principle, they employ a similar technique as is used in the transport and installation of large panes of glass with grips with suction cups. Contrary to the ancient habits of bats, the American disk-winged bats roost head-up in their leaf dwellings in the tropical rainforest.

Unique amont bats, several New World leaf-nosed bats even prepare their roosting quarters by "remodeling." These "tent-building" bats belong to the genera *Uroderma, Ectophylla,* and *Artibeus.* The zoologist Juliane Koepcke has observed the tent-building of *Ectophylla macconnelli* in the Peruvian

rainforest. *Ectophylla* roosts in small groups of two to eight individuals in its daytime quarters, which the animals build themselves by reshaping large leaves of *Philodendron* and similar plants. To build the tent, the bats bite through the leaf tissue in the middle of the bananalike leaves on both sides along the central rib, so that the leaf folds together like a gabled roof. The bats also have several roosting places at all times, which they visit alternately at intervals of a few days. Juliane Koepcke observed that a roost could be used for an average period of four to five months. It began to decay after six months.

The light fur color of *Ectophylla macconnelli* may offer the animals in the roost protection from being detected by diurnal predators. When observed from below, the roof of the roost looks yellowish green in the incident light; the space underneath is diffusely dim. The light gray fur and the yellowish color of the ears, the prominence in front of the external opening of the ear (tragus), and the muzzle area have the effect that the bats more or less blend with this background and are thus camouflaged from detection.

Cracks and hollow spaces between fruits as well as aerial roots and freestanding roots of trees also serve as hiding places for bats. Cracks in the bark and in heartwood are also readily accepted. The most popular roosts of phytophilic bats, however, are tree holes. In the tropical forests, horseshoe bats, leaf-nosed bats, and free-tailed bats use these roosts. In Africa the Greater Slit-faced Bat (*Nycteris grandis*) and the leaf-nosed bat *Hipposideros cyclops* are dependent on tree holes. In the South American rainforests the Spectral Vampire (*Vampyrum spectrum*) and the Common Vampire Bat (*Desmodus rotundus*) readily make their roosts in hollow trees.

European species that use tree roosts are called "tree bats." Upon closer examination, the individual species use their tree roosts in very different ways. Tree holes are only temporary quarters for some, but for others they are important as places for courtship, roosting, and even hibernation. Classic tree bats, which almost exclusively use this type of roost, are Leisler's Bat, Bechstein's Bat, and Natterer's Bat. At most only bird nests and bat boxes are accepted by them as substitute trees. In contrast, the Noctule, the Common Long-eared Bat, the Common Pipistrelle, Nathusius' Pipistrelle, and Daubenton's Bat also accept hollow spaces in buildings as roosts.

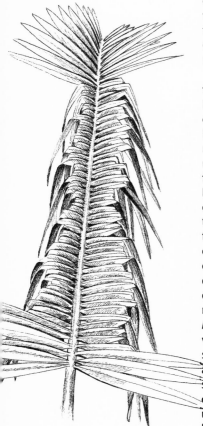

As if in an arbor, the bats hang beneath this palm frond. Although they have no roof over their heads, they do have one over their feet.

THE CAVE-DWELLERS

Considerably more common than plant roosts are roosts of rock. Natural and artificial caves are inhabited by many bats throughout the world, as has long been known. On all continents caves exist that are known to have been occupied by populations of bats since time immemorial. The number of their inhabitants can be in the millions. Approximately 300,000 bats live in Niah Cave in Borneo. One hundred thousand Serotines (*Eptesicus serotinus*) have been counted in the "Cave of Thieves" near Bombay, India. We estimated that the population of bats in a Sri Lankan cave was over a quarter million based on counts taken as

Foliage roosts of bats. Inhabitants as namesakes: Bats like to stay under the dry, downward hanging fronds of the bat palm (Copernicia vespertilionum) (1). The young banana leaves, still rolled up like paper bags (2), are hiding places for bats everywhere. In the Americas, disk-winged bats (Thyroptera

3

spec.), among others, make their roosts in them. Perching head up, they hold onto the smooth walls of leaves by means of the suction disks located on the wrist and ankle (3, after a photograph by Tuttle). "Tent building" is the specialty of several New World leaf-nosed bats (4). Here a small colony of Ectophylla macconnelli has remodeled the tip of a frond of the palm species Geonoma spec. to form their tent roost (after Koepcke, 1984). Ectophylla macconnelli (5) also build their tent roost from the arrowhead-shaped leaf of a plant of the genus Anthurium (Araceae) (after Koepcke, 1984).

they left the roost. Sri Lankan Rousette Fruit Bats (*Rousettus seminudus*) share that roost with thousands of horseshoe bats (*Rhinolophus rouxi*) and leaf-nosed bats (*Hipposideros lancadiva*).

The largest known gatherings of animals are the colonies of the Mexican Free-tailed Bat (*Tadarida brasiliensis*) in a number of caves in Mexico and the southern United States. Up to 20 million animals are estimated to live in certain caves. When the approximately 500,000 Mexican Free-tailed Bats in Carlsbad Caverns National Park, New Mexico, leave their roost in the evening to hunt, their flight is a spectacle. As the park visitors sit in an amphitheater at the entrance to the cave, they are astounded by the unique natural spectacle of shifting clouds of rising bats. (Unfortunately, bat numbers have drastically decreased over the last few decades in such caves, perhaps because of insecticides. For bats there ap-

85

pears to be no safety in numbers.)

In the same way as phytophilic bats divide up their plant roosts, cave-dwelling ("lithophilic," rock-loving) bats also occupy areas and hiding places that meet their individual needs. Many species prefer niches and depressions in the roof of the cave. They either maintain their individual distance or favor body contact and hang in groups.

Bat species that favor body contact with the substrate roost on cave walls with prominences, cracks, and depressions. Only when they can withdraw into a crack do free-tailed bats and several other species really feel at home. With some species the bodies are so flat that they look as if they have been strongly depressed. Bats can even be found under rubble on the floors of caves. Daubenton's Bat occasionally "submerges" in the floor rubble to hibernate.

If conditions such as a supply of hanging places, temperature, humidity, darkness, and lack of disturbance are right, it makes no difference to bats whether they live in natural or artificial caves. Not only mummies were found in Egyptian pyramids and other burial chambers, but very live bats too. Even parts of the Sahara have been conquered by some species, in that they occupied the underground canals of the irrigation systems. Though in central Europe caves, cellars, mines, and bunkers are usually suitable for bats only as winter or temporary roosts, caves in southern Europe also are used as summer roosts and to rear young.

THE SECRETIVE TENANT

Wherever people build, new hiding places are provided for bats. The little house-dwellers use houses, churches, temples, pyramids, towers, and fortresses from the basement to the attic for their purposes. Bats that have more or less become followers of civilization are called "anthrophilic" (man-loving). Nevertheless, this love is usually expressed quite unilaterally. For bats, human structures are only substitute caves, above all in the regions in which natural caves do not meet the bats' need for warmth.

In Africa, species of the genus *Scotophilus* are unequivocal "house bats," as are the free-tailed bats *(Tadarida* and *Molossus)* throughout Africa and Asia and the whole tropical-subtropical region of North and South America.

Of the 22 European bat species, at least 18 are known to roost on and in buildings.

Facing page, top:
Unusual, but
practical: Long-
eared bat roosts!
Top: A Common
Long-Eared bat
(Plecotus
auritus) has
chosen as a
daytime roost the
rubber cover over
a lock on a fence.
Facing page,
bottom: *Here a*
Common Long-
eared Bat
(Plecotus
auritus) hangs in
diurnal sleep
lethargy from the
back of a door
covering a niche
in the wall of a
church.

The closest attachment is shown by the Lesser and the Greater Horseshoe Bats, Geoffroy's Bat, the Pond Bat, the Particolored Bat, the Northern Bat, and the Gray Long-eared Bat. In summer they are found exclusively in these places. Preferentially or regularly, Brandt's Bat, the Whiskered Bat, the Greater Mouse-eared Bat, the Serotine, the Common Pipistrelle, the Barbastelle, and the Common Long-eared Bat make their summer roosts on and in buildings. Rarely, but regularly, the Noctule, Daubenton's Bat, and Nathusius' Pipistrelle are also found there. A few species also like to overwinter in roosts in cracks in buildings; these include the Particolored Bat, the Northern Bat, the Serotine, the Common Pipistrelle, and Nathusius' Pipistrelle, as well as the Noctule, Leisler's Bat, and both species of long-eared bat.

The conception that many people have of bats hanging freely in large clusters is not at all typical of European house bats. Only

This page, top: As
a substitute cave
in the warmth of
summer this
nursery colony of
the Greater
Mouse-eared Bat
(Myotis myotis)
uses the hollow
space of a pre-
stressed concrete
bridge in Upper
Bavaria.
This page,
bottom: *Noctule*
(Nyctalus
noctula) leaving
its tree-hole roost,
an old
woodpecker hole.

the Greater Mouse-eared Bat as well as the rare horseshoe bats and Geoffroy's Bat offer (or more accurately, offerred) such sights. That they prefer churches, castles, and country houses as domiciles has nothing to do with piety or possible aristocracy. The free-hanging species are true traditionalists that usually inhabit for many generations spacious, undisturbed attics as warm substitute caves. The majority of the native tenants, on the other hand, live extremely secretively and often betray their presence only by a few droppings. Where the suspected perpetrator actually is can become a detective game even in single-family houses. Our idea that bats usually live in old, dilapidated structures is also wrong. Some of the little house-dwellers move into a newly built bungalow just as quickly as the human inhabitants.

NOT ALL ATTICS ARE CREATED EQUAL

To find out what demands bats make on their roosts, we studied in detail colonies of the Greater Mouse-eared Bat, Geoffroy's Bat, and the Lesser Horseshoe Bat. The Mouse-eared Bats by no means hang randomly anywhere in their attic roost in the church in Au in Upper Bavaria. The rafters, because of their size and the existing tem-

perature ranges, offer innumerable possible hanging sites because they are almost exclusively made of unplaned wood from which the bats can hang easily with their sharp claws.

Our measurements made it clear what enormous demands were placed on the thermoregulation systems of the Mouse-eared Bats, especially since the variations in temperature even in summer are much greater than in warmer climes. They spend their daily resting phase in a subtropical microclimate (warming of the attic on a "normal" summer day). The ambient temperature in which they live out their natural active phase at night corresponds to the polar summer day. During the time they spend in the roost, the Mouse-eared Bats skillfully make use of the most comfortable temperature for them in the attic. Depending on temperature and season, they change their hanging locations.

Susanne Vogel found two different strategies with which the Mouse-eared Bats in Au reacted to the warming of their roost. When the temperature rose slowly, the Mouse-eared Bats dispersed their large cluster on the roof ridge and formed small groups that distributed themselves in the same hanging field on lower-lying beams

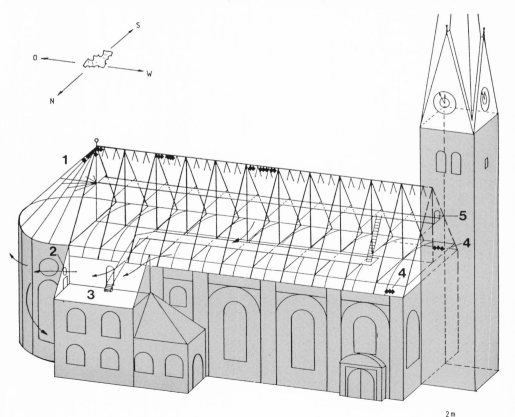

The utilization of a church attic as a nursery colony of the greater mouse-eared bat (Myotis myotis), using the example of the church in Au, Upper Bavaria. 1. Apse field, 2.Exit opening, 3. Exit space, 4. Hanging place in hot weather, 5 . Entrance to the attic (arrows show direction when leaving roost, solid diamonds show principal hanging places of the colony) (from Vogel, 1988).

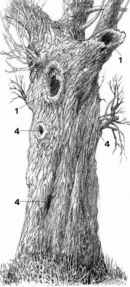

and especially on the diagonal rafters. They did not seek out the cooler hanging sites by flying, but rather climbed down to them. When the temperature rose drastically in the morning, however, the Mouse-eared Bats gradually flew away from their hanging site to form into a large group again in a cooler location. The temperatures in these alternative hanging sites were much lower than the ridge temperature and reached a maximum of 32° C (90°F).

The seasonal changes in hanging sites, on the other hand, are characterized by an apparently "spontaneous" movement of the whole colony to a different area of the roof ridge that showed no measurable difference in microclimate compared to the previously used site.

During pregnancy the animals prefer a very specific hanging site and later disperse over several areas of rafters during the rearing of the young. In the main rearing season, they avoid the mass hanging places, but toward the end of the nursery roost season, when the young can fly, these places become very attractive to all of them again. Felix Heidinger found through precise temperature measurements the reason for this behavior. The pregnant females press close together at the mass hanging place. As a result of the social thermoregulation achieved in this manner the body tempera-

ture remains high, which reduces the expenditure of energy for rapid embryonic development.

The Geoffroy's Bat colony makes completely different demands on its summer roost. Dorothea Krull showed that the Geoffroy's Bats prefer an attic roost that stores heat and acts as a temperature buffer. In contrast to the nearby Mouse-eared Bat roost in Au, the temperatures in the attic of the church in Detterdorf are relatively cool, but also are very constant. Because the rafters warm up very slowly, the roost, which is very cold in the winter, does not reach an average temperature that is comfortable to the Geoffroy's Bats until May. The opposite is true in August and September, when the temperature of the rafters, which release their heat only slowly, is still relatively high. As a result of this progression of temperatures, the Geoffroy's Bats, in contrast to the Mouse-eared Bats, use their summer roost for only about ten weeks. Where the animals stay when they are not in the winter or summer roost remains a mystery for the present. Lesser Horseshoe Bats in turn use different criteria to evaluate the suitability of a roost. Our extremely unusual resettlement action showed that the absolute size of the space is not decisive. Instead, the entire spatial complex, in the manner of a suite of rooms, with variations

Natural and artificial roosts: attics (1) correspond to warm caves in summer in southern Europe (1) and large tree holes (1); cellars, subterranean passages, and so forth (2) correspond to cool, damp caves (2); cracks and fissures in walls (3) correspond to floor rubble in caves (3); hollow spaces (indoors and outdoors) (4) correspond to crevices in rocks (4) and old woodpecker holes or loose bark (4).

*Top: Nursery colony of Geoffroy's Bat (*Myotis emarginatus*). Geoffroy's Bat, extremely rare in Germany, prefers attic roosts with cooler but very constant temperatures.*
*Bottom: Lesser Horseshoe Bats (*Rhinolophus hipposideros*) in the nursery roost. The two German species of horseshoe bat prefer as summer and nursery roosts attics consisting of several room complexes and exhibiting clear differences in microclimate.*

in microclimate are necessary for Lesser Horseshoe Bats. Anyone who wants to make a closer study of the housing requirements of "house bats" will soon also have to learn about architecture and will determine that our little tenants are often living witnesses for particular traditional, stylistic, and landscape-determined building forms. In this way bats have taken part and continue to take part in our cultural history.

BUILDERS AND TENANTS—BATS IN ANIMAL STRUCTURES

Besides human structures, bats also use the dwellings built by other animals as a supply of roosts. This ecological parasitism can be ingenious. African bats of the genus *Kerivoula*, for example, seek out the nests of weaver birds as daytime roosts. The American Cave Bat (*Myotis velifer*) has been found under bridges in the nests of swallows. In England, nest holes of Sand Martins (called Bank Swallows in North America) have been used as roosts by the Whiskered Bat (*Myotis mystacinus*). Round-eared Bats (*Tonatia minuta*) share termite nests in Trinidad with small parrots. Where there is a shortage of roosts, the dens of foxes, badgers, rabbits, and porcupines can become bat lodgings, alway assuming that the excavators have already moved out or tolerate the tenants.

Even spider webs provide roosts for bats. In Gabon, the painted bat *Kerivoula barrisoni* appears to roost fairly regularly under the web of funnel spiders. It uses as a hanging place the thin branches to which the spiders attach the threads of their webs. Small holes in bamboo stalks, which were originally made by insects, are used by the tiny bamboo or club-footed bats, *Tylonycteris*, as entrance holes to their daytime roosts. Finally, the preferred accommodations of European "tree bats" are woodpecker holes. Old Greater Spotted Woodpecker holes, the ceilings of which have been enlarged through fungus attack and decay, are especially coveted bat roosts. The frequent change in roosts of the tree bats probably increases their knowledge of the available supply of holes, but also has hygienic or climatic causes (for example, soiling, valley fog).

Energy Conservation Programs—

Temperature Regulation

The majority of animal species cannot raise their body temperature much above the ambient temperature. When it turns cold around them they are sentenced to inactivity. Largely dependent on the ambient temperature, such species are called "cold-blooded" or poikilothermic ("variable temperature") animals. The cold-blooded animals include not only invertebrates, but (with few exceptions) fishes, amphibians, and reptiles as well. Only mammals and birds can regulate their body temperature at a nearly constant level. For this reason they are also called "warm-blooded" or homoiothermic ("constant temperature") animals.

Because the production of heat, as well as cooling, requires a great deal of energy and demands a good food supply, energy conservation measures are particularly important in times of cold. Through the molting of hair and feathers, a better level of insulation is achieved. Additional energy-saving tricks used by warm-blooded ani-

The lesser horseshoe bat (Rhinolophus hipposideros) wraps itself almost completely in its wing membranes during diurnal sleep lethargy.

The free-hanging flying foxes (Pteropus giganteus) use their wing membranes for protection against wind and weather and can also regulate their temperature with them.

Energy-saving tricks of pregnant female greater mouse-eared bats (Myotis myotis, above and right). When sufficient food is available, the pregnant females press close together in the roost and in this way maintain their body temperature as high as possible to promote rapid embryonic development .

their body temperature day and night at a virtually constant level. Measurements of the body temperatures of these species usually exhibit only slight changes in the alternation of rest and activity. Erwin Kulzer has investigated intensively the temperature regulation of bats from various climatic zones. The researcher recognized at least three different patterns of temperature regu-

mals include reducing the blood supply to the skin and rolling into a ball to reduce the body's surface area.

Some mammals, like hedgehogs and hamsters, allow themselves to cool at certain times and through hibernation save the costly expense of generating warmth in the body. Heterothermic ("unequal temperature") is the term used to describe these animals. By increasing their own production of heat, they wake from hibernation. The body temperature during hibernation lies only slightly above the ambient temperature and can sink almost to the freezing point. In so doing, all metabolic processes are so greatly reduced that the animals can survive the winter without food intake by converting into energy the fat deposits that were accumulated under the skin in the summer.

As a consequence of their body structure and their habits, bats are particularly obliged to conserve energy and have therefore evolved the greatest diversity of temperature regulating mechanisms of all mammals. Because of the heat-radiating surface area of the blood-filled wing membranes, the amount of heat lost is much greater than in other mammals of comparable size. In addition, bats live in spaces with the most variable ambient temperatures, ranging from damp, hot tropical climates to subarctic cold. Finally, many species must be able to survive long periods without food.

The larger flying foxes as well as the medium-sized to very large bats regulate

VENTILATORS, RAINCOATS, AND THERMOSTATS

The large *Pteropus* species, which roost in the open in trees, use their wings very skillfully to protect themselves against wind and weather as well as for temperature regulation. As the temperature rises in the daytime, they unfold their wings and start to fan them. If this "ventilation" is insufficient to prevent overheating, the flying foxes also use their saliva for evaporative cooling. They wet their fur and wings with it and through vigorous wingbeats promote evaporation. In rain and stormy weather the wing membranes are used as protection against rain, the wings being wrapped like a jacket around the body.

Warm body air can accumulate under the wings, which guards against undercooling in occasionally bad tropical weather. As Erwin Kulzer discovered, the small and medium-sized species maintain their body temperature during the active phase at the high level of 36 to 38° C (96 to 100°F). During the resting phase, however, their body temperature sinks, depending on the ambient temperature, to lower values of 18 to 26° C (65 to 79°F). Many bats of the tropics and subtropics belong to this group. Although the lowered body temperature makes the bats sluggish, it contributes greatly to energy conservation.

Several free-tailed bats represent the transition to true hibernators. Their representatives, which range into the temperate zones, can, particularly in the winter months, lower their body temperature by up to 10° C (18°F). In this state they are absolutely lethargic. Nonetheless, this lethargy does not last long. At the beginning of the active phase, free-tailed bats regularly waken from their torpid condition.

The temperature sinks the lowest in a third group of bats. In the waking state these small to medium-sized species regulate their body temperature at a high operating level. In the resting state the body temperature approaches the ambient temperature and readings of just above the freezing point can be achieved. At refrigerator temperatures they rest in the deepest lethargy (torpor) and even begin to hibernate. Some species of the common bat and horseshoe bat families are true "heterotherms" and can withstand unusually great fluctuations in body temperature.

DIURNAL SLEEP LETHARGY—ENERGY CONSERVATION AS OCCASION DEMANDS

The difference between the waking and resting temperatures in bats of the temperate climatic zone was first noted by the bat researcher Martin Eisentraut. In the 1930's he discovered that bats he examined in May in their summer quarters exhibited too low body temperatures (16 to 18° C, 60 to 65°F) during the day to still be able to fly. In the evening and nighttime hours, in contrast, they reached their working temperature of between 35 and 42° C (95 and 108°F). Eisentraut called the lethargic state during the daytime sleeping phase "diurnal sleep lethargy." Many laboratory studies of this phenomenon have shown that the sleeping temperature is largely dependent on the prevailing ambient temperature. Bats are able to end their diurnal sleep lethargy at any time and can warm themselves to "operating temperature" again in less than 30 minutes. Furthermore, the lowering of the body temperature occurs only when the bats are undisturbed and the ambient temperature is substantially below the waking temperature. Finally, the animals can dispense entirely with diurnal sleep lethargy when, for instance, young must be cared for and when it is essential not to delay embryonic development. Bats always use this ability to regulate their body temperature to save energy. In diurnal sleep lethargy the body temperature is maintained between 10 and 28° C (50 and 82°F). The lower it is, the more it limits the bats' ability to move. Thus, at 15° C (59°F), their movements are reduced to slow motion.

HIBERNATION—A MASTERFUL ACHIEVEMENT OF MEASURING AND REGULATING TECHNIQUE

To survive the long, foodless winter in temperate latitudes, there are only two alternatives for bats: migrating to warmer regions with a sufficient food supply or persisting without food. Like migratory birds,

North American populations of the Mexican Free-tailed Bat (*Tadarida brasiliensis*), for example, migrate to warmer regions.

Many species, however, survive the winter in a state of extended lethargy. In so doing, their body temperature falls far below the values achieved in diurnal sleep lethargy. Hibernating bats can cool their bodies almost to the freezing point. Their metabolic processes are so greatly reduced that they can survive for months without food intake. With the help of the energy reserves stored in the summer alone, they survive the period of cold. A special fatty tissue, brown fat, which is located in thick deposits between the shoulder blades as well as on the neck and the flanks, serves the bats as an energy store. Particularly in late summer—in good weather extending into November—bats add to their stores of fat. By employing diurnal sleep lethargy, they keep their daily energy use particularly low during this "storage period." With the addition of the stores of fat, the bats weigh 20 to 30 percent more than in the spring. The hibernating bats must tap this supply for up to six months.

The cells of the brown fatty tissue are surrounded by a network of hair follicles and nerve fibers. Erwin Kulzer described the release of the energy reserves as follows: "In the cells (of the fatty tissue) themselves are contained small fatty droplets that contain the oxidizable substances (neutral fats). On a signal, which reaches the cells via the sympathetic nervous system, rapid heat production begins inside them, which is achieved through a biochemical trick. All

. . . in times of food shortage, energy conservation by moving apart is the only remaining helpful tactic; in this way the body temperature sinks, to be sure at the expense of rapid birth (slowed down embryonic development).

93

Members of a nursery colony of the greater mouse-eared bat (Myotis myotis) hang in a dense cluster in diurnal sleep lethargy.

Overwintering lesser horseshoe bats (Rhinolophus hipposideros) always hang freely from the roof of their winter roost: completely wrapped in the wing membranes, viewed from the side (right) or from behind (above), the hibernating bats look like small, shrivelled fruits.

studies up until now have shown that this tissue is used for the rapid production of heat, which is therefore also called the 'chemical and shiver-free' type of heat production in the body. Through the blood the warmth generated is rapidly transported to the rest of the body. In addition, shivering of muscles also contributes to the rewarming of the body; it is evident in the 'vibration' of the whole body."

In hibernation, bats are almost completely "frozen." With a body temperature of 0 to 10°C (32 to 50°F), they are capable under certain circumstances of only a few life-saving reflex movements: spreading the wings (in falls from the resting position), closing the mouth, screeching, defensive bites, climbing "hand over hand," and searching movements.

LIFE'S FLAME ON PILOT LIGHT

Bats stay in a state of cold-induced lethargy longer than other hibernating mammals. A period of deep sleep can last longer than a month before a hibernating bat warms up again either spontaneously or through an external stimulus. But the hibernating bat maintains control over its temperature regulation only as long as sufficient energy supplies are available. If the energy reserves are consumed prematurely, the bat is thrown into a dangerous undercooling and dies of hypothermia. So that the stored energy reserves will last, all life processes run very economically. Breathing can be interrupted by pauses lasting for minutes. In deep hibernation the oxygen consumption at a body temperature of 5 to 6° C (41 to 43°F) is extremely low and amounts to between 0.02 and 0.07 milliliters per gram an hour. This corresponds to only about one percent of the consumption in the waking state. The heart rate also decreases. In the Greater Mouse-eared Bat, for example, at 15 to 20 beats a minute it amounts to only about one-fortieth of the highest value in the waking state. The heart rate decreases as soon as the bat falls asleep, before reaching minimal values gradually. In general, the switch to "winter operation" does not occur suddenly. Rather, the metabolism of the bat slowly changes over to the "hibernation mode" when nights become increasingly colder in the fall. Bats seek out their winter roosts starting in October and November. The exact time apparently is determined both by the ambient temperature and an internal clock. The onset of lethargy is most easy to recognize by the change to regular breathing with long pauses. In this phase the slightest noise acts as a waking signal, causing the bat to accelerate its breathing.

Erwin Kulzer described the way in which bats regulate their production of body heat: "In the hibernating bat the regulator is located in the middle brain; it consists of hundreds of nerve cells, of centers that are responsible for heating and those that are responsible for cooling. The signals from the temperature sensors of the skin constantly feed into here and give the regulator 'early warning' in the event that greater temperature changes have occurred in the environment. Minute changes in the blood temperature are also measured here. From the regulator the information is transferred to the 'adjusting mechanisms' (sites of heat production, blood vessels in the skin, provisions for increasing or decreasing the release of heat)."

The regulation of the body temperature of bats is also subject to a program for day and night. Additional programs are invoked during lethargy and hibernation. It is possible that in hibernation not only is heat production checked, but that the mechanism that protects warm-blooded animals against cold (retention of body heat) is also suppressed. In this way the body cools in a deliberate manner to a new, lower level that corresponds to the ambient temperature. Bats seek out the most favorable temperature conditions within the winter roost to keep energy consumption as low as possible. The control of this state must not be allowed to lapse for even a moment. The "cold warning" is the last safety device built in for this purpose. In reaction to the entry of cold into the winter roost, hibernating bats immediately go into a state of alarm and increase their production of heat. The heart rate increases so that the blood can rapidly reach the vital organs. This continues until the "all clear signal" is given by the body or the bat wakes up.

Hibernating Daubenton's bat (Myotis daubentoni). It prefers crevices as a winter roost.

page 95 Common long-eared bats (Plecotus auritus) also overwinter at suitable ambient temperatures in above-ground spaces of buildings. Here four hibernating bats are hanging in a niche in a wall behind the choir stall of a church.

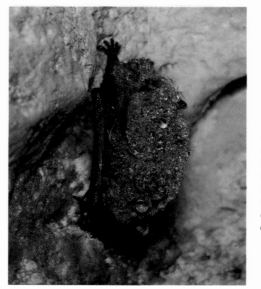

Whiskered bat (Myotis mystacinus) in hibernation. Because of the high humidity in the winter roost, its fur is covered with large drops of dew.

Winter Roosts—Each Species Has Its Own Requirements

Each fall the great movement of bats from their summer roosts to suitable winter housing is repeated. How they find the winter roosts is still largely their secret. Because echolocation functions only at close range, the migrating bats seem much more likely to navigate with the aid of visual landmarks such as mountains, rivers, and valleys, as well as by the position of the sun and stars. Rocky caves, mines, crevices, joints in outside walls, separate beer and ice cellars, basements, as well as holes in large old trees, hiding places in apertures on and in houses, and even the gaps in stacks of firewood in airy sheds or outdoors serve as winter accommodations that the different species use in a typical manner and that are dependent on availability. Most European bat species, however, prefer moist, cool winter roosts of the "cave" type with constant low temperatures and high humidity. In winter roosts of this kind it is often possible to find several bat species at the same time occupying species-specific sleeping places.

MOVEMENT IN AND OUT OF THE WINTER ROOST

Depending on the species and sex, bats seek out winter roosts at different times. As the zoologists Daan and Wichers, for example, determined in their studies in the Limburg limestone caves in the Netherlands, throughout the month of October Whiskered (*Myotis mystacinus*) and Daubenton's Bats (*Myotis daubentoni*) arrived.

Mouse-eared Bats (*Myotis myotis*) arrived in mid-October, Natterer's Bats (*Myotis nattereri*) toward the end of October, and Common Long-eared Bats (*Plecotus auritus*) did not enter the winter roosts until early November. Females arrived before males, but in turn left the roost earlier in the spring. For a winter roost in Deister, Lower Saxony, Germany, Ehlers gave the following times for the movement from the roost: Natterer's Bat early March to late March, Daubenton's Bat early March to late April, Common Long-eared Bat early April, and Greater Mouse-eared Bat mid-April to early May. During cold snaps in late April/early May, we observed Lesser Horseshoe Bats changing quarters, which after moving into the summer roost again sought shelter under winter roost conditions. It is possible that bats move back into nearby winter roosts during cold spells in the spring.

WHAT MAKES WINTER ROOSTS ATTRACTIVE?

Depending on the preferred winter roost, we distinguish between "tree" and "cave" bats. In general, caves in rock offer more constant and more favorable overwintering condtions than do tree holes. Tree bats must therefore be hardier than cave bats because of cold and low humidity.

A number of criteria must be fulfilled for a cave or tunnel to be accepted as a winter roost:
1) Safety from predators.
2) Minimal light levels.
3) The suitability of a cave as a winter roost also depends on its length: The longer it is, as a rule the more bats will be found in it.
4) Temperature regime: depending on ventilation, location, form, and size of the cave, different temperature conditions prevail. The measurements of bat researchers show that the individual bat species prefer particular temperature ranges.

In Polish winter roosts, Kowalski found seven species of hibernating bats in the temperature range of 0 to 8° C (32 to 46°F). The individual species preferred the following temperatures:

Barbastelle, 0-4° C
Whiskered Bat, 2-4° C
Northern Bat, 0-5.5° C

Common Long-eared Bat, 0-7° C
Greater Mouse-eared Bat 2-7° C
Geoffroy's Bat, 7-8° C
Lesser Horseshoe Bat, 6-7.5° C.

Temperature measurments made by Günter Hansbauer in the winters of 1985/86 and 1987/88 at hanging places of six bat species in caves in the Bavarian Alps showed the same result. Whereas Barbastelles stayed in the coolest places (1 to 5° C), Lesser Horseshoe Bats overwintered under the warmest conditions (6 to 8.3° C). Therefore, the species are not distributed uniformly in space throughout the whole cave, but rather there are centers of distribution. Because of their preference for cool temperatures, Barbastelles are principally found in the entrance region; on the other hand, Lesser Horseshoe Bats occur more commonly in the deepest parts of the cave.

Not just particular temperature values but also a specific range of variation of temperatures in the winter roost are critical for certain bats. In his studies of the hibernation behavior of the Greater Horseshoe Bat (*Rhinolophus ferrumequinum*) in England, Ransome found that conspicuously few bats overwinter in caves with very small temperature fluctuations (less than +/-1° C). When he moderated the temperature fluctuations in heavily populated roosts, the number of overwintering bats was greatly reduced. Only after the researcher restored the original conditions did the number of winter visitors increase again.

The altitude of a winter roost also influences the temperature conditions and is therefore likely also a criterion for roost selection, as bat researchers in the Swabian Alb and the Bavarian Alps observed. In otherwise identically furnished roosts, bats prefer winter roosts that offer the most favorable overwintering temperatures for them.

5) Humidity: Loss of water is just as perilous as energy loss for overwintering bats. The delicate wing membranes can dry out rapidly under conditions of excessively high evaporation. Long-eared bats have found an elegant solution for their huge ears, which are additional problem surfaces. They fold their external ears together and tuck them back under the wings. For exposed hanging species, such as horseshoe bats, high humidity is particularly important. The Lesser Horseshoe Bat, in particular, does not fold its wings together in hibernation, but rather wraps them around its small body as an insulating coat. Most species require a minimum humidity of 85 percent in the winter roost.

6) Suitable hanging places: Because central European species overwinter in quite variable sleeping positions, suitable hanging places for them must be available in the winter roost. Based on their body contact to the hanging place, we distinguish three categories of hibernating bats. While some hang completely freely at their hanging places (usually the roof of the cave) and

Hanging place distribution and preferred temperature of several Central European bat species that overwinter in caves. Whereas the barbastelle (1) prefers cooler temperatures, the common long-eared bat (2) exhibits a wide tolerance with respect to hanging place and ambient temperature. Daubenton's bat (3) likes to hide in crevices in ceilings and walls and in the ground rubble. The "free-hangers," such as the lesser horseshoe bat (4), require the most constant temperatures.

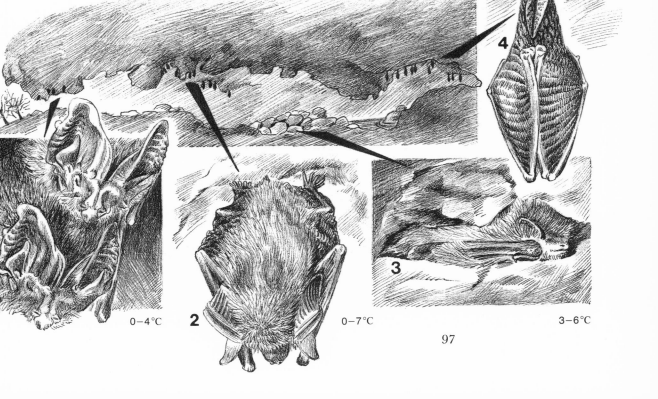

6–8°C

4

1   0–4°C

2   0–7°C

3   3–6°C

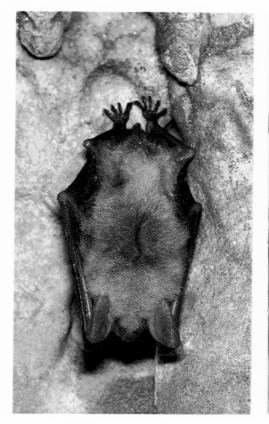

Hibernating greater mouse-eared bats (Myotis myotis) are quite variable. They can hang individually on walls (right) or from the roofs of caves, but also hibernate in small groups (below) and even individually in crevices (center right).

maintain contact only with the claws of their feet, others seek out additional shelter in recesses. They sleep, so to speak, in a "microbiotope" and in this way also protect themselves against small temperature changes in the environment. The third category contains species that seek out, as far as possible, contact on all sides with the substrate. These bats sleep only in crevices, cracks, or tubelike holes in the rock. Because of this secretive behavior, they inadvertently present the greatest problems for bat researchers and conservationists. Often they can be found in their winter hiding places only with great effort, with tricks such as the use of mirrors to investigate hollow spaces, and with a good nose for finding them. According to their increasing need to hide, the most common European cave hibernators can be arranged in the following sequence: Lesser Horseshoe Bat > Greater Horseshoe Bat > Greater Mouse-eared Bat > Geoffroy's Bat > Whiskered Bat > Pond Bat > Common Long-eared Bat > Daubenton's Bat > Natterer's Bat.

Species that are variable in their selection of hanging sites often prefer unprotected sleeping places in the inner parts of caves in which slight climatic variations prevail. In

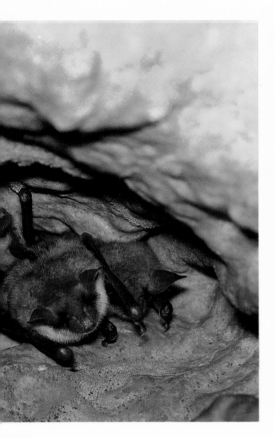

Long-eared bats fold their huge ears together and place them under the wings in hibernation. By decreasing the surface area the evaporation losses are reduced.

*Whiskered bat (*Myotis mystacinus*) in the winter roost. It has "turned a silvery color" because of the dew drops on the fur.*

the exposed entrance region they usually hide in cracks. Some bats can even hide themselves in rubble on the bottom of caves to overwinter. Mouse-eared Bats, Whiskered Bats, and Daubenton's Bats have been found in inhospitable places of this kind.

With the exception of horseshoe bats, which always maintain a distance from their neighbors, probably all other European bats can form clusters in the winter roost. The advantage of sleeping groups lies in the reduction of heat loss and thus energy loss. By hanging close together or even on top of one another like roof tiles, the animals inside the cluster in particular experience less heat loss as a result of social thermoregulation. In cluster formation, a considerable interspecific tolerance generally prevails. Up to five species have been found sleeping together peacefully.

The relative activity of the hibernating bats never ceases to offer surprises. For example, they change their hanging places and occasionally even their roosts. Interruptions in sleeping and changes of position are triggered by changes in the preferred temperature, but can also be purely a matter of choice as is known of Daubenton's Bat.

Laurent Perrin was able to collect revealing data at a crevice roost of the Noctule (*Nyctalus noctula*) in the vicinity of Basel, Switzerland. The crevice roost exhibited a microclimate that differed from that found in two other types of Noctule roosts (tree, building). In the fall it was significantly

Documentation of decline: Where in 1957 a whole colony of hibernating lesser horseshoe bats (Rhinolophus hipposideros) overwintered, today only one hibernating bat remains.

warmer in the crevices, for which reason the bats arrived there later than usual. In the system of cracks of the Jurassic rock formation, Perrin found temperature differences between the outer and inner zones. The overwintering Noctules used this temperature gradient cleverly, in that they moved their hibernating places in the system of cracks and thus largely determined their microclimate themselves. The advantage of the crevice roost above all lay in safety from frost. This was ensured in crevices starting at a depth of one meter (a yard), yet all tree and building roosts in the vicinity could be penetrated by frost.

Human disturbance in the winter roosts is especially dangerous for bats. Slight touching, prolonged illumination with a flashlight, repeated flash photography, and even an extended stay in close proximity to the hibernating animals (due to temperature elevation through the radiation of heat) act as a waking stimulus. The animals wake up and may even seek out different sleeping places. Fairly long waking phases are dangerous, however, because the stored energy reserves are rapidly used up. This increases the danger that the bats will not have the energy to awaken in the spring or that they will not be strong enough to hunt. Therefore, winter roosts require special protection. As late as the 1950's there were mass gatherings of bats in German overwintering roosts. Both sociability as well as better temperature regulation might cause the hibernators to gather in numbers in this way. The hibernating gatherings (for example, in Bavaria of 100 Greater and 200 Lesser Horseshoe Bats in the Grossen Schullerlock at Kelheim, Bavaria; of 7500 Mouse-eared Bats in the Hohlloch at Weissenberg; and the 3000 Barbastelles in the Bodenmaiser mines) were famous. Such an abundance of hibernating bats in Germany has long since been a thing of the past. Today mass winter roosts are found in Europe only in the eastern areas. But the same rules apply whether in the mass winter roost at Nietopererk in western Poland with over 20,000 bats or a few bats in a small beer cellar: Because we know the dangers to which they are exposed, we should grant all hibernating bats an undisturbed sleep.

Bats Migrate Too

Even early naturalists noted that bats in the temperate climatic zones did not appear at the summer roosts until the warm season and left them again in the autumn. Like migratory birds, it was assumed that bats also spent the winter in southern lands. Yet the majority of bats do not migrate in search of an abundant food supply; instead, they look for suitable winter roosts. Long-distance migrants, however, are found among North American and Russian bats. All members or at least some individual species of the genera *Nyctalus*, *Vespertilio*, *Lasiurus*, *Lasionycteris*, *Miniopterus*, *Pipistrellus*, and *Tadarida* undertake seasonal migrations, principally in a north—south direction, of medium (300 to 500 kilometers, 180 to 300 miles) to long distances (1000 to 1500 kilometers, 600 to 900 miles).

LORDS OF THE RINGS

To examine the migratory behavior of bats, experience gained in ornithology was called into play. For the first bat banding in 1916, the American zoologist Allen put bird bands around the legs of bats. In Europe, Eisentraut in 1932 began the first bat banding in Germany. Eisentraut developed special aluminum clamps that are applied to the forearm of the bat in such a way that the bat still has freedom of movement. Banding centers were established in many countries to coordinate the rapidly increasing marking activity. The bands issued from these places contained a band number and the abbreviation of the center. With weights of between 0.10 and 0.19 grams, the bands do not hinder the flying ability of their carriers. However, bats often bite around

*Long-distance migrations of the noctule (*Nyctalus noctula*) in Europe. The seasonal migratory behavior is clearly directional. Animals banded in the summer roost (solid circle) migrate in the fall principally in a southern or southwestern direction. The noctules marked in the winter roost (open circle) in the spring fly correspondingly to the north or the northeast (from Hill & Smith, 1984).*

*Greater horseshoe bats (*Rhinolophus ferrumequinum*) banded by the Hoopers in Devon, England, frequently returned (thicker lines with double arrows) to the banding site (central dot). Some of the short-distance migrants, however, also went "on tour" (thinner lines), probably to check out more distant roosts (from Hill & Smith, 1984).*

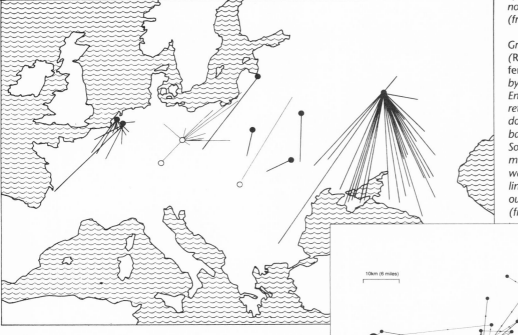

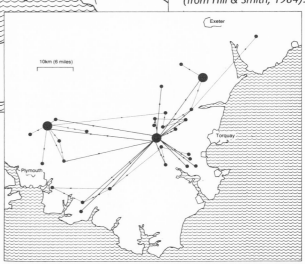

101

Leisler's bat (Nyctalus leisleri) with an aluminum band. Recoveries provide information on migrations, population biology, and roost behavior.

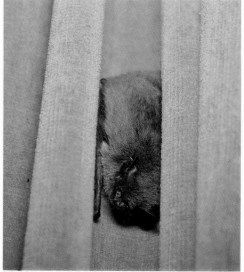

During their change in roosts in late summers, common pipistrelles (Pipistrellus pipistrellus) frequently fly into homes and readily accept curtains as hiding places.

Colony of Schreiber's bat (Miniopterus shreibersi) in a cave in southern Europe. These typical cave bats are the most widely naturally distributed mammal species in the world and occur from Europe through Asia to Australia.

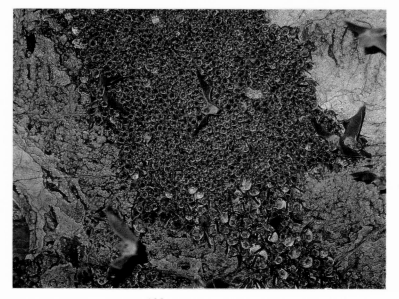

these foreign bodies, which can lead to injuries to the wing membranes when the bands are not properly applied or are made of too soft a material.

Today the great "banding boom" is over. Special permits for the banding of bats are issued by conservation officials only when scientific questions can be answered through banding, the results of which directly or indirectly benefit the conservation of the animals. Up to 1945, the Zoological Museum of the University of Berlin was the German banding center. For the new German federal states in what was formerly East Germany, the Institute for National Research and Nature Conservation of the Academy of Sciences, Dresden branch, has authority. In the old German federal states (West Germany), Hubert Roer of the Zoological Research Institute and the Alexander Koenig Museum in Bonn is the "lord of the rings." This method of marking helped to answer many questions, from migratory behavior through population biology to roost behavior.

DIFFERING TENDENCIES TO MIGRATE

The zoologist Roer from Bonn, Germany, divides the European bats—based on banding results—into migrants, partial migrants, and permanent residents. With an average distance of migration of more than 250 kilometers (150 miles), Noctules, Schreiber's Bats, Leisler's Bats, Nathusius' Pipistrelles, Sari's Pipistrelles, and Northern Bats belong to the long-distance migrants. Medium-distance migrants (partial migrants) such as Common Pipistrelles, Pond Bats, Daubenton's Bats, and Serotines travel average distances of between 20 and 250 kilometers (12 and 150 miles), whereas the permanent residents, such as Grey Long-eared Bats, Common Long-eared Bats, Geoffroy's Bats, Greater Horseshoe Bats, and Lesser Horseshoe Bats, which usually travel distances of less than 20 kilometers (12 miles), are decidedly sedentary.

The Soviet zoologist P. P. Strelkov studied the migratory behavior of eastern European Noctules, which doubtless avoid the cold mainland winter through long migrations. Their migration takes place in the autumn primarily in a southerly or southwesterly direction. In the spring, on the other hand, they move to the north or northeast. It is suspected that the Russian noctules overwinter in southeastern Europe or in eastern central Europe, possibly also in the Caucasus

Miniopterus
schreibersi
migrate 100 to
350 kilometers
during their
seasonal change
in roosts.

or on the Crimean Peninsula. The record-holder is a Noctule banded in August, 1957, at Voronezh, Russia, which turned up in southern Bulgaria in January, 1961. The animal had traveled a distance of 2347 kilometers (1408 miles) as the crow flies.

American long-distance migrants include the Mexican Free-tailed Bat (*Tadarida brasiliensis*). Different populations of these animals exhibit quite distinct migrating behavior. While two populations do not undertake a proper migration at all and during a mild winter merely briefly become lethargic or simply seek out warmer quarters, the population living in southeastern Utah, southwestern Colorado, eastern Arizona, and western New Mexico migrates annually up to 1000 kilometers (600 miles) to the south in western Mexico. The fourth group embraces the population of Oklahoma, eastern New Mexico, Texas, and the southeastern states. To this population belongs the animals of the famous Carlsbad and Bracken Caverns. This population, numbering upward of a million individuals, also spends the winter months in food-rich Mexico.

The migrations of the Greater Horseshoe Bat in Devon, England, have been particularly well documented through the work of the Hoopers. Their seasonal migrations extend scarcely further than 30 kilometers (18 miles).

Partial migrants and permanent residents have in common that they do not prefer a particular migration direction. The path they take is generally in the direction of suitable roosts.

The North American Gray Bat (*Myotis grisescens*) is very strictly bound to a few overwintering caves. Merlin D. Tuttle studied this species for many years and was able to prove that more than 95 percent of all animals overwinter in only nine caves. Of these caves, two located in eastern Tennessee have a combined winter population of about 375,000 animals. The majority of Gray Bats overwinter in a cave in northern Alabama (approximately 1,500,000 individuals). Uniformly cool temperatures and high humidity make this winter meeting

103

place attractive. Independent of how they spend their summer season, almost all of the Gray Bats return to their respective original winter roost. As Tuttle determined, they do not change quarters in winter. Of 3220 animals banded in the winter roost, in 14 years of research activity the researcher was unable to find a single one in a different winter roost. The roost fidelity of the Gray Bat, however, holds a grave danger: The loss of a single winter roost would seriously threaten the survival of the entire species.

SMALL INVADERS

Bats make newspaper headlines most frequently in August and September. Every year small bats are found in town X in house Y hanging in the folds of drapes or fluttering around in a room. If the fire department or police is able to remove the little invader without bloodshed, the bat is lucky. Of all the European bats, the Common Pipistrelle, the smallest species, causes the most bewilderment. Based on the studies of various bat researchers, it is known that invasion-like mass flights are typical for this species. The casual house visitor is most likely an animal from a dispersed summer roost that has ended up in temporary quarters. It is possible that once they have visited a temporary roost, they will continue to seek it out in coming years.

Invasions can also end in death without outside influence. Sometimes bats that have found their way into buildings can no longer find their way out or even fly into a real trap. Roer, for example, found 1180 dead Common Pipistrelles in the air vents of a hospital located in the middle of Bonn, Germany. The animals had entered the open ducts and had died there. The gregarious animals apparently do not have any warning behavior that could have alerted members of the same species that arrived later.

TROPICAL WANDERERS, BIRD ACCOMPANIERS, AND STRAYS

Tropical bats also migrate. Their migrations are governed by the food supply, such as the time of ripening of fruits. Australian Big-headed Flying Foxes (*Pteropus poliocephalus*) feed on cultivated fruits only when their natural foods are in short supply. Flowers and nectar of eucalyptus and wild fruits are preferred. In March and April these foods become scarce in the southern part of their range. Then the Big-headed Flying Foxes move to the north (winter migration) and in a few weeks can cover distances of up to 1000 kilometers (600 miles), reaching far up the coast of Queensland.

The African Straw-colored Fruit Bat (*Eidolon helvum*) also undertakes long migration flights of about 1000 kilometers (600 miles), although the reasons for their migration behavior have not yet been fully explained.

The American *Lasiurus* species *L. cinereus*, *L. borealis*, and *L. seminolus*, as well as the American Northern Yellow Bat (*Lasiurus intermedius*), even migrate together with birds or use the same migration routes. Sometimes they meet with the same misfortunes as their feathered colleagues in the course of their journey: They may collide with the Empire State Building in midtown Manhattan or a tall television tower in Florida, as well as other obstacles standing in their migration path.

When the wind is particularly strong, long-distance migrants become involuntary travelers to new shores. The Australian Big-headed Flying Foxes have reached Tasmania in this way. *Lasiurus cinereus* has even reached the Hawaiian Islands, located 4000 kilometers (2400 miles) from the American mainland, and there in isolation has developed the characteristics of an island race. Sometimes bats become stowaways and travel on ships or planes to distant lands. None of these travelers has as yet succeeded in becoming established, as have, for example, their rodent colleagues the house mouse and rat.

Bats and Humankind

Bats have never been a matter of indifference to humankind. Their peculiar form and their mysterious lives have always stimulated the human imagination. The origin of all of the tales of horror, myths, and superstitious ideas associated with bats is no doubt their secretive and silent, nocturnal way of life. Whatever largely escapes the human eye and understanding soon receives the stamp of the weird, dangerous, and, yes, even evil. *The Pocket Dictionary of German Superstition* offers a wealth of citations concerning all that mythologists and weavers of legend have composed about bats in all ages and cultures. Although evil clearly dominates, the reputedly demonic animals are also used to ward off evil and are sometimes even thought of as lucky mascots. The peculiar dualism in the way bats are viewed is in the final view a reflection of our own human soul. Torn to and fro between good and evil, life and death, luck and misfortune, bats must stand as a symbol for the many facets of our own fickle lives.

THE DUAL NATURE OF THE BAT

"The bat, the bat, she pulls the stockings off the bride . . . ." That the bat turns up in the old folk song of the "bird wedding" is no accident. Its roots go back to the year 1530, a time in which the bats were officially still classified with the birds. "The bat is not only forbidden as an unclean bird in Judaic law, but should also be thought of as an abomination," writes the naturalist Conrad Gesner in 1581 in his great animal book. Gesner was able to rely on the Book of Moses, in which the bat in the Bible was numbered among the unclean birds. The bat also appears in Homer as a bird, and in old zoology texts is presented as the "bird with no tongue, which nurses its young." Because of its bare wing membranes, it is called "leather woodpecker" in Westphalian.

Aesop describes in two fables the encounter of bats and weasels. When a weasel has seized a fallen bat and says to it that he is an enemy of all birds, the bat, with a quick wit, answers that he is not a bird but a mouse. On another occasion the bat talks its

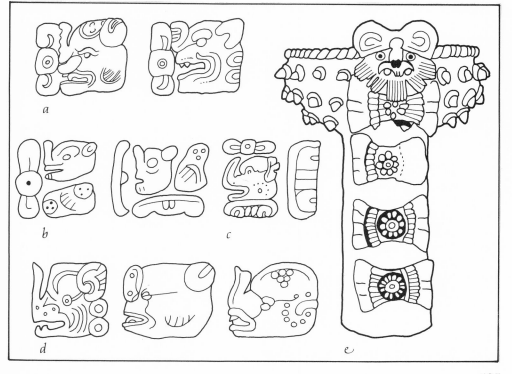

a

b

c

d

e

Mesoamerican "bat spirits" show bats as life givers: a. Classical Mayan hieroglyphs of the "horseshoe bat"; b. "Bat formulas"; c. "Birth of the bat"; d. Classical standard forms of bat hieroglyphs; e. Zapotec pipe, "bat with rosette attributes" (from Dobat, 1985).

way out of trouble with a mouse- hunting weasel by saying that he has wings and is thus a bird. Such ambiguity has its consequences. For example, the Alsation term "fledermüsle" is used in the sense of "to speak or act ambiguously." "Bacon mouse" is another common name for bats, because it was believed that the animals that were often encountered in chimneys ate the bacon hanging there. There also existed an explanation for their metamorphosis: According to a Carpathian popular belief, each mouse that has gnawed at consecrated bread must become a bat.

DEATH AND THE DEVIL

Death and darkness stand in close relationship in the human world of the imagination. As the night warned of the extinction of life, so too the nocturnal bat, in the same way as the owl, became a bad omen, even a symbol of death. The appearance of bats in a dream was considered to be an omen of threatening illness or loss, of a storm on the ocean, or of a surprise attack by bandits. Illness is often the harbinger of death, approaching in bat form. Accepted as demons of fever in India and Sri Lanka, among the southern Slavs bats embodied the plague. Bat droppings on the head signified an ensuing illness. Even more frequently, however, the bat is a messenger of death in that it flies over the head of the person doomed to die or pulls his hair out.

The association with hell becomes particularly clear through a custom of the Gypsies in Siebenbürgen. They protected themselves against a bat that had flown into the room by as quickly as possible throwing out of the window or door as many glowing coals as the house had family members. In many cultures there prevails the belief that human souls fly around at night as bats, whether it be those of the dead who can find no peace or those of sleeping persons before they awake, as is claimed in Finland. The metamorphosis into a bat often occurs as punishment for a life of sin.

According to an old popular belief, with the aid of bat magic it is possible to take something away from the Devil: As many drops of blood from a killed bat that are allowed to fall onto silk, as many souls are wrested from the Devil. Superstition establishes a close connection between bats, witches, and the devil. "Flittermouse" (tinsel-mouse) is one of the most common names for the Devil. According to a popular

belief of Gypsies, the bat was created from a kiss given to a sleeping woman by the Devil. Satan is also said to fly into the house after bats. This, of course, takes place on membranous wings. In sacred art as well, good and evil are distinguished on the basis of the flight apparatus. Whereas angels always float on bird's wings, the creatures of hell always have bat's wings. Bats also play a role in satanic incantations: pacts with the Devil are preferentially signed in bat's blood. If you wanted to make a girl dance (dancing was considered a devilish enticement to lust) you wrote the girl's name in bat's blood on a scrap of paper and tossed it to the ground. If the girl stepped on it she had to dance, whether she wanted to or not. In exorcisms the evil spirit was supposed to fly from the possessed's mouth "like a bat." In some Italian dialects the bat is named after the Devil, as in Brindisi in which it is called "diaulicchiu" (the "little Devil").

Among the Mayas of Central America the bat god Camazótz (the bat of death) held a position of great reverence. In Mayan representations it has human form, bat's wings, and the lanceolate nasal process exhibited by many American leaf-nosed bats. Yet Camazótz was not only the "vampire of death," it was also a symbol of resurrection. In the highlands of Guatemala an entire clan named itself for this god: "Zotzil" (those belonging to the bat). More recent interpretations of the hieroglyphics

Death and the devil with bat symbols. In a representation of the devil in a small Upper Bavarian church, the devil has bat wings (left). Father Time as Death grasps an hour glass, as a symbol of the finiteness of life (right).

and art of the Mayas, Zapoteks, and other peoples in southern Mexico and northern Central America, however, put the representations of bats in a totally different light. Assuming that the ancient peoples were familiar with flower-feeding bats, the ancient artists could have been portraying bats visiting flowers and feeding on nectar instead of bloodthirsty bat doings such as "tearing off heads" or "tearing out hearts."

As a demonic animal, the bat has been used homopathically to ward off demons, and in Christian times witches and devils too. The custom described by Plinius of protecting the house against the influences of evil demons by carrying a living bat around the house three times before hanging it on the door or window has its parallel in Bavaria as well. In Swabia, bats were nailed to house doors for protection against witchcraft. In the Allgau the same thing was done on barn doors. In the vicinity of Landhut, a bat above the door of the house or barn was supposed to protect against fire and lightning. There they even impaled them on the horns of cattle so that the cattle would not be cursed. In the stall this was supposed to keep away vermin. Though dead bats make their contribution to this end only in the human imagination, living bats actually produce the desired effect. Finally, the Siebenbürger Saxons and Slovaks buried bats as a building sacrifice in the foundation of the house or barn.

LUCK AND LOVE

In China the bat is called "fu," which also means luck. In the Cantonese dialect it is called "Fuk-shi," or "rat of luck." Bats often adorn Chinese flags as lucky symbols. One Chinese hieroglyph of luck, which portrays the tower of the moon as a round opening with five stylized bats flying around it, has become particularly well known.

In European culture we also find lucky bats; however, here the portrayal is usually a dualistic clear reference to evil.

The superstition that bats bring luck in games of chance was very widespread: Whether at cards, ninepins, dice, or the lottery, bat fetishes helped to win. To bring good luck, you needed the head, the right eye, the blood, or most often the heart of the bat. Clerics also played along diligently. Often the monks who banned card playing publicly as the "Devil's prayer book" continued to play inside the walls of the monastery. They tried—as did many lay players—to free themselves from "the Devil, who sits at the gaming table" by means of a ruse: A bat's heart carried on a red thread on the right forearm was considered to be a "dependable measure."

It would sometimes be an advantage in our efforts to protect bats had something from the old superstitions of Bosnia and Herzogovina gotten around to us. In about the same way as people everywhere enjoy swallows, bats are held in high esteem

Bat plane type number 3 of Clement Ader, which is still preserved in its original state.

there. If they nest with their young in a house, they bring luck and must be protected. If a bat comes down the chimney, this means an abundance of cattle for farmers. In shops they attract customers.

As is known, luck and love go hand in hand. Therefore, it is not surprising that bats also are used in love potions. Thus the reputedly blind animals, which are also supposed to be sleepless at night, can be turned into all possible forms and mixtures for awakening a blind, sleepless love. The sexual organs of the bat in pulverized form—their hair and blood, however, also work—mixed in drinks are irresistible to reluctant lovers. Being touched by bat bones and claws is supposed to make the potential lover submissive. Even when love has died, the bat is still helpful. Jealous wives roasted a live bat in a covered pot, through which the unfaithful husband was said to feel the same pain as the tortured animal.

HUNTING POTIONS AND FLYING PHARMACY

"To shoot, and hit, what you please. Take the heart and liver of a bat, put it under the lead when you pour bullets, in this way you can hit what you please. This would be a wonderful trick for the hunter, too bad that they have a low opinion of it," is written in an "encyclopedia of magic" from 1759. The unerring aim of bats in darkness was supposed to be transferred to the marksman through shooting magic. To this end not just bat organs were added under the lead or carried along by the huntsman, but a bat's eye (the right one) was inserted in the rifle barrel. At the height of gruesomeness, live bats were poured into molds along with lead to make bullets.

Witches also gained their advantage through bats. They achieved their ability to fly by rubbing themselves with "flying fat," which they prepared from bats.

Bats are very frequently used in folk medicine. Pliny (23-79 AD) knew of their use against various ailments such as enteritis, snake bite, skin wounds, stomach ache,

bleary eye, and as a depilatory. The latter use no doubt was associated with the hairless wing surfaces of bats. Furthermore, bats were used in human medicine for the treatment of ailments ranging from diseases of the eye to corns. Bat ashes were said to promote the production of mother's milk.

The nocturnal animals were considered to be good remedies against drowsiness and insomnia. Bats were even used in popular veterinary medicine. A bat tied to a sick ox was supposed to rid the animal of pain. Gypsies swore by bats as cures for flatulence in horses. Finally, in the Middle Ages falcons suffering from the "falling disease" (epilepsy) were cured with cooked bats, which they had to eat.

BATS AND HAIR—A CHAPTER IN ITSELF

The superstition that bats fly into the hair seems to be almost impossible to eradicate. In Austrian dialect, "hair snatcher" is a name for the Common Pipistrelle. When a bat becomes entangled in the hair, according to an old popular belief it is supposed to be hard to remove, and even then only with the loss of hair. In the Tirol, girls who had had a bat by chance fly into their hair had to remain single. "Bat, bat, don't pull out my hair, leave my pigtails alone, so that I can go to the dance," was written by girls in Mecklenburg, Germany. It was even supposed to be possible to get an "elf lock" from bats, a pigtail-like matting of the hair, and to die from it. Dandruff and hair loss due to festering head wounds were the consequences of contact with a bat on the head, but also could occur through bat droppings or urine. It is therefore called "pissorato" in southern France. Given these abilities attributed to the bat, some have even tried to use bat blood as a depilatory.

WARDING OFF OF TRUE AND FALSE VAMPIRES—BLOOD-SUCKING WITCHES AND POSTMEN OF THE DEVIL

Among the peasants of Mexico, in some places even today vampire bats are considered to be witches who suck the blood of sleeping people. To ward off harm, the people carry into the caves sacrifices in the form of food, flowers, and copper coins. Simultaneously, however, vampire bats are also used as representatives of Lucifer, in that letters to the Devil are placed in the caves.

Of the "true" or human vampires, things are carried as far as the cult figure of Count Dracula, whom the English novelist Bram Stoker immortalized in his novel *Dracula* (1897). The subject of Bram Stoker's novel was Prince Vlad Tepes, who ruled from 1452 to 1462 in Tirgoviste, Walachia (the region of Romania including both Bucharest and the Transylvanian Alps). The gruesome specialties of the man, who numbered among the founding fathers of Romania, included impaling thousands of Turks and criminals. Tepes, by the way, learned about impaling from the Turks, against whose foreign rule he fought with a people's army. Bram Stoker named the hero of his novel Dracula after investigating the story of Vlad Tepes. Vlad's father was called "Dracula," which in Romanian means both dragon and the Devil. Furthermore, in Slav superstition the vampire is a mystical creature, half man, half bat, which as punishment for its gruesomely sinful existence on Earth remains complete in body and soul after it dies and taps people as a blood bank at night. In this way a literary figure arose which has provided virtually inexhaustible material for horror stories and films.

BATS AS "SPECIAL EFFECTS" AND REAL BOMBERS

When suspense and horror are to be produced today in comics or movies, bats often turn up symbolically. At one time they nearly became real bringers of death. During the Second World War, the American military experimented on a secret weappon, which was named "Project X-ray." The plan was to release large numbers of Mexican Free-tailed Bats (*Tadarida brasiliensis*), which were to be equipped with small time-fused incendiary bombs, over enemy territory from planes. It was hoped that the "free-tailed bombers" would then seek out hiding places in buildings as fast as possible, before blowing up along with them. The military strategists failed to consider, however, that the social animals gather in only a few roosts. When several hundred of the little bombers finally escaped in the desert in the Southwest, they sought refuge in a fuel depot, which they proceeded to blow up along with nearby military buildings.

SUPPLIERS OF REAL EXPLOSIVES

Bats supply true explosives as "breech loaders," in a manner of speaking. Their droppings—guano—contain saltpeter (sodium nitrate), which is used in the manufacture of gunpowder and explosives. During the Civil War the Confederates mined bat guano in caves in Texas and Tennessee for that purpose. On Sri Lanka we learned that the bat caves we studied had at times been seized by the British to prevent rebels from

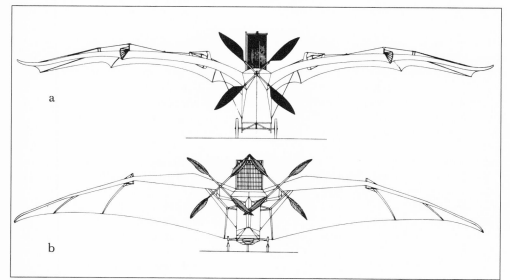

Bat plane number 3 of Clement Ader (about 1890) as a construction drawing (a) and in actual front view (b) (from Nachtigall, 1986).

obtaining "munitions" in the form of bat droppings.

Bats were used for peaceful means by the British Army during the desert campaign from 1940 to 1942 in the Middle East. The military blood transfusion service of the army chose a bat silhouette as its emblem. The three-ton refrigerator cars of the blood transfusion units, which were employed on the European continent to ensure the delivery of the blood supply to the front-line surgical units in the Reichs forest and for the crossing of the Rhine River at Brussels, also carried a bat emblem as a symbol of aid.

Something was even left over from the World Wars for bats: bunker installations in many parts of the world serve many a bat population as a winter or nursery roost.

All the superstitious ideas of the past, and the recipes resulting from them, certainly have had far less effect on bats than the consequences of more recent human greed.

Top: Bats as tolerated temple and palace dwellers: tomb bat colony (Taphozous spec.) in an Indian temple. **Bottom:** *The Indian False Vampire (Megaderma lyra) also inhabits such roosts. Here a colony hangs in the foundation wall of an Indian palace tower.*

FLYING MACHINES BASED ON THE BAT MODEL

Several pioneers of manned flight viewed bats not as representatives of dark powers, but rather as a source of ideas for their dream of flying. In the same way as they borrowed from the bird and insect worlds for their gliders and powered planes, bats also served as models for their clever constructions.

Around 1500, the genius Leonardo da Vinci sketched the wings of a flying machine based on the bat wing. In France, Clement Ader did not store the arm and finger bones of a *Pteropus* flying fox in the drawer of his desk for nothing. The airplane builder, in his patent of 1890, secured the rights to a number of airplanes: "Wings for low speeds in the manner of the bat, wings for high speeds in the manner of the bird." True to the animal model, Ader constructed his flying machines and probably came closest to the "bat construction plan" with his "airplane number 3," which is still maintained in the original today. The prototype he built in the years 1893 to 1897 even completed successful attempts at flight. Clement Ader built the wings of his airplane exactly like the arms and fingers of the bat down to the smallest detail. With a wingspan of 15 meters (47 feet), it was powered with the aid of two propellers and a 40-horsepower alcohol motor.

It is all too easy to ridicule the exact copying of the natural model, which even took into account the mechanics of bat flight. Nonetheless, experts increasingly are amazed by the many original technical innovations thought up by Clement Ader. Although our modern airplanes are constructed along totally different lines, Ader's "giant bat" of fabric and wood is still the most interesting failure of airplane construction.

Rhinopoma
microphyllum
*has a foothold on
a palace
ornament.*

*Bat as a safety
symbol: In Iceland
- where there are
no bats at all - a
security company
uses the bat
trademark!*

Dark times for bats

Today scientists the world over are registering the endangerment of bats. In 1986 only 12 species turned up as endangered worldwide on the "red list" of the International Union for the Conservation of Nature (IUCN), but in the 1990 edition 26 species of flying foxes and 28 species of microbats are listed, the future of which is uncertain in the opinion of experts. Of these, four flying foxes and one microbat species have already become extinct, and one flying fox and two microbat species most likely have disappeared. With the worldwide destruction of nature, bats are losing more and more living spaces and roosts, and their dietary necessities also are shrinking steadily. Wherever bats collide with agricultural interests they are persecuted directly as rivals or pests. The roost caves are dynamited or the animals are killed with poison gas. The "good taste" of many species of flying fox has been their undoing. The small island populations, in particular, often end up in human cooking pots down to the last individual.

With the ban on commercial trade in these species, conservation achieved an important partial success. But restrictions on trade as a result of CITES, no matter how good, cannot stop the further destruction of living space. As before, this development is proceeding at breakneck pace, particularly in the tropics. With the disappearance of large regions of the tropical rainforests, the fate of many fruit- and nectar-eating bat species, in particular, is sealed.

A TRAGIC "GOAL"

The change from "natural" to "plantation" fruit does little to help the fruit-eaters. Wherever fruit plantations appear the bats are persecuted as "harvest pests." The devastating effects of random methods of control against fruit-eating bats are particularly well documented for Israel. There a campaign to smoke out the African Rousette Fruit Bats (*Rousettus aegyptiacus*) from its roost caves was begun in the 1950's. The poisons ethylene dibromide and the particularly long-lasting lindane were used against the fruit bats, which were declared to be pests, in conformity with Israeli conservation laws. The fruit bats withstood the control efforts well, for they breed readily and can move to substitute roosts.

Instead, the campaign affected above all their co-inhabitants in the caves, namely insectivorous bat species. Within 15 years their numbers declined by about 90 percent, even though all Israeli bat species are considered to be protected.

In consequence, several insect species increased explosively and in this way actually did threaten the harvest. The sensitive ecosystem had fallen apart. In the meantime, international protests and a better understanding of the ecological relationships have led Israelis to show more regard for bats.

THE CEMENT INDUSTRY VERSUS THE GIANT FALSE VAMPIRE BAT

The Australian Giant False Vampire Bat (*Macroderma gigas*) has become severely threatened by the destruction of its roosts because of limestone mining. In November, 1988, two of its important roost caves on Mount Etna, Queensland, were dynamited legally by the cement industry with the approval of the Queensland government. However, subsequent resolutions of the IUCN have had an effect, and the Queensland government has incorporated a 15-hectar region around Mount Etna in the Fitzroy Caves National Park.

CONTROL, YES, EXTIRPATION, NO

The unsystematic control of vampire bats also seriously depleted many other Latin American species. The eradication campaign began when the connection between rabies and vampire bats was recognized around 1930. Hollow trees were burned, several thousand caves were destroyed with dynamite, and poisons were sprayed in bat caves. Besides the vampires, in the process thousands and thousands of other bats also were destroyed.

Today the vampire bats are systematically captured or poisoned in seconds by strychnine syrup, which is spread on the cattle hide. Anticoagulants—injected into the cattle or carried on captured vampires, which are licked by conspecifics—kill vampire bats by internal bleeding.

Vampire controls are no doubt necessary. Nevertheless, it is to be hoped that sufficient niches will remain for these interesting and highly specialized animals to survive.

"ALL CLEAR SIGNAL" DESPITE HORROR STORIES

Though in the United States and   in tropical countries the potential transmission of rabies and other diseases by bats has prompted control measures, for a long time no health risk was attributed to European bats. Only very recently have conservationists and bat lovers been made uncertain by sensational headlines concerning rabid bats. But the reality is far less dramatic than is presented in the sensationalist press. It has in fact been possible to demonstrate the presence of a rhabdovirus in European bats, but this virus is not identical with the one that causes rabies in game and domestic animals. Bat rabies is not completely new either. From 1954 to 1988 a total of 345 cases of rabies were described for European bats, 97 percent of which were found in the Serotine (*Eptesicus serotinus*). The majority

of cases were reported in Denmark, northern Germany, and Holland. The virus apparently is present in less than one half of one percent of European bats.

The risk of being bitten by a virus-infected bat is extraordinarily small. Hunting bats and bat roosts are no danger at all. Only those who regularly handle bats—and because of conservation laws all but bat experts must be ruled out here—should wear gloves and for safety's sake should be immunized against rabies. For the bat lover—and those whom it is hoped will become one—there is no reason for concern!

Bats as a delicacy: In Thailand skinned flying foxes (here Eonycteris spelaea) *are put up for sale on the market.*

Collecting bat guano in Thailand: In caves with large bat colonies (Asia, South America) the mining of the valuable fertilizer is still profitable today.

Flowering wild (unpruned) orchards around an Upper Bavarian village. Structure-rich agricultural landscapes in Central Europe are among the most valuable bat biotopes.

Clearing of wild orchards. Because wild orchards unprofitable, in many places the tall fruit trees are cut down. With their destruction bats (and other animals) lose their most valuable hunting biotopes and roosts.

Facing page, top:

The heat-retaining, dry slopes (used extensively for the grazing of sheep) in the Franconian Jura are an indispensible biotope for the resident bat population.
Bottom, right:
Through the felling of old, rotten trees in parks and forests, many bat tree roosts are destroyed. Because the trees are often felled in winter, in many cases hibernating bats are also killed at the same time.

Common long-eared bat (Plecotus auritus) flies to a bat box (of the Issel type). Hung in suitable places (above all in forests with few tree holes), bat boxes increase the roost supply for "tree bats."

FIRST BATS, THEN PEOPLE?

Insectivorous bats, as final links in the food chain, are particularly susceptible to the effects of prey animals contaminated with insecticides. Wood preservatives work in the same way. They are taken up by bats, which make their roosts in contaminated buildings, through the wing membranes and respiratory system, thus damaging their internal organs. Sterility and increased mortality are the results of severe contamination.

The chlorohydrocarbons (such as lindane, hexachlorobenzol, DDT, DDD, and DDE) as well as polychlorinated biphenyls (PCBs) present in the insecticides are very difficult to break down and excrete. Because these substances are readily fat soluble, they can easily accumulate in the organism for years. When bats draw on their stored fat reserves in winter, the toxins concentrate in the reserve fat and in other tissues. In the brain, when in suitable concentration, they have a fatal effect. Even in young bats that have not yet begun to feed independently, chlorohydrocarbons have been detected. The toxins are probably transmitted to the offspring during pregnancy through the placenta and later through the mother's milk. That the population decline of bats is much higher than that of comparable groups of mammals doubtless has something to do with the longer life expectancy of the nocturnal hunters. The effects of pesticide-induced declines in bats are a grave warning signal for people. Wherever bats and people share the living space, Man—also a mammal—could be the next in line.

116

THE THINGS THAT HARM OUR BATS

There are many reasons for the decline in our bat populations. Almost all damaging factors have in common that they are "home-made." Northern bats need at least three living spaces, and this immediately makes them three times as sensitive in our poorer and poorer environment. In summer the nocturnal hunters need warm and dry roosts and nurseries; in winter, in contrast, their hibernation places should be cool, damp, and frostfree. Furthermore, all species are dependent on richly structured hunting territories. But precisely these places have been swept away in the course of changes to the landscape and with them the food of the bats: the abundant insect supply. The decline of the bat population in central Europe was noted by Eisentraut as early as 1937.

The list of detrimental factors can be expanded. Ulrich Jüdes proposed the following overview of the manmade reasons for the decline of bats.

Detrimental factors and their anthropomorphic causes

FOOD SHORTAGE

· Standardization and mechanization of the landscape (creation of huge monocultures, accumulation of fertilizers, paving of open spaces);

· Changes in microclimate brought about by alterations to the landscape;

· Destruction of hunting habitats (rows of trees, ponds, and so forth);

· Agricultural practices that disturb the life cycles of important food insects (use of herbicides, "care" of fallow land and lawns, and so forth).

POISONING OF THE FOOD SUPPLY

· Use of insecticides in agriculture and forestry;

· Use of poisons in towns (particularly in home gardens);

· Other toxins of diverse origins in the environment.

CHANGES TO AND DESTRUCTION OF ROOSTS

· Modern building practices (tongue-and-groove siding, insulation in hollow spaces, and so forth);

· Razing of old buildings;

· Sealing of cracks in walls and joints in buildings (particularly to improve insulation);

· Covering of holes in roofs, closing of owl holes, as well as replacing missing glass (for example, in churches for protection against pigeons);

• Construction of rooms in attics with bats;

• Sealing and drying of damp basements, of ice and potato cellars;

• Impregnation of rafters with wood preservatives in houses and churches;

• Felling of old trees with knot holes and holes (particularly in old orchards);

• Sealing of old pits and bunkers;

• Removal of old stone walls with deep, open cracks;

• Curious "conservationists" who "control" roosts (for example, early control of artificial caves), animal photographers, and banders.

DIRECT INJURY OR EXTERMINATION

• Killing, drowning, or poisoning through the use of wood preservatives and other chemicals;

• Energy loss in hibernation as a result of frequent disturbance;

• Banding;

• Cats (at entrance holes to caves and in attics);

• Owls (for example, nesting of owls in attics with bats);

• Tree Martens (for example, with incorrectly constructed artificial caves and in roosts).

PROTECTIVE MEASURES FOR BATS

The most important provision for protection is not to disturb the animals. Therefore, four basic rules must be followed:

1. Every protective measure is based on intensive observation, which must not be allowed to become harmful to the animals.

2. When it is a question of the control and protection of bat roosts, experts should always be consulted.

3. Nursery roosts must be left completely undisturbed in June and July, because bat mothers with small young are particularly sensitive to disturbance.

4. Visiting summer and winter roosts must be kept to a minimum. Any control also means disturbance for the bats living in the roosts.

These four rules for the protection of bats naturally also apply to experts.

Protecting "house bats"

The survival of the bat species that occur in buildings is always dependent on the degree of understanding the owners or occupants show them. To awaken this understanding and to explain about the lov-

Nursery colony of the greater mouse-eared bat (Myotis myotis). Top: During the nursery season, the animals must not be disturbed. Here the youngsters are already relatively large, but are still darker in color than the adults. Left: Members of the same colony at a different hanging place.

(bottom): A few bat species also rear their young in bird nests or bat boxes. Here a colony of common long-eared bats (Plecotus auritus) in a bird nest box.

*Greater mouse-eared bats (*Myotis myotis*) flying from their nursery roost.*

*(*Vespertilio murinus*) with twins.*

able fellow lodgers is therefore the most effective aid for house bats. Renovations (reconstruction and renovation of attics, treatment of the rafters with toxic wood preservatives) represent a special danger for house bats. If renovations are planned, experts should always be consulted and the following points should be considered:

• If possible, postpone construction in attics until late summer and fall (from September on).

• Retain entrance holes; slits 10 centimeters high and 30 centimeters wide in general are sufficient for bats and simultaneously also keep out undesirable pigeons. Provide additional entrance facilities by removing the screen from ventilation openings or constructing openings in the roof shingles or tiles for bats. (Beware: The addition of new openings can produce detrimental changes in the microclimatic conditions of the attic, for example, by causing a draft.) In inaccessible attics, add only a few openings that bats can pass through, ideally in the middle of the roof, so that the warm air can continue to rise to the peak of the roof. If at all possible, retain the old openings that have been used previously by bats. These can be detected easily by observing the bats flying out of them.

• Retain tin roofs whenever possible (they produce higher temperatures in the roost). When the temperatures in the attic are changed drastically because of renovations, under certain circumstances the warmth-loving animals can be helped by a heat lamp (thermostatically regulated black light).

• Do not cover the roof with impregnated concrete tiles, but rather with ceramic tiles (or nonimpregnated concrete tiles).

• Wood-preservative measures are a critical point. First determine whether a wood-preservative treatment is even necessary. If it is necessary, as far as possible use the nontoxic hot-air treatment. Definitely avoid all of the usual chemical treatments with poisonous wood preservatives. Never use preparations containing lindane. As a substitute for products containing lindane, wood preservatives with synthetic pyrethroids (Permethrin), which are tolerated by bats, should be selected.

Recently, however, these pyrethroid products have fallen into disrepute as nerve poisons. Despite their toxicity, they are still recommended when nontoxic procedures, such as hot air or boric acid, cannot be used.

118

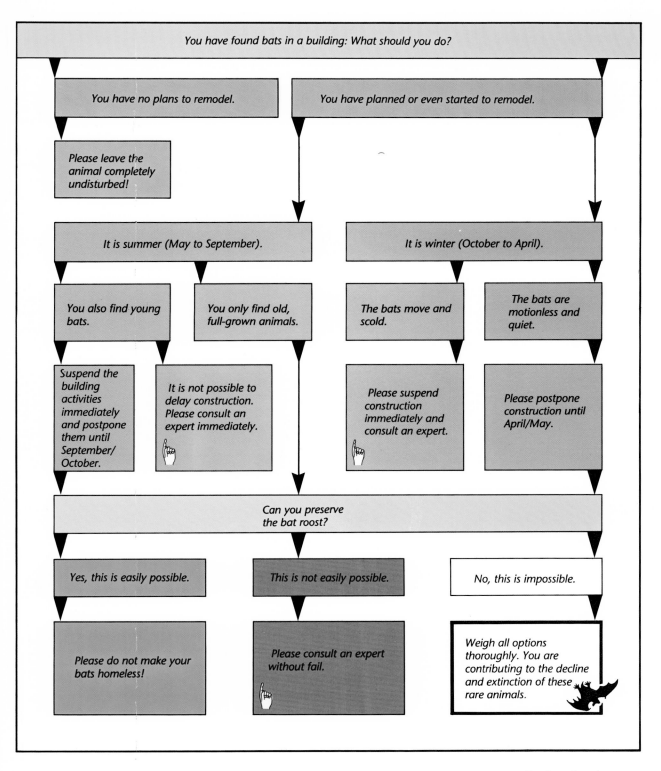

You have found bats in a building: What should you do?

You have no plans to remodel.

You have planned or even started to remodel.

Please leave the animal completely undisturbed!

It is summer (May to September).

It is winter (October to April).

You also find young bats.

You only find old, full-grown animals.

The bats move and scold.

The bats are motionless and quiet.

Suspend the building activities immediately and postpone them until September/October.

It is not possible to delay construction. Please consult an expert immediately.

Please suspend construction immediately and consult an expert.

Please postpone construction until April/May.

Can you preserve the bat roost?

Yes, this is easily possible.

This is not easily possible.

No, this is impossible.

Please do not make your bats homeless!

Please consult an expert without fail.

Weigh all options thoroughly. You are contributing to the decline and extinction of these rare animals.

The wood treatment should be completed at least four weeks before the bats enter the summer roost.

If wood preservatives were used or new rafters or lumber were employed, untreated boards should be nailed over the treated rafters at the preferred hanging places of the animals. If possible, use the old hanging boards—they can be recognized by their dark color, which is produced by the body fat of the bats.

• In attics with bat colonies, do not try to attract Common Barn Owls. Common Barn Owls sometimes learn to prey on bats.

You have found bats in your house - this chart shows you what to do.

(left):
Natterer's bat
(Myotis
nattereri) with
young.

(center):
Cave entrance in
southern Europe.
Only in out-of-the-
way caves left
undisturbed by
tourists do bats
still find sufficient
peace to rear their
young and to
hibernate.

(right):
Grated
overwintering
cave. In this
Upper Bavarian
cave, a good
dozen of the very
rare barbastelle
(Barbastella
barbastellus) still
overwinter
regularly.

wood and stands of old trees are more valuable to tree bats than any nest box. Therefore, locate and mark hollow trees and preserve them by consulting with the owners.

• Protect old hollow trees with known bat roosts. If necessary, make trees in parks and along paths "climb-proof," such as by sawing off individual branches.

• Augment the supply of holes through nest boxes and special bat boxes. The direction of the opening of the box is not critical as long as rain cannot enter. On the other hand, the location plays a large role: Bat boxes must have an open approach (flight)

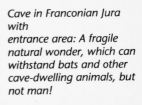

Cave in Franconian Jura with
entrance area: A fragile
natural wonder, which can
withstand bats and other
cave-dwelling animals, but
not man!

Bat conservationists and their charges

WILLI AND BRIGITTE ISSEL

Because of the silent and secret habits of bats, these animals are far less accessible than are birds, for example. Though today interested persons can join active bat preservation groups in conservation societies, our early developers of bat science mostly broke new ground. Among the true "bat pioneers" is the married couple Drs. Brigitte and Willi Issel. These two zoologists began their joint studies about 40 years ago.

Willi Issel (b. 1915) had his first contact with bats as a student, when he undertook adventurous tours of discovery in the ancient bronze mines of the Wester Forest. Among his first successes was the rediscovery of the Greater Horseshoe Bat in the Rhineland.

Before he became a recognized bat expert, however, he took a roundabout way. Willi Issel first studied medicine before finally ending up in his passion, zoology. After his doctoral studies had fallen victim to the war, Issel considered his bats and began a comparative population study of the Lesser Horseshoe Bat in Munich under Prof. Kahmann. At least as significant as the new doctoral research was that he also met his wife there. Brigitte Issel worked with mice under Kahmann at the same time, so it was only natural that the young pair would work together from then on.

(left):
The Drs. Issel, the Bavarian pioneers of bat research.

(right):
Willi Issel is not only a bat researcher, but a bat fancier too. Here he tenderly cares for an injured noctule (Nyctalus noctula).

Even before his work at the ornithological station in Garmisch, Germany, Willi Issel had had the idea of colonizing forest bats in bat boxes. In Countess Goertz of Schlitz, Hessen, Germany, the Issels found a friend and patron who supported the efforts of the young married couple. They even wanted to engage the perfume industry to determine the composition of the pheromones of bats, which are doubtless important for roost acceptance. For analyses of that kind, however, too many animals would have had to be sacrificed, so the idea was soon rejected. A stipend from the German research society and collaboration with the forest zoologist Zwölfer, Sr., ultimately led to the final breakthrough for the first large-scale attempts to establish forest bats in special boxes. During his time as the director of the natural history museum of the city of Augsburg from 1954 to 1977, Willi Issel and his wife also devoted attention to bats during their free time and vacations. Today the Issels, with their vast experience and cordiality, continue to make it easier for budding students of bats to enter the field.

JÜRGEN GEBHARD, THE "ADAMSON" OF BATS

When Joy Adamson published her book *Born Free* in 1960 and it soon became famous throughout the world, the story of the

lioness Elsa exploded like a bomb. The married couple Joy and George Adamson were gamekeepers in northern Kenya. They reared the lion cub Elsa by hand and released her into the wild at the age of three. Although Elsa established contact with free-living lions, she returned again and again to her foster parents and later even presented wild-born offspring to them. Through the close personal contact with Elsa, the Adamson's were able to make remarkable insights into the "private lives" of lions. The animal researcher Jane Goodall became just as intimate with her "wild" animal partners, the chimpanzees of Gombe, as did Dian Fossey with her mountain gorillas.

That something comparable could also be possible with such shy and secretive nocturnal hunters as bats probably was unthinkable, particularly since many serious researchers have a real "fear of contact" with their objects of research. The modern scientific industry seems no longer to have any room for feeling, and someone who talks to the animals and birds is likely to be ridiculed in this age of the computer, telemetry, and statistics, even if his name is Konrad Lorenz. Gebhard ignored such misgivings. He even admitted publicly his subjective love for his objects of research. In his first occupation, Jürgen Gebhard prepared animal specimens in the natural history museum of Basel. His passionate work on the lives of bats brought him fame as an internationally known and recognized zoologist. The sympathetic native of Basel with the Swiss accent is probably the only researcher in the world who works with finger-tame wild bats. The unusual "cooperation" between researcher and subject began when he, as had happened so often before, reared by hand bats that had met with an accident. Two rooms under the museum roof serve as a care and rearing station. But Jürgen Gebhard is also the proud owner of a separate bat research station. Through his popular publications and presentations, Gebhard's bat station "Hofmatt" has already become an institution in expert circles. In a room in the tower of a transformer station, cleverly constructed bat accommodations were built for finger-tame Noctules (*Nyctalus noctula*). Through a "door to freedom" the animals made contact with wild conspecifics and lured them right in front of the researcher's nose. In this way, Jürgen Gebhard, when he drives to his "Hofmatt" after work and

climbs up a steel fire ladder to the research cell on the second floor, can observe the life of the Noctule from his "box seat." Jürgen Gebhard's animals are not primarily research objects, but rather "free collaborators." What "Ala," "Apus," "Artus," and "Coco" experience, the researcher records exactly on paper and thereby astounds us. Besides many amazing details from the intimate life of the Noctule, Jürgen Gebhard also found an interesting variation with the young: they tend to "kleptolactia"; that is, the little bats steal milk by rounding off their meals with dessert from an unrelated female's breast. "Basel's batman," as Jürgen Gebhard has been called, is now recognized by virtually every child in Switzerland. And this is good for all bats.

HOW TO BECOME A GUARDIAN OF BATS

In many respects Switzerland seems to be the "promised land" for bat conservation. Besides Jürgen Gebhard, there is the "Coordination Center East for Bat Conservation" in Zürich. The zoologists Marianne Haffner and Hanspeter Stutz are the founders and driving force of this exemplary institution. Besides their scientific basic research and professional projects, Marianne Haffner and Hanspeter Stutz also understand how to bring bat conservation to man/woman/child. Today many Swiss take part enthusiastically as bat observers or roost guardians. Besides the "bat gazette," which has appeared regularly since 1984 in the *News,* an exchange of information also takes place at participant's meetings.

The enthusiasm of the daily participants, which struck me during a visit, encouraged me to make an attempt with roost guard-

*Noctule (*Nyctalus noctula*) with telemeter. With the aid of the miniature transmitter, some secrets of bats are revealed.*

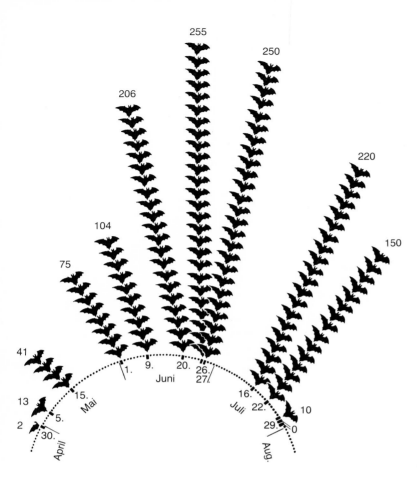

255
250
206
220
104
75
150
41
13
2

1. 9. 20. 26. 27.
Juni
15. Mai
5.
30.
April
16. 22.
Juli
29. 0
10
Aug.

Flight numbers of a summer colony of male parti-coloured bats (Vespertilio murinus), which live under a garage roof in Raisting, Upper Bavaria (counts taken in 1988 by Josef Sporrer). In late April the roost is first occupied by a few males. In late June/early July the colony reaches its maximum population, before then falling off rapidly again by late July. From August on the colony is deserted again. At that time the males probably undertake their migrations and seek out courtship sites (after Richarz et al., 1989).

ians in Germany. Our man of the hour is Josef Sporrer of Raisting on the Ammersee, Germany. Since 1983 not only has he cared for his "tenants," he has also collected data and given advice on roost protection in his home town of Raisting. Through his efforts not only was he able to find and protect roosts effectively, but he contributed substantially to a better appreciation by the inhabitants for bats. Sporrer's bat roost even made its way into the specialist journals. Behind the attic of Sporrer's garage roof lives the largest known summer colony of the Particolored Bat. Thanks to his regular counts of bats leaving the roost, for the first time we have more precise information on the duration of occupation and the change in roosts of such gatherings. Quite unusually for European bats, the migratory particolored bats form large colonies of males in the summer. Apparently as time goes by more and more males are attracted to such a "men's club." When it reaches a certain number of animals, however, the group starts to break up again. After a neighbor's garage, into which Sporrer's bats regularly flew, was equipped with a diagonal roof

attachment that was provided with an extra hiding place according to Josef Sporrer's blueprint, the number of inhabitants increased to 311 Particolored Bats! Such a number of animals simultaneously flying out from two roosts simply can no longer be managed by a single counter. Since then Josef Sporrer counts along with his neighbors.

BRITISH TRADITION—IN BAT CONSERVATION, TOO

Bat conservation enjoys a lofty position in Britain based on the long tradition of field biology there. Years of experience and an exemplary organization made the British bat guardians respectable. In many regions "bat groups" have formed that are led by licensed bat guardians. The headquarters of the bat groups is in the hands of Anthony Hutson, who is employed as bat conservation officer by a conservation organization, the Vincent Wildlife Trust. Hutson coordinates and advises the individual bat groups. Members are trained at regular meetings. A newsletter, the *Bat News*, which is edited by the bat conservation officer and published by the influential Fauna and Flora Preservation Society, also appears quarterly. Another leading figure within the organized bat guardians, Anthony Mitchell-Jones, is employed by the Nature Conservancy Council, the government conservation board. Among other things, he compiles the range maps of bats on the basis of the roosting data of bat guardians and has published an exemplary handbook, *The Bat Worker's Manual*.

Two other leaders, Robert E. Stebbings and Paul A. Racey, work scientifically with bats and have many years of experience in field work. Bob Stebbings wrote the first review of bat conservation in Europe. Paul Racey is chairman of the Bat Specialist Group of the IUCN, which publishes the *Red Book* of species threatened throughout the world and develops plans for their protection.

ON THE DECLINE OF ISLAND-DWELLING BATS

If a beauty contest for bats were held, the flying foxes doubtless would have the best prospects for the top places. With their foxlike and doglike faces, large button eyes, and sometimes even a colorful pelt, according to human perceptions of beauty they are certainly among the most attractive bats. For these reasons (among others), the international bat conservation organization Bat Conservation International, headed by Merlin D. Tuttle, chose a flying fox to grace its emblem. Placed on its feet, and thus brought 180 degrees out of its normal hanging position, it looks dowright trustingly at the observer and thereby provides an excellent advertisement for its bat brethren.

Flying foxes range from Africa across the entire Indo-Pacific island world, but they have not reached South America. There leaf-nosed bats take over the ecological function of plant pollinators and dispersers. In the ecosystem of the tropics of the Old World, flying foxes play a leading role in this task. It is estimated, for example, that about 40 percent of the tree species occurring on the island of Guam in the Pacific Ocean can survive only when their seeds are dispersed by flying foxes. As pollen transporters, flying foxes have a key role in the pollination of many rainforest tree species. If a species of flying fox disappears, an entire food chain can collapse and thus a number of mutually dependent animal and plant species could die out. Measured by this enormous ecological significance for the topical forests, flying foxes have so far been treated by zoological research and international conservation more like stepchildren. Scarcely any notice was taken of the decline and even the complete extinction of several species.

The bat researchers and guardians P. Mickleburgh, Paul A. Racey, and Anthony M. Hutson have for the first time developed an action plan with essential guidelines for the protection of threatened species of flying foxes for the international conservation organization IUCN. Roland Wirth and Michael Riffel, friends from the Zoological Society for Species and Population Conservation who also work for the IUCN, for the first time compiled a summary of rare species and named the reasons why they are endangered. Although the flying fox species that are endangered or that have already become extinct occur or occurred in widely separated regions, Wirth and Riffel are of the opinion that the causes of the decline are the same everywhere.

Owing to their ability to fly, the larger forms of flying fox have been able to colonize even the smallest oceanic islands. Often only a few animals reached an island, so that founder populations were small. This led to the rapid evolution of new forms.

Often the islands were colonized accidentally, which is why individual genera and species of flying foxes exhibit a mosaiclike distribution today. If a species occurs only on islands, its existence is particularly threatened. Everywhere, whether on the Comoros, the Philippines, Mauritius, or Samoa, people destroyed the forests or have almost completely transformed the original vegetation into cultivated land. Where flying foxes survived these changes to their living space and switched to a plantation diet, they are persecuted as pests.

Furthermore, in some regions flying foxes are considered a delicacy. That people have developed a taste for them has led to the virtual extirpation of several species. Some subspecies of the Marianas Flying Fox (*Pteropus mariannus*) and the Guam Flying Fox (*Pteropus tokudae*) have disappeared almost completely. So as not to have to do without the delicate roast, rare species of Flying Fox are being imported from other South Sea islands. Particularly hard hit by the trade as a delicacy is the Samoan Flying Fox, *Pteropus samoensis*, which occurs only on Samoa and Fiji. In contrast to the other

(top):
Male parti-coloured bats (Vespertilio murinus) in crevice hiding place behind the mezzanine of the garage studied by Sporrer.

(bottom):
The parti-coloured bat (Vespertilio murinus) is in many respects one of our most unusual species. The females form only small nursery colonies and can give birth to up to four young. In summer males form unusually large associations.

Right: Rodrigues flying fox (Pteropus rodricensis). A zoo breeding program of the Jersey Zoo signifies last-second salvation for the species.

Bottom: For the conservation of the Pemba flying fox (Pteropus voeltzkowi) the zoological society has started a conservation and publicity project for species and population protection.

members of its genus, the very large Samoan Flying Fox lives solitarily and appears to be diurnal. It is reported to fly like a raptor above the canopy of forested regions. Because it is more dependent on the presence of fairly large forested areas than most other species of flying fox, it has been hit particularly hard not only by hunting but also by the deforestation of its living space. Although the large Samoan Flying Fox seemingly would be particularly interesting for zoos on account of its diurnal habits, up to now no zoo in the world has made an effort to keep it.

The story of the Rodrigues Flying Fox (*Pteropus rodricensis*) shows that a successful zoo breeding program may mean that a species can be saved from extinction. This medium-sized, silvery and blackish brown species lives only on the 100-square-kilometer (40-square-mile) Rodrigues Island

OKOA POPO MNYAMA
SAVE THE PEMBA FLYING FOX

near Mauritius. In the 1950's the Rodrigues Flying Fox population still numbered at least 1000 individuals; in 1974 scientists were only able to find about 70 animals. The living space of the species had decreased greatly because of deforestation. The remaining population was in constant danger of literally being "blown away by the wind." Because the last animals were concentrated in a few roost trees, a severe hurricane of the type that not infrequently sweeps across the island could have wiped out the flying foxes. In 1978 an expedition captured 18 animals, of which eight were sent to a breeding enclosure on Mauritius and the remaining ten were brought to the Jersey Zoo on the British Channel Island of Jersey. The Rodrigues Flying Fox reproduced so successfully in both breeding stations that by the end of 1988 not only did 60 animals live there permanently, but it proved possible to establish additional breeding colonies in three other zoos. Field observers in 1981 and 1982 counted 350 wild flying foxes on Rodrigues. Their future is tied closely to the reforestation program on the little tropical island. Equally important is the appreciation of its inhabitants for the significance of their unique flora and fauna. With the captive-bred animals it should also be possible to fill in gaps produced by future hurricanes.

Two additional species live on the other Mascarene islands of Mauritius and Réunion. Though *Pteropus niger* has already disappeared on Réunion, a small population of fewer than 3000 individuals lives on Mauritius. The second species, *Pteropus subniger*, has been extinct since 1875. These flying foxes apparently roosted during the day in hollow trees, where people, as well as introduced cats and rats, could get at them easily.

Of the two species of flying foxes of the genus *Pteropus* that live on the Comoro Islands, the future prospects are especially grim for *Pteropus livingstonei*. Livingstone's Flying Fox lives only on the Comoro Island of Anjouan and is limited there to the evergreen forests of the montane region. Because the forests are being cut all the way up to the mountain peaks, the extinction of the last 100 inhabitants of this cold and wet mountainous region is only a question of time. The Jersey Zoo is planning a breeding project for Livingstone's Flying Fox. It is possible that keeping it could prove impossible because of dietary problems, for more than other flying foxes, *Pteropus livingstonei* seems to be specialized on a diet of leaves.

The situation is also particularly grim for the flying foxes of the Philippines. Massive environmental destruction as a result of deforestation is causing the extinction of the species. The Panay Fruit Bat (*Acerodon lucifer*) has not been seen since 1988. The Philippine Bare-backed Bat (*Dobsonia chapmani*) was not discovered until 1952 and has been considered extinct since 1964. Of the Philippine Tube-nosed Fruit Bat (*Nyctimene rabori*), which was first described in 1983, small, constantly endangered remnant populations live in the mountainous region in the southern part of the island of Negros. The protected areas that have been established there are of little use to the fruit bats, because even in the reserves uncontrolled and unpunished deforestation continues.

Especially tragic is the story of the Fossil or Bulmer's Fruit Bat (*Aproteles bulmerae*). Initially known only from fossils and considered to be extinct for 9000 years, living

(Pteropus mariannus) feeding on pollen.

representatives were found in 1975 in a cave in the highlands of Papua New Guinea. Yet scarcely had they been rediscovered when native hunters there apparently wiped out the entire population. The only hope for Bulmer's Fruit Bat and perhaps also a few other lost species is that somewhere undiscovered small populations still exist.

THE BUMBLEBEE BAT—NOT ONLY PARTICULARLY SMALL, PARTICULARLY RARE, TOO

There are two common names to choose from for the little tongue-twister Craseonycteris thonglongyai: Bumblebee Bat or Hog-nosed Bat. The first refers to its small size, the second to the little bat's face. At a weight of 2 grams (0.07 ounce) and a head-body length of just 3 centimeters (1.2 inches), this dwarf is the smallest mammal

in the world. The species was discovered in October, 1973, by the famous Thai mammal researcher Kitti Thonglongya in western Thailand near the River Kwai. Kitti immediately recognized that his find differed from all of the bats known to him and subsequently sent several specimens to his colleague John E. Hill at the British Museum of Natural History in London. The confirmation of his sensational discovery was never known to Kitti, who died suddenly in February, 1974. Hill was able to describe the bat not only as a new species and genus, but because of its unique traits was even able to erect a new family for it and simultaneously honored its discoverer with the specific name: family Craseonycteridae with one genus and one species, Craseonycteris thonglongyai Hill, 1974. It is most closely related to the families of the sheath-tailed bats (Emballonuridae) and mouse-tailed bats (Rhinopomatidae). Besides the small size, the most conspicuous features of the Bumblebee Bat are the absence of a tail and spur. The extensive tail membrane and a large gland on the throat of males call to mind certain sheath-tailed bats. The ears and the form of the tragus, however, cannot be confused with those of other species. The skull characters in particular justify the separate taxonomic classification of the Bumblebee Bat. When all its measurements are combined, it defeats all other contenders for the title of "world's smallest mammal."

Almost nothing is known so far about the habits of this midget. All observations and collected specimens have originated from a small area on the River Kwai, which achieved unhappy fame in the Second World War. The Bumblebee Bat lives there in limestone caves. In small groups of four or five animals, they always occupy the deepest and darkest chambers. The animals take flight at the slightest disturbance. The dwarfs become active around 6:00 p.m. They apparently prefer rock chimneys and crevices as exit openings, for they have never been observed leaving their daytime roosts through the main entrance. They hunt in thick bamboo forests, carried by long and broad wing surfaces that also permit them to hover. Tiny (2-3 mm) flies, parasitic wasps, and bark lice, which occupy the air around the tops of trees and bamboo, are their principal prey. How the miniature bats meet their energy requirements and how tiny their young must be are still unknown.

Maybe we will never learn much more

about this species. Scarcely were they discovered when the smallest mammal made another, much less welome "hit parade": The IUCN placed the Bumblebee Bat on the list of the 12 most endangered species. Today scarcely more than 200 Hog-nosed Bumblebee Bats flutter around the strictly guarded caves in a region that because of deforestation, road construction, and tourism is scarcely still able to offer even the world's smallest mammal enough living space.

BARBASTELLES—SOME LIKE IT COLD

With its compressed little pug face and the silky, blackish brown, shiny pelt, the Barbastelle (*Barbastella barbastellus*) is unmistakable. It is found in Europe from southern England to the Caucasus. The Barbastelle reaches its northern limit in Norway and Sweden at approximately 60° latitude, and it occurs only sporadically in the Mediterranean region. Of all the European species, Barbastelles tolerate the lowest temperatures. In the winter roosts the animals can be found in the coolest parts of caves, cellars, and mine shafts. Even temperatures just below freezing do not seem to bother the hibernating bats.

Present-day inquiries into bat populations in Germany indicate a rapid downward trend of this never very abundant species in central Europe. Only a few confirmed nursery roosts of the Barbastelle have ever been reported there. Above all, the findings of declines or even the complete disappearance of formerly relatively large winter roosts are alarming. The only winter roost that has not been subject to serious disturbance at present is the bat reserve Nietoperek in western Poland. In the former fortifications from the Second World War, over 1000 Barbastelles still overwinter regularly.

Otherwise the present-day balance looks very modest. In northern Bavaria, 31 barbastelles were recored during winter-roost counts in 11 roosts. In southern Bavaria we currently know of five winter roosts with a total of 22 animals. According to

The barbastelle (Barbastella barbastellus prefers cooler temperatures in the winter roost and is often even found free hanging in the entrance region of caves. It ranks among our most severely threatened species.

(top left):
Through the introduction of nontoxic hot air, all pests in wood on and in the rafters are killed by the heat.

(bottom left):
The mouse-eared bats that have returned after the renovation avoid the fresh roof covering as a hanging place.

Bodenmais, in the second largest Bavarian Barbastelle roost, the Angerloch in Upper Bavaria, Brigitte and Willi Issel found 75 hibernating bats in 1953. In the 1980's, only six animals on average could be found there in winter. And, as was confirmed by the speleologist Günter Hansbauer through a study, even these bats are extremely threatened by visitors to the cave. Formerly only a few spelunkers turned up in the Angerloch, but today the cave, with more than 1000 vistors yearly, has become almost a vacation spot for the adventuresome. Although the Angerloch is off the beaten path and visitors must put up with a rather strenuous climb, Günter Hansbauer has counted up to 60 persons in the cave on a single winter's day. More than 95 percent of those questioned had not seen any bats at all. Several Barbastelles hanging in narrow places near an entrance of the Angerloch were in constant danger of being pulled off or injured by passing visitors. Furthermore, remains of fireworks and traces of fires were evidence that some "romanticists" like to cap their visit to the cave with a private fireworks display in the entrance region.

These findings had the result that starting with the winter season of 1989/1990, the entrances to the Angerloch have been sealed with bat gratings. Since then the Barbastelle population has increased to 11 animals. The consistent protection of all known winter roosts of this very site-faithful species is certainly particularly important.

We still know very little about the summer and temporary roosts of the Barbastelle. Apart from records in tree holes (Denmark and Poland) and nest boxes (Poland, sporadic finds also in Baden-Württemberg, Germany), summer roost records of Barbastelles in Germany almost exclusively refer to crevice-like hiding places on buildings. Nursery roosts were found almost exclusively behind window shutters. It took almost 30 years before we discovered another Barbastelle nursery colony in 1987 in Bavaria. The approximately 15 females occupied a roost behind the wind screen on the roof of a house, which was revealed to us by three youngsters that had fallen from the roost.

Rescue Actions

Whoever want to successfully help bats must understand that, despite all rules and recommendations, unforeseeable difficulties and problems can turn up that often can be overcome only with the aid of experts. What roost preservation during renovations can look like in practice is shown in the following examples.

HOT AIR HELPS BATS

In the summer of 1982 it was planned to sanitize the roof timbers of the famous monastery church in Benediktbeuern, Germany, because of an infestation of pests. The attentive director of the sanitization company that won the contract called us and reported that he had seen bats during an inspection of the church roof. Once we knew that a large Mouse-eared Bat nursery colony had lived there for years, we made an appointment with the local authorities to discuss protective measures. We advised the owners of the church, the archbishopric in Augsburg, to sanitize the roof with the nonpoisonous hot-air procedure, after the animals had departed for their winter roost. Moreover, no changes were to be made to the hanging places of the bats, which were distributed throughout the entire attic. The church administration immediately agreed

(top

Under experimental supervision even extensive renovations can be carried out without the loss of animals (church in Au, Bavaria).

(bottom

The mouse-eared bat colony in the Auer church was even able to increase in size after the renovation.

to our proposals.

After a thorough inspection of the church attic in late fall showed that all of the Mouse-eared Bats had left their roost, the sanitization work could begin. A few damaged beams had to be replaced, then hot air was blown through large pipes into the attic until all pests in the wood, even those in the thickest beams, had been killed by the heat.

For the bats, which returned punctually to their nursery roost in the spring, nothing had changed. On July 6, 1983, we were able to confirm that youngsters were being reared without problems at the old hanging places. In the census three years later, we noted the impressive total of 320 Mouse-eared Bats in Benediktbeuern.

Though in Benediktbeuern the roost preservation proceeded unproblematically because of the timely information and the good cooperation of all parties, the preservation of a Mouse-eared Bat nursery roost in the Upper Bavarian community of Rohrdorf was to be considerably more dramatic.

SAVED AT THE LAST MINUTE

In this case nobody bothered to inform the conservation authority in time about the planned replacement of the church roof. Not until June, 1983, after the renovations had already begun, did we learn of the bats. On our first inspection in mid-June we found female Mouse-eared Bats with newborn young in a wall niche in the facade of the church attic. It would have been impossible to postpone the renovation work at that point, because a large portion of the roof had already been removed and the extensive construction work with the replacement of beams and refurbishment of the facade would have been delayed into the winter. A spontaneous solution had to be found that would give the bats a chance without materially affecting the construction work. Because the only exit hole for the animals luckily was located directly by their hanging place near a rotten door in the masonry gable end, we decided simply to separate the hanging place with the exit hole from the rest of the attic. This was accomplished by hanging a large canvas sheet diagonally in the attic space. Because a section of the roof of the "roost compartment" created in this fashion had already been sheathed, an additional water-tight plastic membrane was also nailed onto the outside of the roof. Finally all of the carpenters were shown the nursery colony. I told the men that each of them was responsible for the preservation of the animals and that the only way the colony could be saved would be by proceeding as carefully as possible.

In the bat-free section of the attic, work could proceed without interruption. When I saw the construction site again in late July, the first part of the experiment fortunately was over. The youngsters in the roost compartment had been reared successfully by their mothers and could already fly.

The last critical construction phase, however, was yet to come. Starting in early August, work on the roof of the roost compartment was to resume. How could it be explained to 300 bats that, because of the renovation of their home, they should move? The only gentle means of persuasion we could think of was to open the canvas sheet in the attic and to make it somewhat uncomfortable for the animals. So that the renovated section of the attic would be somewhat familiar to the bats, we nailed a few old boards—to which much bat scent clung—in the new apartment they were to occupy. After the carpenters began the renovation on the outside of the roost compartment, the bat colony moved out completely and the curtain (canvas sheet) could be closed again before the last act, the renovation of the roost compartment. Up until then the difficult production had run almost perfectly.

But then the stage managers (bat experts) made a serious mistake. Whoever directs should not only explain how the production is to be completed according to his wishes, he must also watch over the piece until its conclusion. However, we only gave the instruction that all of the old hanging boards should be saved and nailed to the new rafters. But as is proper for an orderly construction site, by our next visit all of the old wood had been carted away as scrap wood. This error in direction continued to affect the bat colony in the following years. To be sure, all of the bats returned to the renovated roost the following season, but the animals almost exclusively chose as hanging places the few remaining old boards in the attic and for years still avoided the new rafters—this comparison is allowed in a church attic—like the Devil avoids holy water!

DETAILED KNOWLEDGE PAYS OFF

When we began to be interested in 1984

in another nursery colony in the attic of the church in Au at Bad Feilnbach, Germany, the first thing we did was to obtain complete data on the roost behavior, rearing of the young, development of colony size, length of stay in the nursery roost, as well as on flights by the Mouse-eared Bats from the roost. The detailed knowledge of the roost behavior of the Au bats was to become very important the following year. Their roost had to be renovated, some of the rafters and the entire roof covering replaced. Because we knew the temporal and spatial distribution in the attic, with the cooperation of church authorities it was possible to draw up a precise working plan that would take into account the animals' needs. Thus, only the facade at the base of the roof was renovated while the bats were present. The building engineers were amazed that we were able to predict when and where the females would give birth to their young. The work on the church roof was postponed so the Mouse-eared Bats in the apse, the roof section above the altar space, could bring their young into the world without disturbance. Because all of our predictions came to pass, it was easy to convince the carpenters to postpone further renovations until the young were able to fly. After this critical phase had passed, we gave the green light so that the apse as well could be finished by the fall. Although all of the participants were happy with the success, the scaffolding outside the church, which was kept in place longer than usual, was considered an eyesore by a few residents of the village. They spoke with the construction supervisor and accused him of showing too much consideration for a few bats. After they heard our bat presentation in the town hall and observed the evening flight of the colony, however, even the construction supervisor had been "rehabilitated."

A SUCCESS THAT SHOULD NOT SERVE AS A MODEL

In successful conservation actions, normally you hope for as many imitators as possible. An exception to this rule is our resettlement of a nursery roost of the Lesser Horseshoe Bat. On the "hit list" of endangered speces, the Red List of Germany, the Lesser Horseshoe Bat together with its close relative the Greater Horseshoe Bat, as well as the Barbastelle and Geoffroy's Bat, hold the unfortunate top positions. All four species are placed in the highest category of

A common pipistrelle (Pipistrellus pipistrellus) urinating.

endangerment, containing those species that are threatened with extinction. To find any reports of nursery roosts of the Lesser Horseshoe Bat in Germany, it is necessary to go back many years in the relevant bat literature. All the greater was the surprise when in the spring of 1983, in the attic of a former hotel in Peissenberg, Upper Bavaria, we discovered an up to then unknown colony of the Lesser Horseshoe Bat. Once again our publicity work had paid off. Our first hint of the presence of the roost came from a Peissenberg electrician, Leo Weissenbach, at a bat seminar in Wolfratshausen, Germany. Although he had not seen any bats in the hotel attic, during his electrical work he had noticed a large amount of old bat droppings. Our great enthusiasm about the unusual find, however, was soon followed by great disillusionment. The structural condition of the roost building made us fear the worst. First we visited the local government in Peissenberg. The good news that the former hotel was owned by the town was promptly folowed by the bad: The town had already sold the building and property to a residential construction company, which planned to build an apartment building at the same location. Mayor Führler, whom I dealt with, must have noticed my disappointed face, for he spontaneously offered me the attic of a nearby building, which was being renovated as a mining museum, as a replacement roost for the Horseshoe Bats. Despite the generous offer, what were we to do now? All of the specialist colleagues we asked unanimously advised us to not even attempt a completely hopeless resettlement. In this case our alternatives were to do nothing and to try the impossible. In evaluating our prospects of success, the only thing that came to mind was the aphorism of the lifeguard in Achternbusch: "You have no chance, so use it!" So we started with our experiments.

Our first success was to postpone the demolishing of the old building until the

133

(top):
The former Sulz hotel in Peissenberg, Upper Bavaria, harbored one of the last German nursery colonies of the lesser horseshoe bat (Rhinolophus hipposideros) *in the angled attic under a tin roof.*

(center):
We were offered the attic space of the nearby mining museum as a replacement roost for the horseshoe bats.

planned resettlement action was complete. That was the beginning of my "summer in Peissenberg." Whenever I had free time I drove to Peissenberg to learn as much as possible about the roost requirements of the Horseshoe Bats through observations and measurements. Finally we believed that we knew what made the old hotel attic so attractive to the animals. A tin roof provided comfortable temperatures when the sun was out. Through two built-in walkways, a gable, and eight chimneys, the attic space was divided into a whole "spatial complex," which the Horseshoe Bats could use in many different ways. Depending on the weather and the outside temperature, the animals could use different hanging places. Because the inhabitants of the building still cooked with coal-burning stoves, even in summer a few of the chimneys gave off heat. The Horseshoe Bats liked to seek these out when it was temporarily uncomfortably cold. All of the animals then hung in the vicinity of the hot chimney. In contrast, the mining museum that was to serve as the replacement roost had a tile roof that warmed up more slowly. To be sure, as in the bat roost, a wooden floor was present. Otherwise, however, the attic had scarcely any nooks and crannies. If the new roost was to be to the bats' liking, it would have to be furnished in a Horseshoe Bat-friendly manner. Therefore, we had two important tasks to deal with in the winter season of 1983/84. First, we wanted to know where the Peissenberg Horseshoe Bats hibernated. Despite the most diligent search, to this day their winter roost is still a mystery to us. Second, we had to build a home for the bats in the attic of the future roost.

For this purpose we used parts of the floor from the hotel attic to build the replacement roost. An old hayrick with untreated wood was purchased and used to make the wooden partitions with openings for the bats to fly through. Two heated chambers were built. In the heated chambers of the future "luxury penthouse for Horseshoe Bats" we installed two separately controled floor heaters. With these built-in heaters as well as supplemental black-light radiators, from the formerly bare attic a room complex with sections of variable temperature was created. Finally, an infrared light cabinet was added to record the comings and goings of the future inhab-

134

itants.

The actual experiment began in May, 1984, after up to 11 Horseshoe Bats were encountered again in their roost in the hotel attic. We planned to try the resettlement on a cold day, but when we approached we found that up to five of the Horseshoe Bats apparently had wandered off because of the cold. The remaining animals hung with lowered body temperature in deep diurnal sleep lethargy from their hanging places and were easy to pluck from there and store in small linen sacks. We had not expected that the animals would hardly notice the first part of the resettlement. The animals woke up immediately again in the heated replacement roost and were irritated by their new surroundings.

So we changed our battle plan and used a cool mine shaft next to the mining museum as "temporary storage" for the torpid animals in their small linen sacks. A Horseshoe Bat, which we found there deep in sleep, was also put in a sack and was hung alongside its colleagues. After we had turned off the floor heating and had aired out the space thoroughly, it took five hours for the replacement roost to cool down. Then we

hung the six Horseshoe Bats in the unheated chambers. After briefly spreading their wings, they wrapped themselves in their wing membranes again and remained hanging lethargically as we left the involuntary transplants on tiptoes. Beforehand we had spread Horseshoe Bat droppings from the hotel attic on the floor heater, so when it was turned on the animals would be exposed to the "smell of home." We kept

The former deep mine shaft behind the mining museum served as "temporary storage" for the collected horseshoe bats.

(bottom): A picture of success: Six of the approximately 13 lesser horseshoe bats in one of the two warm chambers. Since 1985 the entire colony has occupied their "luxury penthouse" for the whole summer season.

(bottom): So that the animals met with conditions similar to those in their original roost, in the future replacement roost we added insulation, niches, and even floor heating.

A Bechstein's bat flies just above the water's surface to drink.

the exit opening of the new roost closed for two days. On the following day we had a surprise: two animals hung sleeping in a different spot. The four remaining Horseshoe Bats, after they woke up, must have escaped through a narrow crack in the roof ridge that we only now discovered. The only thing we could do was to heat the warm chambers and to open the exit hole. As our infrared sensors showed, the two remaining bats stayed in the replacement roost four more days before, as expected, returning to the other bats in their old roost. But after only 12 days the completely unexpected happened: The counter of the infrared sensors regularly registered individual bats entering and leaving. By the fall of 1984 two of the Horsehoe Bats had accepted the replacement roost and even had their preferred hanging places there.

After the colony had left the hotel attic in the fall of 1984, the roost building was demolished. The following spring would show whether our efforts had paid off. In fact, at first two Horseshoe Bats returned to the replacement roost. In the course of time the new abode filled up, as was registered by the infrared sensors. We suspect that the two "regular tenants" of the previous summer had attracted the other colony members to the new roost. Since then the small colony has returned to its "luxury apartment" each summer season.

This kind of success cannot be kept secret, especially since many helpers had taken part in the good fortune. After newspapers, radio, and television had reported it, home owners who were not thrilled with their secretive tenants called up in the belief that the animals could be removed and resettled. Our standard answer to such an undertaking must continue to be, "Resettlement is out of the question!" Despite all the strategic discussions in the case of our Peissenberg Horseshoe Bats, a substantial portion of luck and accident also played a part in the successful resettlement—not to mention the 560-work hours and the considerable expense the action had cost. Through our efforts we learned more about the roost requirements of the Lesser Horseshoe Bat, but as a method for practical bat conservation, resettlement must remain the absolute exception. In consideration of the site faithfulness of many species and their general endangerment, these kinds of experiments are much too risky. Successful roost protection always means to preserve and possibly to improve existing roosts. Furthermore, our studies of the Lesser Horseshoe Bat show that this species faces imminent extinction. Even in our Peissenberg nursery colony we have only been able to confirm two young since 1983. This is particularly depressing. In the end, with the replacement roost we could no longer ensure the survival of the population, but rather merely grant the animals a pleasant "old-age home."

The bats of Europe—
Their appearance and Lives

Bats are principally found in the warmer regions of Earth. Accordingly, Europe is hardly one of their main areas of occurrence. Still, 30 species from three families live in Europe, 21 species of which have been documented in Germany. All of these species belong to the suborder of the insectivorous bats (Microchiroptera). The most well-represented family, with 24 European representatives, is that of the common bats (Vespertilionidae). Five species of the horseshoe bat family (Rhinolophidae) occur in Europe. The free-tailed bats (Molossidae) are represented by one European species.

Within the common bats there are unmistakable representatives, but there are also externally very similar species. This suggests that even with the small number of bats in Europe it is possible that some so-far unrecognized species exist.

In Europe bats find their prey, namely insects and spiders, through the use of their echolocation system. The foodless season is survived through migration and hibernation. Because flying uses up a great deal of energy, even during the hunting season energy is saved through all kinds of tricks, such as lowering of temperature during inactive and sleeping phases.

The flying foxes (Megachiroptera) would too seldom find enough fruit, pollen, and nectar to eat in the European realm. Hence, only one species has managed to gain a toehold in Europe: There is an enclave of African Rousette Fruit Bats (*Rousettus aegyptiacus*) on Cyprus. All of the European bats are portrayed in the following brief descriptions. Their habits and the type of living space they require largely determine their degree of endangerment, but also suggest ways to protect our little sprites of the night.

We usually see photographs of bats with wide-open mouths and sharp teeth bared; nevertheless, with closed mouth the same bat looks much quainter.

Lesser Horseshoe Bat
Rhinolophus hipposideros (Bechstein, 1800)

BODY SIZE: HBL 37-45 (47) mm; TL 23-33 mm; FL (34) 37-42.5 mm; WS 192-254 mm; Wt (4) 5.6-9 (10) g.

CONSPICUOUS CHARACTERS: Smallest European horseshoe bat. Delicate build. Median keel of the nasal process is tapered from bottom to top; rounded upper process is lower when viewed from the side. Fur light gray toward base. Brownish smoky colored without reddish tint, underside gray to gray-white. Fur soft, sparse; juveniles dark gray.

REPRODUCTION: G approximately 75 days; Y 1 (2); BW approximately 1.8 g.

LIFE CYCLE: W at about 6-7 weeks, SM at about 1-2 years, LS maximum age 21 years, average 3-4 years.

DIET: Small insects (moths, flies, craneflies, beetles), also spiders.

ENEMIES: Man.

HABITS AND LIVING SPACE: Gregarious, always hangs singly. Short migrations between summer and winter roosts. Warmer regions in foothills and subalpine mountain ranges, in part in forested landscapes, chalk formations. House bat in the north, cave bat in the south! In the north, summer roosts (nursery roosts) in warm attics, often near chimneys, in drains and shafts of heated cellars; relatively modest demands with re-spect to space; roosts must be draft-free, but can be lighted; attics are either strongly niched or consist of several rooms; these kinds of "room complexes" exhibit clear microclimatic differences, which are used according to weather and outside temperature; often leaves roost through a window. In the south, roosts in caves and tree holes. Winter roosts in caves, tree holes, cellars, temperature 6-9° C (43-48°F), high humidity. Always free-hanging in the winter roost and maintains distance to neighbors. Very sensitive to disturbance in the roost. Hunts in open forests, parks, among undergrowth. Flight altitude low, up to 5 meters. Whirring flight. Can also take prey from substrates.

ABUNDANCE/ENDANGERMENT: Severe decline since the mid-1950's in central Europe. Numerous populations have already died out. Threatened principally by loss of and changes in habitat, disturbance, destruction of roosts, use of insecticides. In the north, decline possibly also because of climatic changes for the worse.

PROTECTION: Systematic protection of summer and winter roosts (preservation and improvement of the roost situation). Protection, care, and development of hunting habitat.

page 139 (bottom right):
Greater noctule (Nyctalus lasiopterus). The range of the largest European bat is incompletely known. This migratory bat species occupies nursery and winter roosts in tree holes.

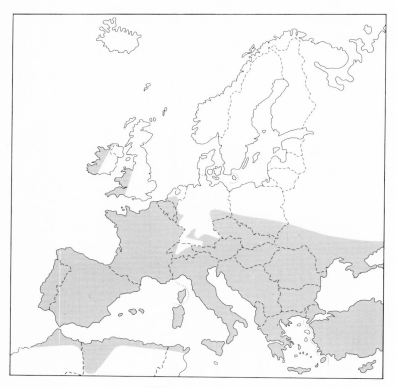

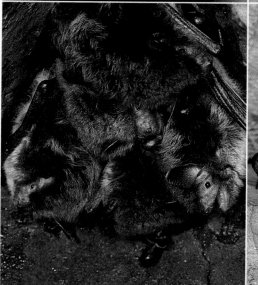

(top left):
The greater horseshoe bat (Rhinolophus ferrumequinum) is the largest of the five species of European horseshoe bats.

(top right):
The Mediterranean horseshoe bat (Rhinolophus euryale) prefers limestone regions with an abundance of caves.

(center left):
Daubenton's bat (Myotis daubentoni) is widely distributed in Europe and prefers to hunt just above water surfaces.

(center right):
The warmth-loving Geoffroy's bat (Myotis emarginatus) is found in Central Europe only in regions with favorable climates. This species has soft, cilia-like hairs on the free edge of the wing membrane.

(bottom left):
Bechstein's bat (Myotis bechsteini) holds the record for the longest ears of all the Myotis species of approximately the same size. The fur of this typical forest bat is relatively long.

139

Greater Horseshoe Bat
Rhinolophus ferrumequinum (Schreber, 1774)

BODY SIZE: HBL (50) 57-71 mm; TL (30) 35-43 mm; FL (50) 54-61 mm; WS 350-400 mm; Wt 17-34 g.

CONSPICUOUS CHARACTERS: Largest European horseshoe bat. Upper saddle process of the nasal leaf short, rounded; lower part pointed in profile. Fur soft, sparse, light gray toward base. Back gray brown or smoky gray, more or less tinged with red. Underside gray white to yellowish white. Juveniles more ashy gray on the back. Wing membranes and ears light gray-brown. Large ears.

REPRODUCTION: G approximately 75 days; Y 1 (2); BW unknown.

LIFE CYCLE: W at approximately 7-8 weeks; SM at approximately 2-3 years; LS maximum age 30 years.

DIET: Small to medium-sized and larger insects (June beetles, carrion beetles, grasshoppers, moths).

ENEMIES: Man.

HABITS AND LIVING SPACE: Leaves roost at nightfall. Flight low, butterflylike, with short stretches of gliding, usually at low altitude (0.3-6 m). Little flight activity in unfavorable weather. Prefers to hunt in country with open stands of trees, along slopes and rock faces, also in gardens. Hunts from ambush and also takes prey on the ground. Uses feeding places. Short migrations between summer (nursery) and winter roosts. Roost requirements as for Lesser Horseshoe Bat.

ABUNDANCE/ENDANGERMENT: Severe decline in England, Belgium, Luxembourg, and Germany. Threatened mainly by changes (deterioration) in habitat, use of insecticides, disturbance, and destruction of roosts. In England, Switzerland, and possibly the border region between Germany and Luxembourg still stable remnant populations

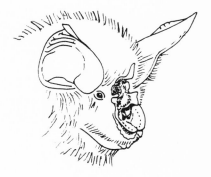

(a tiny remnant population also exists in the Oberpfalz, Bavaria) that require comprehensive total protection as a priority.

PROTECTION: In regions that still have remnant populations, comprehensive total protective measures based on the English model (see Stebbings, 1988).

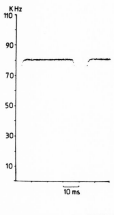

Mediterranean Horseshoe Bat
Rhinolophus euryale (Blasius, 1853)

BODY SIZE: HBL 43-58 mm; TL 22-30 mm; FL 43-51 mm; WS 300-320 mm; Wt 8-17.5 g.

CONSPICUOUS CHARACTERS: Medium-sized species. Nasal process (median keel) with pointed upper process when viewed from the side. Bare facial area (horseshoe, lips) light brownish, ears and wing membranes light gray. Fur sparse. Fur light gray toward base. Back gray-brown with light reddish or pinkish tinge, underside gray-white to yellowish white. Boundary between back and underside indistinct. Often a few dark hairs around the eyes; juveniles altogether more gray colored.

ABUNDANCE/ENDANGERMENT: General population decline, particularly in the northern part of the range. Threatened in part by disturbances in the roosting caves (tourism).

PROTECTION: Systematic protection of roosts and biotope urgently needed.

REPRODUCTION: G unknown; Y 1 (2); BW approximately 4 g.

LIFE CYCLE: W at approximately 6-7 weeks; SM at 1 year; LS unknown.

DIET: Moths and other insects.

ENEMIES: Man.

HABITS AND LIVING SPACE: Cave bat, in the north also occupies summer roosts, rarely in warm attics. Lives gregariously, with animals in active state frequently in body contact, embracing one another with the wings and licking one another's head and face. Often roosts together with other bats (horseshoe bats, Geoffroy's Bat, Schreiber's Bat). Natural caves, grottoes, tree holes; warm, forested regions in foothills and mountains, prefers cave-rich chalk formations with water nearby. Sedentary with only minimal tendency to wander. Leaves roost in late evening. Flight slow, fluttering, also hovers, very agile. Hunts low on warm slopes, but also in dense foliage. Sometimes visits feeding perches.

141

Blasius's Horseshoe Bat
Rhinolophus blasii (Peters, 1866)

BODY SIZE: HBL (44) 46.5-54 mm; TL (20) 25-30 mm; FL (43.5) 45-48 mm; WS approximately 280 mm; Wt (10) 12-15 g.

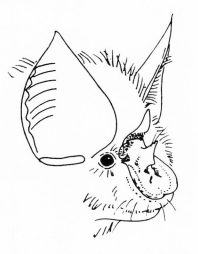

page 143 (top left): Northern bat (Eptesicus nilssoni). This species has gleaming gold tips of the hairs on the back and on top of the head.

page 143 (top right): Portrait of a particoloured bat (Vespertilio murinus).

K Hz

CONSPICUOUS CHARACTERS: Medium-sized species. Nasal process (median keel) with pointed upper process when viewed from the side, tapering to lanceolate point. Horseshoe broad, flesh colored, ears and wing membranes light gray. Fur sparse, very pale, almost white, toward base. Back gray-brown, in part with light pink tinge, underside almost white or with slight yellowish tinge. Boundary between back and underside relatively sharp. Dark "spectacles" around the eyes lacking or only suggested.

REPRODUCTION: G unknown; Y 1 (2); BW unknown.

LIFE CYCLE: W at approximately 6-7 weeks; SM at approximately 1 year; LS unknown.

DIET: Small insects.

ENEMIES: Man.

HABITS AND LIVING SPACE: Little is known about habits. Summer and winter roosts in caves and subterranean passages (cave bat). No precise data on hibernation. Animals always free-hanging, without mutual body contact. Warm chalk formations, with shrubs and open woodland. Apparently a site-faithful species.

ABUNDANCE/ENDANGERMENT: Some populations in decline. Threatened by disturbance and killing in caves (tourism and persecution).

PROTECTION: Protection of roosts (preservation/securing).

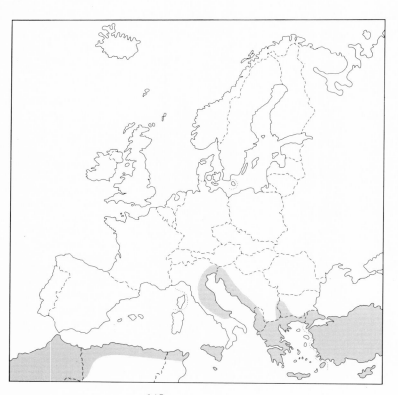

(center left):
*Common long-eared bat (*Plecotus auritus*) at the mouth of a tree hole. Our common long-eared bats accept a wide range of roost types: from attics with hiding places to tree holes and nest and bat boxes.*

(center right):
*Young barbastelle (*Barbastella barbastellus*). The tips of the hairs of the back are already whitish in larger youngsters; this makes the top side look frosted.*

(bottom left):
*Because of its very short muzzle, the bulbous forehead, and the short, triangular ears, which are set far apart, Schreiber's bat (*Miniopterus schreibersi*) is unmistakable in Europe.*

(bottom right):
*In the European free-tailed bat (*Tadarida teniotis*) the tail extends freely up to a third, in part up to a half, beyond the tail membrane. This large bat, with its characteristic face, the large ears projecting over the eyes and face, and the very narrow, long wings, cannot be confused with other species in Europe.*

Mehely's Horseshoe Bat
Rhinolophus mehelyi (Matschie, 1901)

BODY SIZE: HBL (49) 55-64 mm; TL (23) 24-29 mm; FL (47) 50-55 mm; WS approximately 330-340 mm; Wt 10-18 g.

CONSPICUOUS CHARACTERS: Medium-sized species. Nasal process (median keel) with wedge-shaped upper process when viewed from the side. Horseshoe and lips pale, flesh colored; ears and wing membranes gray-brown. Fur relatively dense, gray white at base. Back gray-brown, underside almost white. Boundary between back and underside relatively sharp. Conspicuous dark "spectacles" around eyes comprised of gray-brown hairs.

REPRODUCTION: G unknown; Y 1 (2); BW unknown.

LIFE CYCLE: W at approximately 6-7 weeks; SM at 1 year; LS unknown.

DIET: Small insects (moths and the like).

ENEMIES: Man.

HABITS AND LIVING SPACE: Little is known about habits. Cave bat; summer and winter roosts in caves. Lives gregariously in large roosts. Often shares roost with other horseshoe bats, Lesser Mouse-eared Bat, and Schreiber's Bat. Lives in chalk formations with water nearby. Apparently site-faithful. Leaves roost at nightfall. Hunts low over the ground on warm mountain slopes, also between bushes and trees. Flight slow, nimble, very agile, in part with short stretches of gliding. Because it can easily and effortlessly take off from the ground, it is suspected that Mehely's Horseshoe Bat also captures prey on the ground.

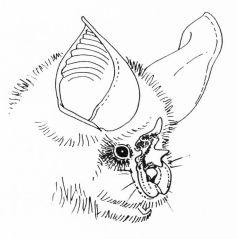

ABUNDANCE/ENDANGERMENT: Rare, possibly in rapid decline due to disturbance and loss of roost caves.

PROTECTION: Protection of roosts (preservation and securing of caves) and biotope protection (reduced use of insecticides) are needed.

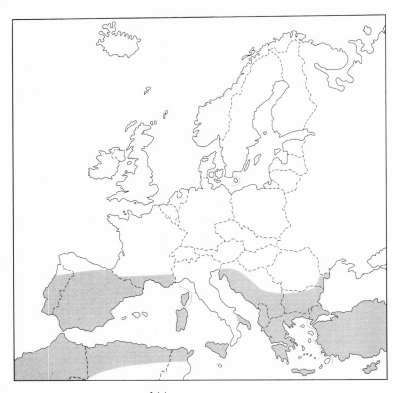

144

Long-fingered Bat
Myotis capaccinii (Bonaparte, 1837)

BODY SIZE: HBL (43) 47-53 mm; TL 35-42 mm; FL (37) 38-44 mm; WS 230-260 mm; Wt 6-15 g.

CONSPICUOUS CHARACTERS: Medium-sized species. Ears of medium length. Large feet with long bristles. Fur dark gray at base. Back light smoky gray, in part with slight

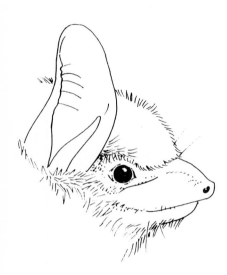

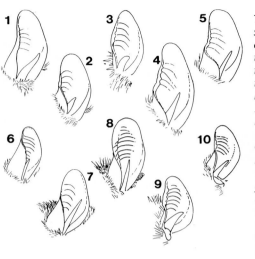

The Myotis species are most easily identified on the basis of ear form: 1. long-fingered bat, 2. Daubenton's bat, 3. pond bat, 4. Brandt's bat, 5. Whiskered bat, 6. Geoffroy's bat, 7. Natterer's bat, 8. Bechstein's bat, 9. greater mouse-eared bat, 10. lesser mouse eared bat. The illustrations of the ears are not to scale.

yellowish tinge, underside light gray. Boundary between back and underside indistinct. Snout reddish brown, ears and wing membranes gray-brown, tail membrane above and below from the legs to about the middle very dark, with downlike hair. Nostrils clearly more protruding than in other European *Myotis* species.

REPRODUCTION: Known only incompletely. G approximately 50-60 days; Y 1 (2); BW unknown.

LIFE CYCLE: W at approximately 6-7 weeks; SM at 1 year; LS unknown.

DIET: Small insects.

ENEMIES: Apparently man.

HABITS AND LIVING SPACE: Incomplete knowledge of range. Summer and winter roosts in caves and subterranean passages (cave bat). Gregarious. Apparently sedentary, but also migrates at times (migrations not understood). Winter roosts often in crevices, chalk formations. Prefers well-watered, forested, or shrubby landscapes. Leaves roost in late evening. Flight similar to that of Daubenton's Bat. Often hunts flying insects over water.

ABUNDANCE/ENDANGERMENT: Little known. Populations rare and possibly declining. Endangered by the destruction of caves, disturbance, and direct persecution.

PROTECTION: Preservation and securing of roosts.

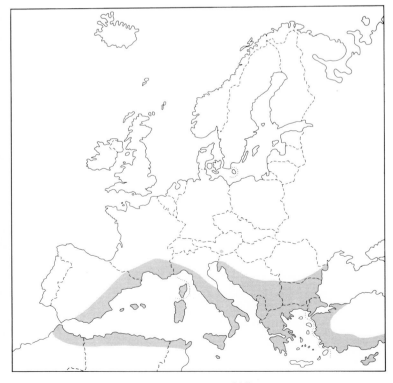

Daubenton's Bat
Myotis daubentoni (Kuhl, 1819)

BODY SIZE: HBL (40) 45-55 (60) mm; TL (27) 31-44.5 (48) mm; FL (33) 35-41.7 (42) mm; WS 240-275 mm; Wt (5) 7-15 g.

CONSPICUOUS CHARACTERS: Medium-sized to small species with rufous muzzle and conspicuously large feet with long bristles. Relatively short tail and short ears. Fur sparse, dark gray-brown at base. Back brown-gray to dark bronze, tips of hairs often glossy, underside silvery gray, in part with brownish tinge. Boundary between back and underside usually sharp. Ears and wing membranes dark gray-brown; juveniles more gray.

REPRODUCTION: G approximately 50-55 days; 1 (2) Y; BW about 2.3 g.

LIFE CYCLE: W at approximately 7-8 weeks (able to fly starting in the fourth week); SM at 1 year; LS maximum age 20 years; average 4-4.5 years.

DIET: Small flying insects (flies, craneflies, moths, and the like) primarily near water.

ENEMIES: Man.

HABITS AND LIVING SPACE: Leaves the roost in twilight. Flight fast, agile, wing beats in part whirring. Primarily in flat country, found there in forests, parks (forest bat) near bodies of water. Migrates between summer and winter roosts. Winter roosts in caves, mine shafts, bunkers, cellars, old wells (tem-

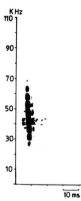

perature 3-6° C, high humidity); usually pressed into a crack in hibernation, but also free-hanging on the wall in large clusters; has also been found up to 60 centimeters deep in floor rubble. Partial migrant, usually roosts in summer in tree holes, but also in narrow cracks in attics, behind shutters, in cracks in walls. Individual animals and small groups of males in summer also in moist, cool cracks in walls of bridges over rivers, rarely in bat boxes.

Roosts in attics or steeples of churches; animals hide there in chinks or in cracks in walls (depending on weather). Daytime roosts more likely to exhibit low but relatively constant temperatures. Often hunts only 5 to 20 centimeters above the water's surface, but also up to 5 meters high in trees. Feeds in flight, rests during breaks from hunting on branches and walls. Hunting grounds are usually located only 2-5 kilometers from the roost.

ABUNDANCE/ENDANGERMENT: A few local populations in central and northern Europe are stable or have increased, otherwise in decline. Threatened by changes in habitat, draining of wetlands, loss of food supply. Individual animals get caught accidentally by fish hooks (with mouth or wings). Disturbance or destruction of winter roosts, shortage of suitable summer roosts (lack of tree holes, changes in building construction without joints).

PROTECTION: Protection of roosts and biotope; food situation evidently often better than with the majority of other species (no use of insecticides over water surfaces). Preservation of old deciduous trees along riparian edges, plantings of soft-wooded trees along bodies of water; preservation of rock faces and abandoned, water-filled quarries, above all near water; preservation and construction of summer roosts on bridges and water tunnels (2-3-centimeter-wide cracks with rough walls, as deep as possible) are urgently needed.

Preserving and guarding mass roosts (winter) in Poland.

Pond Bat
Myotis dasycneme (Boie, 1825)

BODY SIZE: HBL 57-67 (68) mm; TL (39) 46-51 (53) mm; FL (41) 43-49.2 mm; WS 200-300 mm; Wt (11) 14-20 (23) g.

CONSPICUOUS CHARACTERS: Medium-sized species with relatively large feet. Resembles Daubenton's Bat, but obviously larger.

Top side of tail membrane bare, without downy fur. Fur dense, black-brown at base. Back brownish or pale gray-brown with silky sheen, underside gray-white to yellow-

mals also in hollow trees. Partial migrant. Migrations between summer and winter roosts usually more than 100 kilometers. Leaves roost in late evening, in part two hunting periods (evening and toward morning). Hunts over water as well as over meadows and along forest edges. Flight fast, agile, often only 5-10 centimeters above water; also takes insects from the water's surface.

ABUNDANCE/ENDANGERMENT: Very rare species. Decline of populations in all centers of occurrence. Causes include changes in habitat, use of wood preservatives in buildings with roosts, and water pollution.

PROTECTION: Systematic protection of roosts and biotope. Avoidance of toxic wood preservatives!

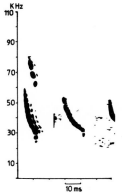

ish gray, relatively sharply demarcated from the back. Muzzle short, rufous, ears and wing membranes gray brown; juveniles altogether darker colored.

REPRODUCTION: G about 50-60 days; Y 1 (2); BW unknown.

LIFE CYCLE: W at approximately 7-8 weeks; SM apparently in the second year (females); LS maximum age 19.5 years.

DIET: Small insects (flies, craneflies, moths).

ENEMIES: Man.

HABITS AND LIVING SPACE: In summer in areas with abundant water, meadows and forests in lowlands, in winter also foothills of medium elevation mountain ranges. Winter roosts in natural caves, mine shafts in chalk formations, cellars, bunkers (temperature 0.5-7.5° C); forced into cracks, also free-hanging on walls and ceilings, forming small clusters in large winter roosts. Summer roosts (nursery roosts) in buildings, usually in attics or church steeples, frequently on roof ridge in large groups (40-400 females) in darker part; individual ani-

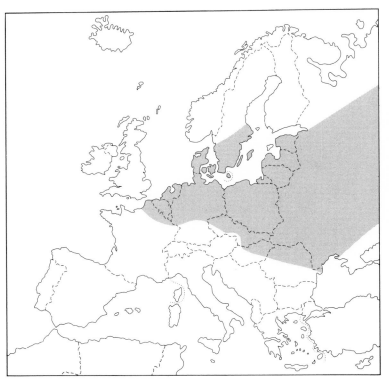

147

Brandt's Bat
Myotis brandti (Eversmann, 1845)

BODY SIZE: HBL 39-51 mm; TL 32-44 mm; FL 33-39.2 mm; WS 190-240 mm; Wt 4.3-9.5 g.

CONSPICUOUS CHARACTERS: Small species. Occurrence in Europe was first documented in 1958 by Topal. Fur relatively long, dark gray-brown at base. Back light brown, usually with a golden sheen, underside light gray, in part with yellowish tinge. Muzzle, ears, and wing membranes medium to light brown. Penis in adult males clearly thickened at the end. Juveniles strongly resemble the Whiskered Bat; the two species are hard to distinguish.

REPRODUCTION: G unknown; Y 1 (2); BW unknown.

LIFE CYCLE: W unknown (able to fly at 3-4 weeks); SM at 2 years (females); LS maximum age 19 years 8 months.

DIET: Small insects (probably small moths and other flying insects).

ENEMIES: Man.

HABITS AND LIVING SPACE: Distribution only incompletely known. Forest bat. More closely bound to forested regions and bodies of water than is the Whiskered Bat. Summer roosts (nursery roosts) in narrow cracks in attics of buildings, behind roof laths, roof coverings outside and inside, in holes in beams, also in bat boxes (of small

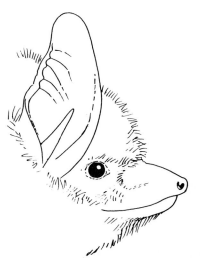

volume). Winter roosts in caves, tunnels, old mines, cellars (temperature [0° C] 3-4° C [7.5° C]), often together with the Whiskered Bat. Rarely in crevices, usually free-hanging on the wall or ceiling, also in clusters. Partial migrant, migrates up to 230 kilometers. Leaves roost in early evening. Hunts at low to medium altitude in not too dense woods and over water. Flight is fast and agile with quick turns in small spaces.

ABUNDANCE/ENDANGERMENT: Only small populations have been found so far. Apparently in decline because of changes in and destruction of habitat, loss of hollow trees, and the use of wood preservatives.

PROTECTION: Avoid use of toxic wood preservatives. Installation of shallow bat boxes in suitable biotopes. Protection of biotopes and roosts (above all through the preservation and protection of suitable winter roosts).

Whiskered Bat
Myotis mystacinus (Kuhl, 1819)

BODY SIZE: HBL 35-48 mm; TL 30-43 mm; FL (31) 32-36 (37.7) mm; WS 190-225 mm; Wt (3) 4-8 g.

CONSPICUOUS CHARACTERS: Smallest European *Myotis* species. Muzzle, ears, and wing membranes blackish brown; base of tragus and inner margin of ear, in contrast to Brandt's Bat, not light. Fur long, somewhat coarse, dark gray at base. Coloration of back varies greatly from dark nut-brown to dark gray-brown, rarely light brown, always darker than Brandt's Bat. Underside dark to light gray. Juveniles darker, fur black at

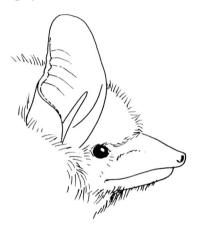

base, back dark gray-brown. Penis thin, not thickened at end. Temperamental and lively in behavior, scolds loudly when disturbed in the roost.

REPRODUCTION: G approximately 50-60 days; Y 1 (2); BW unknown.

LIFE CYCLE: W at approximately 6-7 weeks; SM at 1 year; LS maximum age 19 years, average of 3.5 years.

DIET: Small insects (flies, mayflies, small dragonflies, beetles, moths).

ENEMIES: Man, Common Barn Owl.

HABITS AND LIVING SPACE: Not as closely tied to forest and bodies of water as Brandt's Bat, more in parks, gardens, and villages. More of a house than a forest bat. In southeastern Europe also found in chalk formations. Summer roosts (nursery roosts) usually in cracklike hollow spaces on and in buildings (also in smaller buildings such as single-family homes, vacation homes, hunting lodges, chapels), behind wood siding, between joists and foundations, but also crawlspaces. Usually lives in east- or southeast-facing facades, also behind shutters, seldom in nest boxes. Winter roosts in caves, tunnels, cellars (temperature 2-8° C), usu-

ally free-hanging on walls or ceilings, more rarely pressed into cracks. Predominantly sedentary, but migrations of up to 240 kilometers are also known. Leaves the roost in early evening. Hunts in practically any biotope; belongs to the adaptable species. Flight fast, agile, and twisting. In spring and fall occasionally hunts during the day; hangs from branches during pauses in hunting.

ABUNDANCE/ENDANGERMENT: Some populations in decline in central Europe. Causes include changes in habitat, destruction of roosts, and disturbance in roosts.

PROTECTION: Systematic protection of roosts (summer and winter). Protection of biotope.

149

Geoffroy's Bat
Myotis emarginatus (Geoffroy, 1806)

BODY SIZE: HBL 41-53 mm; TL 38-46 (48) mm; FL 36-41 (42) mm; WS 220-245 mm; Wt (6) 7-15 g.

CONSPICUOUS CHARACTERS: Medium-sized species. Margin of the tail membrane has fine hairs. Top half of the outside of the ears has distinct, close to right-angle indentation. Fur long, light, woolly looking. Hair on the back tricolored, base gray, middle straw yellow, tips conspicuously rusty to rufous, underside yellowish gray. Muzzle rufous, ears and wing membranes dark gray-brown. Juveniles considerably darker smoky gray to brown-gray, without reddish tint.

REPRODUCTION: G approximately 50-60 days; Y 1 (2); BW unknown.

LIFE CYCLE: W at approximately 6-7 weeks (able to fly at about 4 weeks); SM at 1 year; LS maximum age 16 years, average age 2.8-3.5 years.

DIET: Small insects (flies, butterflies, and caterpillars), spiders.

ENEMIES: Man.

HABITS AND LIVING SPACE: Warmth-loving species. In the north primarily a house bat; in the south a cave bat. In lowlands and at lower elevations in mountains, in towns with parks, gardens, and water, as well as in chalk formations. Summer roosts (nursery roosts) in attics (in the north) or warm caves (in the south), also in comparatively bright attics with relatively low but constant temperatures. Pefers hanging sites often in the middle parts of roofs, on beams or boards, usually not in the gable. Gregarious, often sharing attics with other species (mouse-eared bats, Lesser Horseshoe Bat); individual animals also in tree holes and cracks, bat boxes ("temporary roosts"). Winter roosts in caves, tunnels, and cellars (temperature 6-9° C, rarely lower), usually free-hanging singly from the ceiling or wall,

rarely in small clusters or in crevices. Predominantly sedentary, migrations usually under 40 kilometers. Leaves roost in early evening. Hunts in twisting flight, but also harvests prey from substrates and hunts from ambush.

ABUNDANCE/ENDANGERMENT: Very rare. Threatened by changes in habitat, disturbance, and destruction of roosts. Food shortage. In part severe decline in population.

PROTECTION: Systematic protection of roosts and biotope, avoidance of wood preservatives.

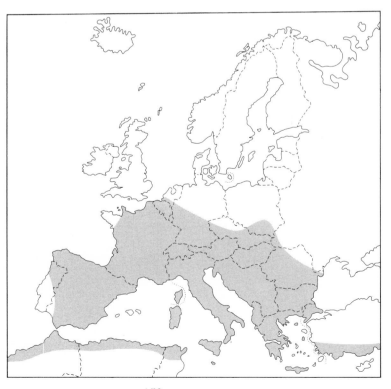

Natterer's Bat
Myotis nattereri (Kuhl, 1818)

BODY SIZE: HBL (40) 42-50 (55) mm; TL 38-47 (49) mm; FL 36.5-43.3 (46) mm; WS 245-280 mm; Wt 5-12 g.

CONSPICUOUS CHARACTERS: Medium-sized species. Rear margin of tail membrane has bent, stiff fringing hairs. Ear relatively long, tragus pointed, somewhat longer than half ear length. Fur long, sparse, dark gray at base. Back light gray, with only slight brownish tinge, underside light gray, sharply set off from back. Muzzle light flesh colored, ears and wing membranes light gray-brown, tragus light yellowish gray, darker toward the tip.

migration 90 kilometers. Flight low (1-4 meters), slow, in part whirring wing beats, very agile, also hovers. Primarily harvests prey animals from substrate.

ABUNDANCE/ENDANGERMENT: Populations are in many parts of Europe. Reductions due to changes in habitat, use of wood preservatives, loss of roosts through the felling of hollow trees, and destruction of winter roosts.

PROTECTION: Protection of roosts and biotope. Preservation of old hollow trees (old tree program).

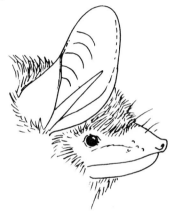

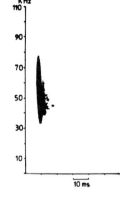

REPRODUCTION: G approximately 50-60 days; Y 1 (2); BW unknown.

LIFE CYCLE: W at approximately 6-7 weeks; SM apparently at 1 year; LS maximum age 17 years 5 months.

DIET: Small insects (primarily diurnal flies and dipterans).

ENEMIES: Man.

HABITS AND LIVING SPACE: Predominantly a forest bat. Forests and parks with bodies of water and wetlands, also in villages. Summer roosts (nursery roosts) both in tree holes and bat boxes in forests as well as in crevices or in buildings (on rafters, less commonly on the ridge). Individual animals also in crevices under bridges and behind shutters. Winter roosts in tunnels, caves, and cellars (high humidity, temperature 2.5-8° C, temporarily also at -0.5° C), usually squeezed into narrow cracks, in part also lying on the back, also in the ground rubble or free-hanging on walls and ceilings in small clusters. Sedentary species, longest

Bechstein's Bat
Myotis bechsteini (Kuhl, 1818)

BODY SIZE: HBL 45-55 mm; TL (34) 41-45 (47) mm; FL 39-47 mm; WS 250-286 mm; Wt 7-12 g.

CONSPICUOUS CHARACTERS: Medium-sized species. Conspicuously large ears, tragus long, lanceolate, reaches about half the ear's length. Ears do not touch at the base. Fur relatively long, dark gray-brown at base. Back fawn brown to reddish brown, underside light gray. Muzzle rufous, ears and wing membranes light gray-brown. Juveniles light gray to ashy gray.

REPRODUCTION: G approximately 50-60 days, Y 1 (2), BW unknown.

LIFE CYCLE: W at approximately 6-7 weeks; SM at 1 year; LS maximum age 21 years.

DIET: Small to medium-sized insects (moths, flies, beetles).

ENEMIES: Man.

HABITS AND LIVING SPACE: Forest bat. Prefers deciduous forests. Summer roosts (nursery roosts) in tree holes and bat boxes (not shallow boxes), more rarely in buildings, there free-hanging, individual animals also in rock cavities. Small nursery roosts (10-30 females), frequent change of roosts. Winter roosts in caves, tunnels, cellars, possibly also sporadically in tree holes (temperature 3-7° C, high humidity), usually singly free-hanging on the ceiling or wall, more rarely in tight cracks. Ears erect even in hibernation (in contrast to long-eared bats). Apparently sedentary, longest migration 35 kilometers. Leaves the roost only after the onset of darkness. Swaying flight, but very agile maneuvers in the most confined space. Hunts low, takes prey from branches, possibly also from the ground.

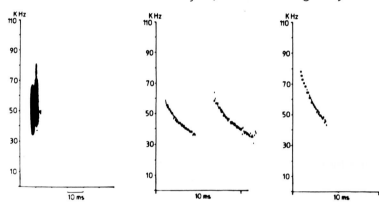

ABUNDANCE/ENDANGERMENT: Not abundant anywhere, small populations in central Europe. Decline in numbers probably because of changes in and losses of habitat and changes in climate.

PROTECTION: Protection of summer and winter roosts. Preservation of hollow trees. Installation of bat boxes. Biotope preservation and improvement.

152

Greater Mouse-eared Bat
Myotis myotis (Borkhausen, 1797)

BODY SIZE: HBL (65) 67-79 (84) mm; TL (40) 45-60 mm; FL 54-67 (68) mm; WS 350-430 mm; Wt 28-40 g.

CONSPICUOUS CHARACTERS: Largest German species. Muzzle short and broad. Ears long and broad, tragus broad at the base, reaches almost half the ear's length. Fur dense and short, blackish brown at base. Back light gray-brown, in part with rusty suffusion, underside pale gray. Muzzle, ears, and wing membranes brownish gray. Juveniles darker, smoky gray without brownish tint.

REPRODUCTION: G approximately 50-70 days; Y 1 (2); BW approximately 6 g.

LIFE CYCLE: W at approximately 6-7 weeks; SM at 1-2 years; LS maximum age 22 years, average 4-5 years.

DIET: Medium-sized to very large insects (predominantly ground beetles, also June beetles, carrion beetles, grasshoppers, crickets, moths) and spiders.

ENEMIES: Man, Common Barn Owl.

HABITS AND LIVING SPACE: Warmth-loving species. A house bat in the north and a cave bat in the south. Prefers climatically favorable valleys, open forest, forest edges, stands of trees, pasture land, and regions with traditional agriculture (organic farming). Summer roosts (nursery roosts) in the north in warm attics, church steeples (temperature up to 45° C), rarely in warm subterranean spaces; in the south in caves. Individual animals (males, which are usually solitary in summer) also in nest boxes or tree holes. Of all attic-dwelling species, Greater Mouse-eared Bats require the most space; small attics are the exception. In cool weather (particularly after arrival in the spring) protected cracks, such as small hollow spaces in rafter braces, are sought out readily. Males prefer to crawl into cracks throughout the summer season, as do juveniles and adults when disturbed. They leave the roost through open windows and gaps in the roof, but may also crawl between loose roof tiles and other openings. When towers offer better conditions, summer roosts are also established in the relatively small spire or bulbous spire, but the entire volume of the church roof is—in so far as it is accessible—also used (significant as a flight space for juveniles before the first flight from the roost). Colonies are rarely found in larger bridge structures (spaces inside piers). Winter roosts in caves, tunnels, cellars (temperature [3] 7-12° C). Usually free-hanging on the ceiling, often in clusters, but also in hollow spaces and narrow cracks. Partial migrant, migrations of more than 100 kilometers are not uncommon. Usually leaves the roost only after nightfall. Slow flight with long wingbeats, 5-10 meters in altitude, in part also hunts just above the ground. Sometimes also locates prey from perch low on tree trunks and also hunts prey "on foot" on the ground.

ABUNDANCE/ENDANGERMENT: Declining in many regions. In central Europe, population declines of about 80 percent or more in the last 20-30 years. Threatened by changes in habitat, destruction of and changes in the biotope, shortage of prey, loss and disturbance of roosts, poisoning by wood preservatives.

PROTECTION: Systematic protective measures for roosts and biotope, above all in areas with populations capable of surviving.

153

Lesser Mouse-eared Bat
Myotis blythi **(Tomes, 1857)**

BODY SIZE: HBL (54) 62-71 (76) mm; TL 53-59 (60) mm; FL 52.5-59 (61.5) mm; WS 380-400 mm; Wt 15-28 g.

CONSPICUOUS CHARACTERS: Very similar to the Greater Mouse-eared Bat, but somewhat smaller. Ears and tragus pointed and narrow. Relatively pointed muzzle. Fur short, dark gray at base. Back gray with brownish tinge, underside gray-white. Muzzle, wing membranes, and ears light gray-brown, tragus light yellowish white.

REPRODUCTION: G unknown; Y 1 (2); BW unknown.

LIFE CYCLE: W at approximately 6-7 weeks; SM unknown; LS maximum age 13 years.

DIET: Medium-sized insects, such as moths and beetles.

ENEMIES: Man.

HABITS AND LIVING SPACE: Warm regions with open stands of trees and bushes, chalk formations, parks, also villages. Habits probably similar to those of the Greater Mouse-eared Bat, differences in ecology with respect to Greater Mouse-eared Bat not precisely known. Both species occur in the same places and can even form mixed colonies (nursery roosts in attics). Summer roosts (nursery roosts) primarily in warm caves, often together with Long-eared Bats and horseshoe bats, but also colonizes warm

attics, free-hanging on the roof ridge, individual animals rarely in tree holes. Winter roosts in caves and tunnels (temperature 6-12° C), principally free-hanging. Partial migrant, longest migration 600 kilometers. Leaves the roost in darkness or in late evening. Flight slow, regular, more agile in confined space than the Greater Mouse-eared Bat. Probably also takes prey from the ground.

ABUNDANCE/ENDANGERMENT: Indications of population decline and disappearance of entire colonies caused by direct persecution

or disturbance in the roosts.

PROTECTION: Preservation and protection of roosts are necessary.

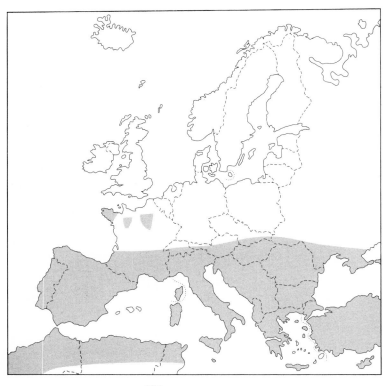

Noctule

Nyctalus noctula (Schreber, 1774)

BODY SIZE: HBL 60-82 (84.8) mm; TL 41-60.6 mm; FL 48-58 mm; WS 320-400 mm; Wt (17) 19-40 (46) g.

CONSPICUOUS CHARACTERS: Large species. Ears short and oval; like all *Nyctalus* species, has a short and mushroom-shaped tragus. Fur short, close-lying, hair monotone. Back with rufous sheen in summer, underside dull, lighter brown; after the molt (August/September) back dull fawn brown, in part with light gray suffusion. Ears, muzzle, and wing membranes blackish brown. Juveniles dull brown above, altogether darker. Wings long and narrow.

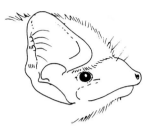

REPRODUCTION: G approximately 70-73 days; Y 1-2 (3); BW approximately 7.5 g.

LIFE CYCLE: W at 7-8 weeks; SM at 1-2 years; LS maximum age 12 years.

DIET: Larger flying insects, such as moths, June beetles.

ENEMIES: Man, birds of prey, parasites.

HABITS AND LIVING SPACE: Originally a forest bat. Prefers lowlands, in deciduous and mixed forest, park landscapes, and thickets in fields with stands of old trees, often in the vicinity of settlements; regionally, particularly in fall and winter, a "city bat." Summer roosts (nursery roosts) usually in old tree holes (holes produced by woodpeckers or rotting, cracks in trunks) that have rotted out above the entrance hole, but also in bat boxes; in summer has also been observed in hollow concrete light poles. Winter roosts in hollow trees or in buildings; roosts in high and very high buildings (multiple family houses, schools, skyscrapers, and factories). Prefers hollow spaces behind facades (facings), also behind shutters of roller doors; facade roosts usually oriented west or southwest, also used as temporary roost. Mass winter roosts in crevices are known in Switzerland (temperature usually low, can even survive 0° C for short periods). Gregarious. In summer, clear separation of the sexes, males then living singly with other males. High losses in hard winters. Migratory species, withdrawing from northeastern to southwestern Europe, longest migration 930 kilometers, in part also migrates during the day. Leaves the roost early to hunt, sometimes before sundown, in the fall some-

times in the afternoon. Flight fast and usually above the treetops, direct flight with quick turns and dives. In suitable weather conditions low-flying insects are also hunted near the ground in the manner of swallows. Hunts over meadows, lakes, garbage dumps, parking lots.

ABUNDANCE/ENDANGERMENT: Decline in many areas as a result of changes in habitat (loss of food supply and roosts). Stable populations still found in eastern Europe; in Germany in some regions one of the most common species at present.

PROTECTION: Protection of roosts through preservation and improvement of the tree hole supply (preservation and increase in stands of old trees, old tree programs, and the like) are urgently needed.

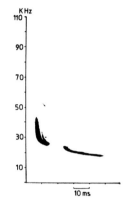

155

Leisler's Bat
Nyctalus leisleri (Kuhl, 1818)

BODY SIZE: HBL 48-68 mm; TL 35-45 mm; FL (37) 39-46.4 mm; WS 260-320 mm; Wt 13-20 g.

CONSPICUOUS CHARACTERS: Medium-sized species. External ear and tragus as in Noctule, muzzle more delicate, more pointed. Fur short, hair bicolored, base blackish brown. Back rufous, usually somewhat darker and less shiny than in Noctule, underside yellow-brown. Face, ears, and wing membranes blackish brown. Juveniles altogether darker. Wings long and narrow.

REPRODUCTION: G approximately 75 days; Y 2 (1); BW unknown.

LIFE CYCLE: W at 7-8 weeks; SM unknown; LS maximum age 9 years.

DIET: Larger insects, similar to Noctule.

ENEMIES: Man.

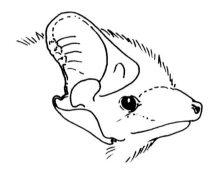

HABITS AND LIVING SPACE: Forest bat. Similar to Noctule. Prefers extensive forested regions, also in mountains, large park landscapes with stands of old trees, more rarely in towns. Summer roosts (nursery roosts) in tree holes and bat boxes, in part together with Noctule, rarely also in cracks in buildings. Winter roosts in tree holes, also in cracks and hollow spaces on and in buildings. Overwinters in large groups. Migratory species, migration path apparently from east to southwest, longest migration 810 kilometers. Leaves roost to hunt shortly after sundown. Flight fast, high, also with dives. Hunts in the manner of the Noctule.

ABUNDANCE/ENDANGERMENT: Threatened through changes in habitat, such as destruction of stands of old trees and tree holes. Rare in the majority of its range, usually known only in small colonies.

PROTECTION: Protective measures similar to those given for noctule. Installation of bat boxes in suitable biotopes.

Greater Noctule
Nyctalus lasiopterus **(Schreber, 1780)**

BODY SIZE: HBL 84-104 mm; TL 55-65 mm; FL 63-69 mm; WS 410-460 mm; Wt 41-76 g.

CONSPICUOUS CHARACTERS: Largest European bat. Similar to Noctule, but noticeably larger. Fur dense and relatively long, hair monochrome. Back rufous, usually darker than Noctule, underside yellow brown. Muzzle and ears blackish brown, wing membranes dark brown. Juveniles darker. Wings long and narrow, with rusty hairs on the underside along the body.

Silhouettes of flying noctules shown to scale: Leisler's bat (black), noctule (gray), greater noctule (white).

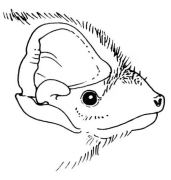

REPRODUCTION: G unknown; Y 2 (1); BW 5-7 g.

LIFE CYCLE: W not precisely known, probably at 7-8 weeks; SM not precisely known, probably similar to Noctule; LS maximum age unknown.

DIET: Unknown, probably similar to that of the Noctule, consisting of large insects (beetles and the like).

ENEMIES: Unknown.

HABITS AND LIVING SPACE: No precise information. Range only imperfectly known, the majority of populations live outside Europe. In Germany one report from the last century. Forest bat, common in deciduous forests. Summer roosts in part shared with Noctule, Nathusius' Pipistrelle, and Common Pipistrelle. Summer and winter roosts in tree holes. Migratory species, migration path to the southeast (in fall). Hunts in the air and on the ground.

ABUNDANCE/ENDANGERMENT: Larger populations only in eastern Europe.

PROTECTION: Possibly the same as given under the other two species of Noctule.

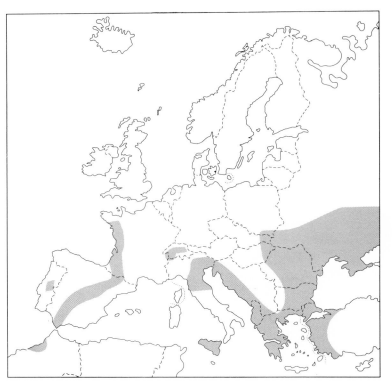

Serotine
Eptesicus serotinus (Schreber, 1774)

BODY SIZE: HBL 62.6-82 mm; TL (39) 46-54 (59) mm; FL 48-57 mm; WS 315-381 mm; Wt 14.4-33.5 (35) g.

CONSPICUOUS CHARACTERS: Large species. Ears relatively short, tragus shorter than in mouse-eared bats, but longer than in Noctule, attains about one-third the ear length. Fur long, dark brown at base. Back dark smoky brown, varies somewhat, tips of hairs in part slightly glossy, underside yellow-brown. Ears and muzzle black, wing membranes dark blackish brown. Boundary between back and underside indistinct. Juveniles altogether darker. Wings broad.

REPRODUCTION: G unknown; Y 1; BW 5.2-6.2 g.

LIFE CYCLE: W at approximately 6-7 weeks (independent from 5 weeks on); SM at 1 year; LS maximum age 19 years 3 months.

DIET: Large insects (moths, beetles).

ENEMIES: Man, cats.

HABITS AND LIVING SPACE: House bat. Principally in lowlands, there in areas settled by man with gardens, meadows, parks, also on outskirts of cities. Summer roosts (nursery roosts) in cracks on and in buildings (in the roof ridge, under roof laths, behind facades of sheet metal and other materials), enters roost between roof tiles or loose tiles or cracks. Individual animals (usually males)

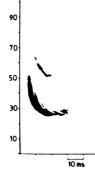

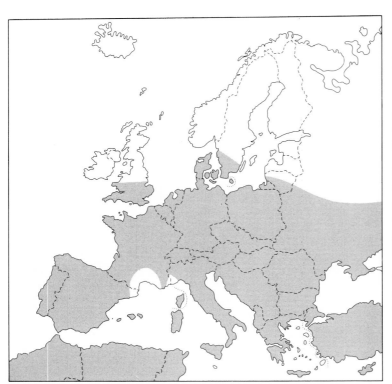

also rest in joists, behind shutters, rarely in bird or bat boxes; in southeastern Europe also in chalk caves. Winter roosts in caves, tunnels, cellars, also deep in beam rafters, behind pictures, in churches, in wood piles. No mass roosts known, usually singly squeezed into cracks or free-hanging on ceiling or wall, also in ground rubble (temperature 2-4° C, humidity relatively low). Rather sedentary, but can migrate up to 330 kilometers. Leaves the roost in early evening; wingbeats are slow and regular (flies at altitude of 6-10 meters). Hunts in gardens, on forest edges, around street lamps, over garbage dumps, possibly also takes prey from branches and the ground.

ABUNDANCE/ENDANGERMENT: Still common in some areas. Population in decline because of destruction of roosts, use of toxic wood preservatives, changes in habitat. Can be attacked by domestic cats while crawling out of the roost.

PROTECTION: Preservation and construction of roosts.

Northern Bat
Eptesicus nilssoni (Keyserling & Blasius, 1839)

BODY SIZE: HBL (45) 54.5-63.5 mm; TL 35-50 mm; FL (37) 38.1-42.8 (44) mm; WS 240-280 mm; Wt (6.5) 8-17.5 g.

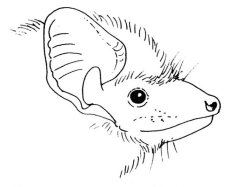

CONSPICUOUS CHARACTERS: Medium-sized species. Ears relatively short, tragus short, broad, curved slightly to the inside. Fur long, dark brown at base, on the back with gleaming gold tips; gleaming gold hairs also on crown of the head. Nape darker, only here a relatively sharp boundary to the yellow-brown underside. Muzzle, ears, and wing membranes blackish brown. Juveniles altogether darker.

REPRODUCTION: G unknown; Y 1-2; BW unknown.

LIFE CYCLE: W at approximately 7-8 weeks; SM unknown; LS maximum age 14.5 years.

DIET: Medium-sized flying insects.

ENEMIES: Man.

HABITS AND LIVING SPACE: The only European bat to reach the Arctic Circle. In central Europe mostly in foothills or at medium altitudes in mountains. Summer roosts (nursery roosts) usually in cracks on and in buildings (behind paneling, shutters, in rafters, behind fireplace facades); frequently on or in houses covered with slate or sheet metal (for warmth). Individual animals also in tree holes and fallen trees. Winter roosts in caves, tunnels, cellars (temperature 1-5.5° C, briefly to -5.5° C!), singly, either free-hanging or in cracks. Apparently chiefly sedentary. Leaves roost in early evening, sometimes only after nightfall. Flight fast, agile, with quick turns. Hunts more in free air space, also in light rain, over water, at street lamps, as well as at treetop height. Hangs in branches during pauses in hunting.

PROTECTION: Protection of known summer roosts. Preserving slate facades on houses.

ABUNDANCE/ENDANGERMENT: Rare in central Europe, possibly expanding its range. Threatened by the destruction of roosts.

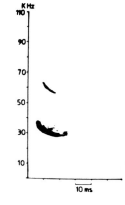

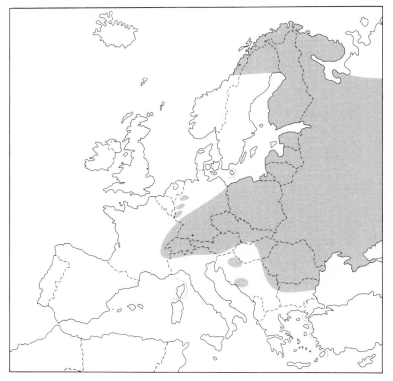

159

Particolored Bat
Vespertilio murinus **(Linnaeus, 1758) =**
Vespertilio discolor
(Natterer, 1818)

BODY SIZE: HBL 48-64 mm; TL 37-44.5 mm; FL 40-47 (48.2) mm; WS 270-310 mm; Wt 12-20.5 g.

CONSPICUOUS CHARACTERS: Medium-sized species. Ears short, broad and oval, tragus short, broader toward the top, rounded at the tip. Fur long, dense, blackish brown at base, on the back with silvery white tips, giving frost-covered or "moldy" appearance. Underside whitish gray, throat almost pure white, sharply set off against back. Ears, wing membranes, and muzzle blackish brown. Juveniles darker, more gray-black, tips of hairs dirty gray-white, belly yellowish white. Wings narrow.

REPRODUCTION: G unknown; Y 2 (3); BW unknown.

LIFE CYCLE: W at approximately 6-7 weeks; SM at 1 year; LS maximum age 5 years.

DIET: Medium-sized to large insects (beetles, moths).

ENEMIES: Little known.

HABITS AND LIVING SPACE: Originally most likely a cliff bat. In forested highlands, plains, also in cities on high buildings (as a cliff substitute?), in mountains. Summer roosts primarily in cracks on and in buildings, behind shutters, in cracks in walls, in joists

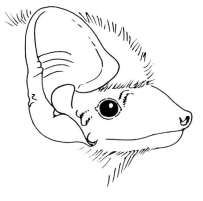

of attics. In central Europe often only single records. Nursery roosts small (30-50 females); the westernmost record for a nursery roost was in Bavaria (roost in the attic of a church steeple east of Munich). In western Europe mostly colonies of males (up to 250 animals). Winter roosts in cracks in walls and cliffs, occasionally also in caves and subterranean passages (there in cracks), possibly also in tree holes. Migratory species (up to 900 kilometers). Leaves the roost in late evening. Usually hunts in fast flight at considerable height (10-20 meters). Very vocal, especially in fall, twittering calls audible from a distance.

ABUNDANCE/ENDANGERMENT: Rare. Only a few fairly large colonies are known.

PROTECTION: Protection of roosts, particularly the securing and protection of known colonies.

Common Pipistrelle
Pipistrellus pipistrellus (Schreber, 1774)

BODY SIZE: HBL (32) 36-51 mm; TL (20) 23-36 mm; FL 28-34.6 mm; WS 180-240 mm; Wt 3.5-8 g.

CONSPICUOUS CHARACTERS: Smallest European species. Ears short, triangular, tips rounded, tragus longer than broad, curved slightly inward, rounded on top. Fur dark to blackish brown at base. Back rufous, chestnut, or dark brown, underside yellow-brown to gray-brown. Muzzle, ears, and wing membranes black-brown. Juveniles darker, more blackish brown. Wings narrow.

REPRODUCTION: G about 44 days (dependent on ambient temperature); Y 1-2 (in Britain only 1); BW 1-1.4 g.

LIFE CYCLE: W at approximately 6-7 weeks (able to fly starting at 4 weeks); SM at 1 year (males in part in second year); LS maximum age 16 years 7 months, average 2-3 years.

DIET: Small and very small insects (small moths, flies, and the like).

ENEMIES: Man, Pine Martens, cats.

HABITS AND LIVING SPACE: Primarily a house bat. In villages, towns, also in the center of cities, in parks, boulevards, orchards, woods. Summer roosts (nursery roosts) in cracks on buildings accessible from the outside; preferred roosts are so narrow that there is contact between the back and belly and the substrate. Usually in attics of smaller buildings, in hollow spaces of facades (wood paneling). Also behind shutters, rarely behind roll-down gates, in shallow bat boxes, behind signs; also colonizes suitable cracks in new buildings (for example, in hollow concrete blocks); also under loose bark and in hollow trees. Winter roosts behind facades, in cracks in cliffs and walls, wood piles, behind pictures in churches, occasionally also in caves; relatively sensitive to cold (temperature 2-6° C). In central Europe usually sedentary, sometimes migrates. Leaves the roost early, in part before sundown and in fall also during the day. Flight fast and agile. Hunts 1-2 kilometers from roost over ponds, along forest edges, in gardens, around street lamps, maintains set flight paths and often hunts its range in a set pattern.

ABUNDANCE/ENDANGERMENT: In northern and central Europe still the most abundant bat species, in part still in stable populations. Animals that "invade" buildings have been and continue to be destroyed. Lamp shades, vases, and pipes occasionally become death traps. Domestic cats and Pine Martens sometimes catch Common Pipistrelles when they crawl from their roosts. Destruction of roosts and dispersal from roosts are problems. Also threatened by the use of toxic wood preservatives.

PROTECTION: Preservation and construction of roosts. Securing and protecting known nursery roosts. Keeping open cracks on and in buildings that lead to the roosts. Avoidance of toxic wood preservatives. Organic agriculture and care of gardens, orchards, parks, boulevards, and woodlands.

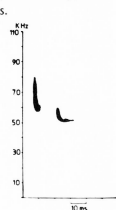

Nathusius' Pipistrelle
Pipistrellus nathusii (Keyserling & Blasius, 1839)

BODY SIZE: HBL 46-55 (58) mm; TL (30) 32.3-40 (44) mm; FL 32-37 mm; WS 230-250 mm; Wt 6-15.5 g.

CONSPICUOUS CHARACTERS: Small species, somewhat larger than the similar Common Pipistrelle. Tragus short, curved slightly inward, tip rounded. Fur darkish brown at base. Back in summer rufous to chestnut brown, after the molt more dark brown, often with distinct gray suffusion, underside light brown to yellow-brown. Tail, ears, and wing membranes blackish brown. Juveniles dark brown without gray tones.

REPRODUCTION: G unknown; Y 2 (1); BW 1.6-1.8 g.

LIFE CYCLE: W at 7-8 weeks (able to fly at about 4 weeks); SM in first year, males in second year; LS maximum age 7 years.

DIET: Small to medium-sized flying insects.

ENEMIES: Man, Common Barn Owl.

HABITS AND LIVING SPACE: Forest bat. From moist deciduous forests to dry pine forests, parks, more rarely in settlements, prefers lowlands. Summer roosts (nursery roosts) in tree holes, shallow bat boxes, cracks in trunks, more rarely in narrow cracks on and in buildings, behind roll-down gates, shutters, wood siding (also cracks between walls

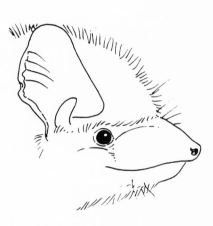

and framing), and the like; sometimes shares nursery roosts with Common Pipistrelles or Brandt's Bats. Winter roosts in fissures in cliffs, cracks in walls, also in caves and tree holes. Migratory species (maximum of 1600 kilometers!). Leaves the roost at early twilight. Flight fast, direct, in part with deep wingbeats. Corridor hunter in clear cuttings, along paths and forest edges, and along and above bodies of water.

ABUNDANCE/ENDANGERMENT: Little known, but possibly increasing in western part of range. Known populations in part stable. Threatened by shortage and loss of roosts.

PROTECTION: Protection of biotope in forests with improvement of the natural and artificial roost supply (installation of bat boxes).

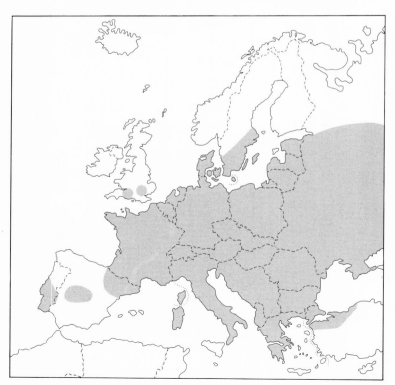

Kuhl's Pipistrelle
Pipistrellus kuhli (Kuhl, 1819)

BODY SIZE: HBL 40-47 (48) mm; TL 30-34 mm; FL 31-36 (37) mm; WS 210-220 mm; Wt 5-10 g.

CONSPICUOUS CHARACTERS: Small species. Ears short, rounded on top, tragus does not broaden above, rounded, curved slightly inward. A sharply demarcated white border usually present on the trailing edge of the wing membrane. Fur coloration highly variable, dark brown at base. Back medium brown to yellow-brown, also light cinammon, underside light gray to gray-white. Ears, wing membranes, and muzzle dark to blackish brown. Wings relatively narrow.

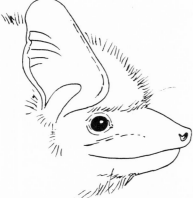

REPRODUCTION: G unknown; Y 2 (1); BW unknown.

LIFE CYCLE: W at approximately 7-8 weeks; SM at 1 year (females); LS maximum age 8 years.

DIET: Small flying insects.

ENEMIES: Little known.

HABITS AND LIVING SPACE: Similar to Common Pipistrelle. Occurs both in lowlands and at low altitude in mountains. Relatively closely tied to human settlement, but also found in chalk formations. Summer roosts (nursery roosts) predominantly in cracks on and in buildings (under the roof, cracks in walls), also in new buildings (like the Common Pipistrelle), individuals also in fissures in cliffs. Winter roosts in fissures, cellars. Apparently sedentary. Leaves roost in late twilight or in darkness. Flight fast and agile. Hunts at low and medium altitude in gardens, around street lamps, over water surfaces. Frequently observed in Mediterranean region.

ABUNDANCE/ENDANGERMENT: Ranges only through the warm regions of Europe, where it possibly often is overlooked. Probably threatened by the same agents as the Common Pipistrelle.

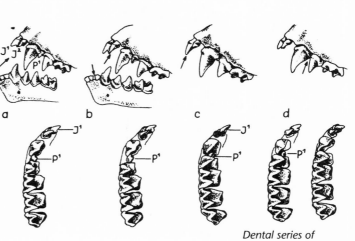

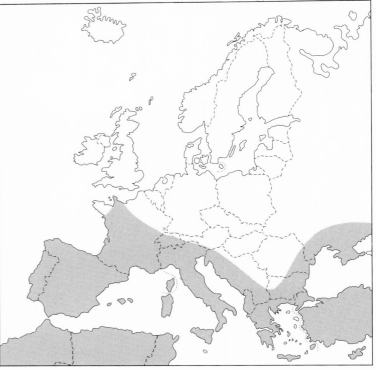

Dental series of the Pipistrellus species (viewed from the outside and above): a. common pipistrelle, b. Nathusius' pipistrelle, c. Kuhl's pipistrelle, d. Sari's pipistrelle, I incisors, P1 premolars in upper mandible.

Savi's Pipistrelle
Pipistrellus savii (Bonaparte, 1837)

BODY SIZE: HBL 40-54 mm; TL 31-42.5 mm; FL 30-36.5 (38) mm; WS 220-225 mm; Wt 5-10 g.

CONSPICUOUS CHARACTERS: Small species. Based on several morphological characters, it is intermediate between the genera *Eptesicus* and *Pipistrellus* and is therefore placed in its own genus, *Hypsugo* Kolenati, 1856, by Horácek and Hanák. Ears wider and rounder than in the other European pipistrelles, tragus short and broad. Fur relatively long, blackish brown at base. Back variable from fawn yellow-brown or golden yellow-brown to dark brown with shiny gold tips, underside light whitish yellow to grayish white, in clear contrast to back. Ears and muzzle blackish brown or black, wing membranes dark brown.

REPRODUCTION: G unknown; Y 2 (1); BW unknown.

LIFE CYCLE: W at 7-8 weeks; SM at 1 year; LS maximum age unknown.

DIET: Small flying insects.

ENEMIES: Unknown.

HABITS AND LIVING SPACE: Principally found in southern Europe. Nursery roosts recorded from Switzerland. Mountain valleys, alpine pastures, chalk formations, on Mediterranean islands and on coasts, also in settled areas. Summer roosts (nursery roosts) often

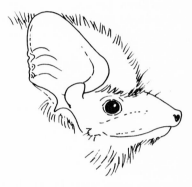

in cracks in and on buildings (rafters, cracks in walls, hollow spaces between bricks, holes in walls), crevices. Up to now only one recorded roost in Germany, in the rafters of a house south of Mittenwald, Upper Bavaria. Winter roosts in low-lying valleys, there in holes and crevices in cliffs, probably also in tree holes. Apparently a partial migrant. Leaves the roost shortly after sunset. Flight is direct, smooth, in part above houses and treetops. Hunts almost the whole night, on islands and on the coast as well as over the ocean. Very lively, calls resemble those of the Whiskered Bat.

ABUNDANCE/ENDANGERMENT: Very little known. Apparently threatened in roosts by toxic wood preservatives.

PROTECTION: Protection of known roosts. Avoidance of toxic wood preservatives.

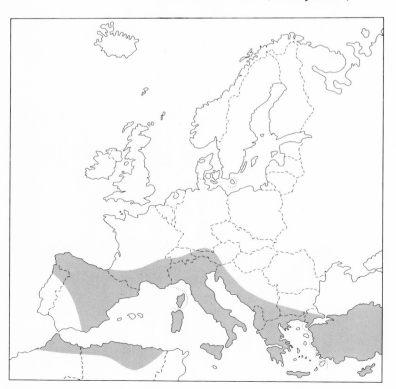

Common Long-eared Bat
Plecotus auritus (Linnaeus, 1758)

BODY SIZE: HBL 42-53 (55.5) mm; TL (32.5) 37-55 mm; FL (35) 37-42 mm; WS 240-285 mm; Wt 4.6-11.3 g.

CONSPICUOUS CHARACTERS: Medium-sized species. Conspicuously long, thin external ears, touching at the base; long, pointed, usually weakly pigmented tragus. Sleeping Long-eared Bats conceal their ears under the forearms (tilted to the back, folded), so that only the tragus, resembling a little ear, is exposed. Fur sparse, long, dark gray-brown at base. Back light brownish gray; at the boundary with the underside on the neck there usually is a light yellowish brown spot; underside light gray, sometimes with yellowish suffusion. Lips pale, nostrils and eye region light brown, ears and wing membranes light grayish brown. Juveniles pale gray without brown tones, face dark. Wings broad.

REPRODUCTION: G unknown; Y 1 (2); BW unknown.

LIFE CYCLE: W at approximately 6-7 weeks; SM in second year (females); LS maximum age 22 years, average 4 years.

DIET: Medium-sized insects (primarily moths and the like).

ENEMIES: Man.

HABITS AND LIVING SPACE: Prefers forested regions in lowlands and mountains at medium altitude (deciduous and coniferous forests), open tree and shrub landscapes, also parks and gardens in villages and towns, but not bound to settled regions. Summer roosts (nursery roosts) in tree holes, bat and bird boxes, on and in buildings, in attics with beams (for hiding). Leaves roost by flying through large openings, but also crawls out through cracks, often in the same building as the Greater Mouse-eared Bat. individuals also in holes in cliffs, behind shutters, in cracks in buildings. Winter roosts in caves, tunnels, cellars, seldom in buildings (joints in walls) or thick-walled tree holes, relatively resistant to cold (temperature 2-5° C, for 1-2 days as low as -3.5° C), usually singly in cracks or on walls. Sedentary. Leaves the roost at late twilight. Flight is slow, low, swaying, can harvest prey animals from substrates (leaves, branches, walls) while hovering. Apparently also detects insect prey visually. Sometimes prey is consumed at permanent feeding places, where food remains (wings, legs, and the like) accumulate.

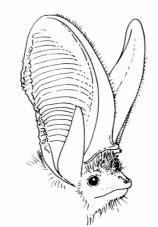

ABUNDANCE/ENDANGERMENT: Still relatively widely distributed in central Europe. Threatened by the use of toxic wood preservatives and loss of roosts.

PROTECTION: Preservation and construction of roosts. Avoidance of toxic wood preservatives. Installation of bat boxes with natural wood construction.

165

Grey Long-eared Bat
Plecotus austriacus (Fischer, 1829)

BODY SIZE: HBL 41-58 (60) mm; TL 37-55 (57) mm; FL (35) 37-44.5 mm; WS 255-292 mm; Wt 5-13 g.

CONSPICUOUS CHARACTERS: Medium-sized species. Very similar to Common Long-eared Bat (not rediscovered as a species in central Europe until 1960). Conspicuously long ears. Muzzle longer and more pointed. Fur long, usually grayer. Thumbs not longer than 6 millimeters (in contrast to Common Long-eared Bat).

REPRODUCTION: G unknown; Y 1 (2); BW unknown.

LIFE CYCLE: W unknown; SM unknown; LS maximum age 14.5 years.

DIET: Principally moths, flies, small beetles.

ENEMIES: Man.

HABITS AND LIVING SPACE: Warmth-loving species. Usually in cultivated landscapes and bound to human settlement. House bat. Avoids extensive forests. Summer roosts (nursery roosts) in buildings, like the Common Long-eared Bat in cracks (beam mortises, rafters, and the like). Nursery roosts usually consist of only 10-30 females and have never been recorded in tree holes or bat boxes. Individual animals also in caves and bat boxes. Summer roosts sometimes in same building roosts as Greater Mouse-eared Bat and Lesser Horseshoe Bat. Winter roosts in caves, tunnels, cellars, sometimes with Common Long-eared Bat (temperature 2-9° C, to 12° C), in cracks and free-hanging on walls. Sedentary. Leaves the roost in darkness. Flight is like that of Common Long-eared Bat. Often hunts in free air space and around street lamps. Has never been observed taking prey from substrates.

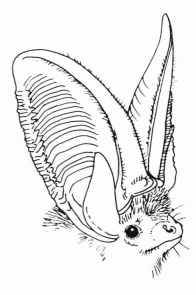

Uses feeding places.

ABUNDANCE/ENDANGERMENT: Only small populations in central Europe, rarer than Common Long-eared Bat. Endangered by destruction of roosts and the use of toxic wood preservatives.

PROTECTION: Preservation and construction of roosts in buildings. Protection of winter roosts. Protection of biotopes.

166

Barbastelle
Barbastella barbastellus (Schreber, 1774)

BODY SIZE: HBL 45-58 mm; TL (36) 38-52 mm; FL 36.5-43.5 mm; WS 262-292 mm; Wt 6-13.5 g.

CONSPICUOUS CHARACTERS: Medium-sized species. Muzzle has a pug-nosed appearance, face unmistakable. Fur long, silky, black at base. Back looks blackish brown with whitish or yellowish white hair tips as if frosted, underside dark gray. Bare part of the face and the ears black, wing membranes gray-brown to blackish brown.

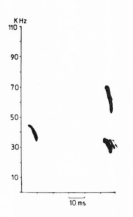

Entranceways should be built for hibernating bats in subterranean passages, frost-free cellars, and caves.

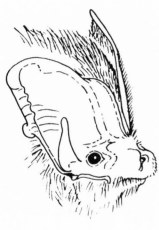

treetops, along forest edges, boulevards, in gardens.

ABUNDANCE/ENDANGERMENT: Very rare. Severe decline in central Europe, already extirpated in many places. Threatened by loss and disturbance of roosts (in winter roost), changes in habitat (reduction of food supply).

PROTECTION: Systematic protection of roosts and biotopes, especially of known nursery roosts and winter roosts.

Fledged juveniles somewhat darker, already with whitish tips of hair on the back. Wings long and narrow.

REPRODUCTION: G unknown; Y 2; BW unknown.

LIFE CYCLE: W at approximately 6 weeks; SM in second year (females); LS maximum age 23 years.

DIET: Small, delicate insects (moths, flies, small beetles).

ENEMIES: Man.

HABITS AND LIVING SPACE: Prefers forested foothills and mountains, also in villages. Summer roosts (nursery roosts) in cracks on buildings, behind shutters. Nursery roosts usually consisting of only 10-20 females. Males separate, in small groups, very sensitive to disturbance. Individuals also in tree holes, nest boxes, and entrance regions of caves. Winter roosts in caves, tunnels, cellars; cold hardy (temperature 2-5° C, more rarely to -3° C), in cracks and free-hanging on walls, in part in large clusters. Partial migrant. Leaves the roost at early twilight. Flight fast, agile. Hunts at the altitude of

Schreiber's Bat
Miniopterus schreibersi (Kuhl, 1819)

BODY SIZE: HBL (48) 50-62 mm; TL (47) 56-64 mm; FL (44) 45.4-48 mm; WS 305-342 mm; Wt 9-16 g.

CONSPICUOUS CHARACTERS: Medium-sized species. Very short muzzle with forehead hump. Ears short, triangular. Wings long and pointed. Fur on head short, erect. Back gray-brown to ashy gray, sometimes with pale lilac suffusion. Juveniles grayer.

REPRODUCTION: G in Europe starting in fall (after copulation—in contrast to all other European bat species—immediate fertilization, embryonic development suspended during hibernation and starting again in the spring); Y 1 (2); females are also said to suckle unrelated young; BW unknown.

LIFE CYCLE: W at approximately 7-8 weeks; SM in second year (females); LS maximum age 16 years.

DIET: Medium-sized insects (moths, flies, beetles).

ENEMIES: Man.

HABITS AND LIVING SPACE: In open, climatically favorable landscapes of the lowlands and mountains. Cave bat. Very gregarious. Summer roosts (nursery roosts) in warm and roomy caves, tunnels, and barbettes, rarely (in northern part of range) in large attics of old buildings. Nursery roosts often of more than 1000 females. Winter roosts in

caves (temperature 7-12° C), free-hanging on ceiling or wall, in part in clusters. Migratory species in the north. Leaves the roost shortly after sunset. Flight very fast, resembling that of swallows or swifts. Hunts in free air space often far from roost.

ABUNDANCE/ENDANGERMENT: Many large colonies in central Europe have declined severely or have died out. Threatened through changes in habitat and disturbance and destruction of roosts.

PROTECTION: Systematic protection of roosts.

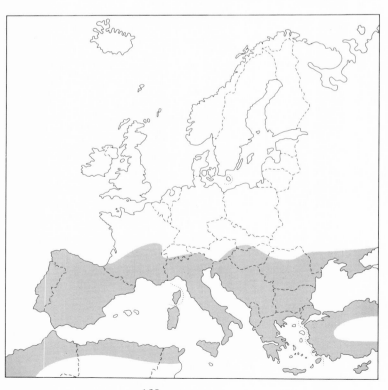

168

European Free-tailed Bat
Tadarida teniotis (Rafinesque, 1814)

Body size: HBL 81-92 mm; TL 44-57 mm; FL 57-64 mm; WS approximately 410 mm; Wt 25-50 g.

Conspicuous characters: Large species. Muzzle long. Ears long and broad, protruding forward over the eyes and face and touching at the base in the front. Tail extends freely up to one-third to one-half beyond the tail membrane. Wings very narrow and long. Fur short, fine and soft, moleskinlike. Back blackish to smoky gray with brownish suffusion, underside lighter

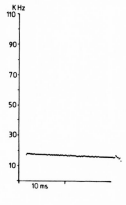

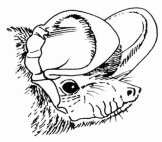

Abundance/endangerment: Little known.

Protection: No detailed advice possible.

The European Free-tailed Bat reaches its northernmost outpost in central Europe in the Walliser Alps (southwestern Switzerland). Though the first animals found were considered to be vagrants, the Swiss zoologist Raphael Arlettaz (1990) demonstrated that *Tadarida teniotis* lives in the Wallis the year round, occupies roosts in vertical crevices, and systematically hunts insects passing through the Bretolet and Balme passes.

gray. Ears, muzzle, and wing membranes blackish gray. Juveniles altogether grayer.

Reproduction: G approximately 77-84 days; Y 1; BW unknown.

Life cycle: W independent at 6-7 weeks; SM at 1 year; LS not precisely known, maximum age over 10 years.

Diet: Large flying insects.

Enemies: Little known.

Habits and living space: Southern Europe, Mediterranean region. Cliff bat. Inhabits warm regions with high cliffs (mountains) or high buildings, bridges. Summer roosts in cracks in cliffs, walls, buildings, in large caves, also in crevices in riparian cliffs. Winter roosts unknown. It is not clear whether this species undergoes a fairly long hibernation. Apparently a partial migrant or migrant. Northernmost record from Basel, Switzerland. Sometimes leaves the roost at early twilight. Flight is high, fast, and direct, occasionally flies in the company of swallows and swifts. Hunts in open air space, in part circling bodies of water. Call is loud and audible from afar with sharp "tsick" notes or whistles. Only forms small colonies.

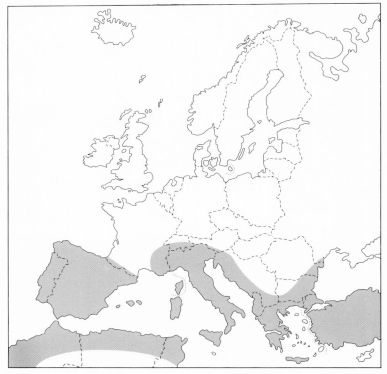

Bats of the world—
The world of bats

To present all of the bat species found in the world would not only require a great deal of space, it also would be simply impossible. The habits of many tropical species are still totally unknown to us. Currently we know some species from only a few, often only a single, museum specimens. Furthermore, some totally undiscovered—and thus nameless—bats will continue to flutter through their tropical world, as long as it exists at all. Precisely because of the monstrous destruction of the tropical rainforests, it can be assumed that with its ultimate destruction many bat species, some of which will never be described, will also disappear from the face of the earth. This is true both of the suborder of the insectivorous bats (Microchiroptera) as well as the flying foxes (Megachiroptera).

The Megachiroptera are a "subject unto themselves." Because the flying foxes differ considerably both anatomically and in their sensory performance (visual searching) from the insectivorous bats (echolocators), some researchers believe that there were two distinct origins of these two disparate groups. Everything that they have in common (flight, nocturnal habits) could have evolved separately (convergence) through similiar habits and use of resources.

Though taxonomists classify the flying foxes, all of which are limited to the Old World tropics, in a single zoological family (Pteropodidae), at present there are 17 families of insectivorous bats. Of these, ten are small families with only one to eight members. The surprises these imps have in store for us is shown by the discovery of the tiny Bumblebee Bat. Not discovered until 1973, a new family had to be erected for this dwarf because of its many unique traits.

No matter how the appearance or habits of the individual bat species may strike us as unfamiliar, exotic, or even grotesque, our world becomes the poorer with the loss of every individual life form of these charming creatures.

In the descriptions of the individual species the following abbreviations are used:

BODY SIZE: **HBL:** head-body length; **TL:** tail length; **FL:** forearm length; **WS:** wingspan; **Wt:** weight.

REPRODUCTION: **G:** gestation period; **Y:** number of young per birth; **BW:** birth weight.

LIFE CYCLE: **W:** weaning; **SM:** sexual maturity; **LS:** lifespan.

Flying foxes, Old World fruit bats

Family **Pteropodidae** with 42 genera and 174 species

BODY SIZE: HBL 50-400 mm; FL 37-230 mm; WS 24-170 cm; Wt 11-1500 g.

CONSPICUOUS CHARACTERS: Head doglike; no nasal process present; eyes large and efficient for twilight vision; ears fully rounded at the base, without a tragus. A claw is usually present on the second finger, and there are large, very movable thumbs. Wings simple; tail membrane narrow, tail very short or absent, when present not completely contained in the membrane. Color usually brownish, with conspicuous color patterns in a few species. Echolocation only in the genus *Rousettus*. Smallest species: three species of *Syconycteris* from Australia and New Guinea (one species with 5 cm HBL).

REPRODUCTION: G 100-150 days; Y 1, rarely 2; BW 13-17 percent of the adult weight.

LIFE CYCLE: W at 4-5 months (medium-sized to large species); SM up to 2 years; LS maximum age 30 years.

DIET: Fruits, flowers, leaves, nectar, pollen, exceptionally also insects.

ENEMIES: Man, diurnal and nocturnal birds of prey, parasites.

HABITS AND LIVING SPACE: The majority of flying foxes roost in trees and foliage; only a few are cave-dwellers. In tropical and subtropical forests, also in agricultural land, occasionally even in towns (parks). The family includes some of the few species that have colonized the islands of the central Pacific Ocean (east as far as the Cook Islands). Some species of the genus *Pteropus* are especially gregarious and form large groups.

Micropteropus

Hypsignathus

Macroglossus

ABUNDANCE/ENDANGERMENT: Populations are in decline in most countries. Persecution as pests and for food.

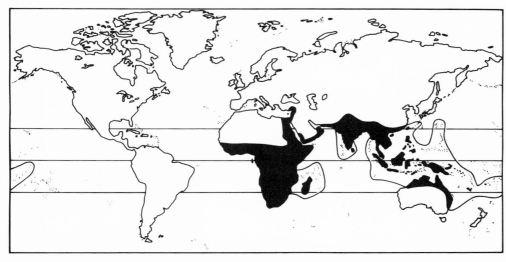

Mouse-tailed bats, Long-tailed bats

Family **Rhinopomatidae** with 1 genus and 3 species

BODY SIZE: HBL 50-80 mm; TL up to 60 mm; FL 55-70 mm; Wt 10-25 g.

CONSPICUOUS CHARACTERS: Tail almost as long as the body, not contained in the wing membrane. Ears connected above the forehead by a band of skin; vertical nose leaf ("snout") present, longitudinal furrow on top of the nose; nostrils can be sealed from sand and dust by the nose leaf; fields of sweat and sebaceous glands in the facial area. Location calls short, emitted through the mouth.

REPRODUCTION: G approximately 3 months; Y usually 1; BW unknown.

LIFE CYCLE: W unknown; SM unknown; LS maximum age several years.

DIET: Small insects.

ENEMIES: Man.

HABITS AND LIVING SPACE: Daytime roosts in caves and fissures in cliffs, for millennia in Egyptian tombs and pyramids. Gregarious, living in colonies. Prefer dry regions. In parts of their range, mouse-tailed bats become torpid for fairly long periods.

ABUNDANCE/ENDANGERMENT: Severe decline in Israel and Egypt because of changes in habitat.

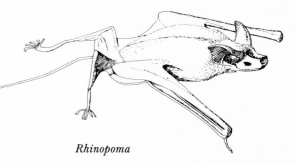

Rhinopoma

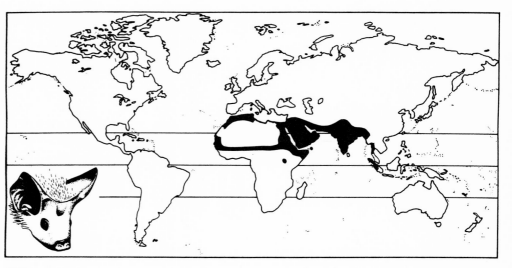

Sheath-tailed bats, Sac-winged bats

Family **Emballonuridae** with 13 genera and 51 species

BODY SIZE: HBL 37-100 mm; TL 6-30 mm; FL 55-70 mm; Wt 3-30 g.

CONSPICUOUS CHARACTERS: Tail always short. Base contained in tail membrane, but end protrudes freely from the back of the membrane. Tail membrane only loosely connected and can easily slide up and down the tail vertebrae; tail membrane strongly developed, can be spread like a sail by stretching the legs. Narrow, long wings. Nose region smooth. Ears often connected to each other on the forehead; tragus present. Usually gray, brown, or black, but several species exhibit a color pattern (camouflage). Ghost bats (genus *Diclidurus*, 4 species) from tropical America are totally white, including the wings. A peculiarity of the sheath-tailed bats is that when folding the wings at rest, the third finger is bent back at the joint between the first finger and the metacarpals. Many of the sheath-tailed bat species of the New World have small pouches or sacs in the antebrachial wing membrane between the shoulder and elbow; these arm pockets are always larger in males than in females and have glands on the inside. The red, strong-smelling glandular secretion probably plays a role in reproduction (territorial marking). Echolocation calls short, emitted through the mouth.

REPRODUCTION: G approximately 3-4 months; Y 1; BW unknown.

LIFE CYCLE: W at approximately 1-4 weeks; SM unknown; LS several years in captivity.

DIET: Insects (especially moths), rarely fruits (based on unconfirmed reports).

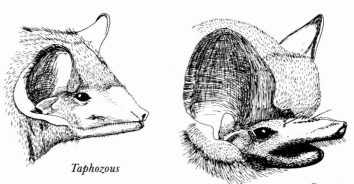

Taphozous

Peropteryx

ENEMIES: Man.

HABITS AND LIVING SPACE: Daytime roosts in caves, crevices in cliffs, foliage, hollow trees, and buildings. The species of the genera *Rhynchonycteris* and *Saccopteryx* from the New World tropics often rest in the open on tree trunks, under bridges, under palm fronds and other foliage; they do not form clumps, but always maintain a distance to their sleeping neighbors. Males form harems, defend roosts and hunting territories. A few species form large colonies, but others live in small groups or are solitary.

ABUNDANCE/ENDANGERMENT: In decline in regions subject to urbanization.

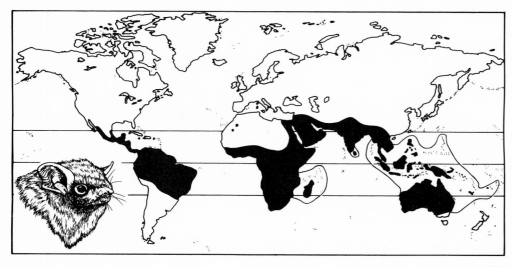

Hog-nosed bats, Butterfly bats, Bumblebee bats

Family **Craseonycteridae** with 1 genus and 1 species

BODY SIZE: HBL 29-33 mm; TL 21-26 mm; FL 15-17 mm; Wt 1.5-3 g.

CONSPICUOUS CHARACTERS: Smallest bat. Nose snoutlike, similar to pig's snout. Large ears with tragus. Wings comparatively long and broad, adapted for hovering flight. Echolocation call short.

REPRODUCTION AND LIFE CYCLE: Unknown.

DIET: Very small insects (small beetles, other small insects, as well as small spiders).

ENEMIES: Man.

HABITS AND LIVING SPACE: Roost in limestone caves on the River Kwai, Thailand (only a few localities have been found so far), in the deeper parts of caves in small chambers on the ceiling. Roost during the day in small groups. Hunt among bamboo stalks and the foliage of trees. Prey animals are also collected from the foliage in hovering flight.

ABUNDANCE/ENDANGERMENT: Extremely rare. Total population only about 200 animals. Changes in habitat, development of tourism in the range.

Slit-faced bats, Hollow-faced bats

Family **Nycteridae** with 1 genus and 12 species

BODY SIZE: HBL 45-75 mm; TL 43-75 mm; FL 36-60 mm; Wt 10-30 g.

CONSPICUOUS CHARACTERS: Cutaneous nasal process, top of nose divided by a longitudinal furrow, nostrils at the front end of the furrow, circumscribed by lateral nasal lobes. Huge ears, joined in the middle of the forehead. Wings broad. Tail long and completely contained in the membrane, the posterior tip of the last caudal vertebra T-shaped, supporting the edge of the wing membrane. Echolocation calls very short, emitted through the nose.

REPRODUCTION: G unknown; Y 1; BW unknown.

LIFE CYCLE: W at 45-60 days; SM and LS unknown.

DIET: Small to large insects, spiders, scorpions (Egyptian Slit-faced Bat).

ENEMIES: Man.

HABITS AND LIVING SPACE: In small groups or singly. In caves, ruins, and buildings, also on shaded twigs and branches, even in aardvark and hedgehog burrows. Live in tropical forests as well as in semi-arid regions in Africa, Arabia, and Palestine; one species lives in Indonesia.

ABUNDANCE/ENDANGERMENT: Shrinking of living space and changes in habitat.

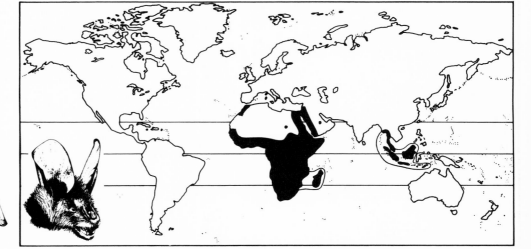

Nycteris

False vampire bats, Yellow-winged bats

Family **Megadermatidae** with 4 genera and 5 species

BODY SIZE: HBL 65-140 mm; TL 0; FL 50-120 mm; Wt 20-200 g.

CONSPICUOUS CHARACTERS: Largest species of microbats. Huge ears, connected above the forehead by a flap of skin. Large, erectile nose leaf. External tail absent. The genera differ primarly in body size. Coloration variable (whitish to blue-gray or pale gray-brown). The African Yellow-winged Bat (*Lavia frons*) is certainly one of the "prettiest" bat species because of its conspicuous coloration: fur light blue-gray or blue-brown, skin of wings and ears yellow. Fly with mouth closed. Echolocation calls very short, emitted through the nose.

REPRODUCTION: G approximately 5 months; Y 1 (2); BW unknown.

LIFE CYCLE: W at approximately 45 days; SM at approximately 2 years; LS at least 18 years in captivity.

DIET: Insects and small vertebrates (mice, birds, lizards, frogs, smaller bat species, and fishes).

ENEMIES: Man.

HABITS AND LIVING SPACE: The genera *Megaderma* and *Macroderma* roost in caves, tunnels, galleries, crevices in cliffs, and hollow trees; *Lavia* prefers hollow trees or shrubs. Roost in small groups or singly. Hunt close to the ground and near trees and bushes. The African False Vampire Bat (*Cardioderma cor*) usually flies to a permanent hunting place, where it hangs and locates insects flying by. False vampire bats usually bring their prey to a favorite feeding place.

ABUNDANCE/ENDANGERMENT: Changes in habitat, in some regions threatened by the spread of civilization. The Australian Giant False Vampire Bat *(Macroderma gigas)* is threatened in the bulk of its range by the destruction of its living space as a result of limestone mining.

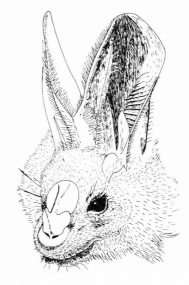

Megaderma

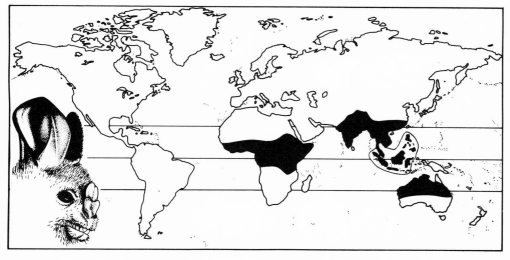

Horseshoe bats

Family **Rhinolophidae** with 1 genus and 69 species

BODY SIZE: HBL 35-110 mm; TL 25-45 mm; FL 35-70 mm; Wt 4-40 g.

CONSPICUOUS CHARACTERS: Conspicuous nose leaf, horseshoe-shaped lower part covers the upper lip and surrounds the nostrils; above is an upright lancet, longitudinal ridge between the horseshoe and lancet. Ears relatively large, very movable, tragus absent. Eyes proportionately small. Usually brown or rufous in color. Females have false

DIET: Insects.

ENEMIES: Man, parasites.

HABITS AND LIVING SPACE: Roost during the day in caves, tunnels, mine shafts, hollow trees. Free-hanging from the ceiling. Many

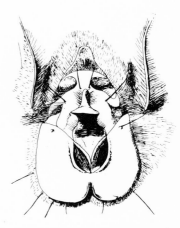

Rhinolophus

teats (like megadermatids) on the lower belly, which the young hold on to during transport. Tail short, placed on the back at rest. Echolocation call long, emitted through the nostrils.

REPRODUCTION: G 60-75 days; Y 1 (2); BW approximately 2-3 g.

LIFE CYCLE: W at approximately 2 months; SM at approximately 2-3 years; LS over 18 years (record age of the Greater Horseshoe Bat 30 years).

species are gregarious. Hibernate in frost-free caves. Hunt among the foliage of trees and shrubs, often close to the ground. Collect food animals from the substrate, hunt from ambush, and in flight can catch insects with the wings and bring them to the mouth.

ABUNDANCE/ENDANGERMENT: Changes in habitat. In all European countries in the range, severe decline because of loss of living space (roosts and hunting grounds).

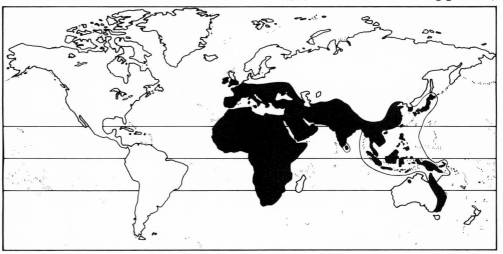

Leaf-nosed bats, Trident bats

Family **Hipposideridae** with 9 genera and 60 species

Body size: HBL 25-140 mm; TL 0-60 mm; FL 30-110 mm; Wt 4-120 g.

Conspicuous characters: Nose leaf horse-shoe-shaped in front, often with additional folds of skin, pointed to the rear, lancet often multiply divided and with spear-shaped tips. Ears well developed, tragus absent. Usually dark brown or reddish brown, but pale reddish or reddish orange individuals also exist. The Orange Leaf-nosed Bat (*Rhinonycteris aurantius*) from Australia is golden yellow in color. Echolocation calls long, emitted through the nostrils.

Reproduction: G unknown; Y 1 (2); BW unknown.

Life cycle: W unknown; SM unknown; LS maximum age over 12 years.

Diet: Insects, also small vertebrates.

Enemies: Man.

Habits and living space: In tree holes and holes in cliffs, also in buildings, occasionally in underground animal dens. In large colonies or singly. Catch insects in flight.

Abundance/endangerment: Changes in habitat. In regions with human settlement, roosting sites are reduced.

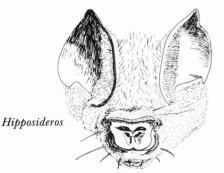
Hipposideros

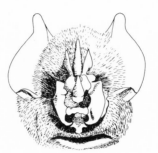
Triaenops

Asellia

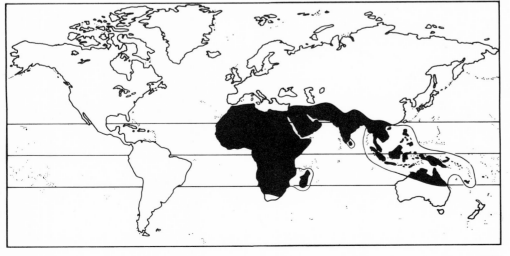

Fisherman bats, Bulldog bats

Family **Noctilionidae** with 1 genus and 2 species

BODY SIZE: HBL 70-132 mm; TL 17-23 mm; FL 54-92 mm; Wt 15-70 g.

CONSPICUOUS CHARACTERS: Upper lip divided by vertical fold of skin. Nose tube-shaped with downward directed nostrils. Ears long and slender, tragus present. Wing membrane reaches only to the knee and not, as is usual with bats, to the ankle. Very long hind legs. Very large claws on the toes. Sex-specific color differences: males reddish or pale orange on the back, females uniform brown or grayish. Echolocation calls short, emitted through the mouth.

REPRODUCTION: G unknown; Y 1; BW unknown.

LIFE CYCLE: Unknown.

DIET: Fishes, small crustaceans, and insects.

ENEMIES: Man.

HABITS AND LIVING SPACE: *Noctilio leporinus*, the larger species, feeds primarily on fishes, which it catches while hunting above the water's surface, dragging the large feet through the water like two grappling irons; fishes up to 100 mm long and up to 25 mm under the water are caught, in addition to crustaceans and aquatic insects that are active on the water's surface. *Noctilio albiventris* (formerly *N. labialis)*, the miniature edition of *N. leporinus*, principally feeds on insects. Both species roost in caves, fissures in cliffs, hollow trees, occasionally also in buildings. Both species live in small groups, *N. albiventris* also in foliage.

ABUNDANCE/ENDANGERMENT: Changes in habitat. Possibly threatened by destruction of living space.

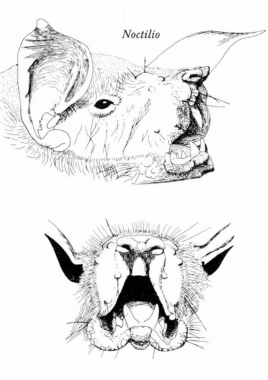

Noctilio

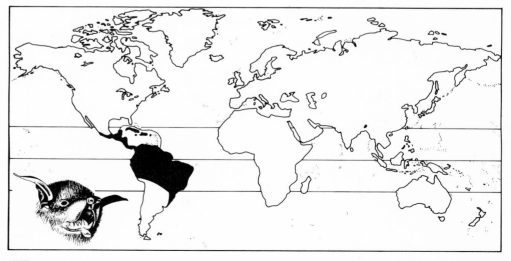

Leaf-chinned bats, Naked-backed bats

Family **Mormoopidae** with 2 genera and 8 species

BODY SIZE: HBL 40-77 mm; TL 15-34 mm; FL 35-65 mm; Wt 7-25 g.

CONSPICUOUS CHARACTERS: The mouth has a funnel-like form because of the leaf formations on the lips. The wing membranes attach far above the flanks; in two species the wing membranes meet in the middle of the back, which gives the back a naked appearance. Ears small, tragus present. Tail barely extends beyond the membrane. Unusually long and narrow wings. Back under the joined wing membranes usually

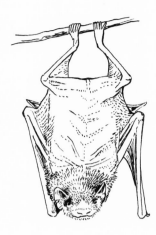

Pteronotus

Mormoops

furred. In general brown or reddish brown; faded fur becomes bright red-orange. Echolocation calls long or short, emitted through the mouth.

REPRODUCTION: G unknown; Y 1; BW unknown.

LIFE CYCLE: Unknown.

DIET: Insects.

ENEMIES: Unknown.

HABITS AND LIVING SPACE: Often occur near lakes and rivers. Almost always roost during the day in caves or tunnels, occasionally also in buildings and in dense shrubbery. Live gregariously in medium-sized to large colonies. Large ecological range, from moist, hot tropical forests to arid zones. Hunt just above the ground in fast flight.

ABUNDANCE/ENDANGERMENT: Unknown.

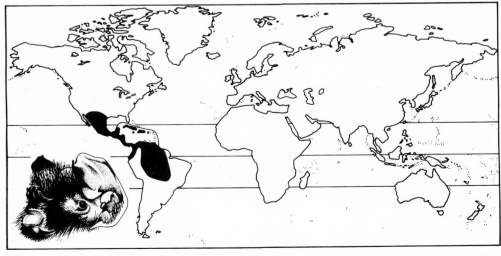

New World leaf-nosed bats, Spearnosed bats

Family **Phyllostomidae** with 50 genera and approximately 148 species

Phyllostomus

BODY SIZE: HBL 40-135 mm; TL 0-55 mm; FL 30-110 mm; Wt 7-200 g.

CONSPICUOUS CHARACTERS: Many species with relatively simple, spear-shaped nose leaf; in a few species the nose leaf is small and reduced, in vampire bats it is extremely rudimentary. Ears usually simple, connected above the forehead, tragus present. Fur color variable; some species have striped fur. Tail length and size of the tail membrane vary tremendously. Subfamily Glossophaginae has very long muzzle and long tongue. Echolocation calls short to very short, emitted through the mouth or nose.

REPRODUCTION: G (longest among the bats!) 220 days (Common Vampire); Y 1 (2); BW up to l14 percent of the adult weight (Common Vampire).

LIFE CYCLE: W 9 months at the latest (Common Vampire); SM at 1-2 years; LS 20 years.

DIET: Phyllostominae: small vertebrates like birds, other bats, rodents, lizards, and frogs; in addition, insects and other arthropods, occasionally also fruits.

Glossophaginae: highly specialized on fruit pulp, nectar, and pollen. Carolliinae: fruits. Stenodermatinae: principally fruits, also insects depending on season. Brachyphyllinae (Phyllonycterinae): fruits and nectar. Desmodontinae: blood (of warm-blooded animals).

ENEMIES: Man, diurnal and nocturnal birds of prey.

HABITS AND LIVING SPACE: In keeping with the size of the family, the individual species inhabit a wide variety of living spaces. Day-

Pteronotus

time roosts in caves, mine shafts, tree holes, animal burrows, dense foliage, and buildings. Hunting grounds in hot tropical lowland forests or in moist, cool montane forests to dry plains and semi-arid landscapes. Some species "build" tents of (palm) leaves. Found in large colonies to singly.

ABUNDANCE/ENDANGERMENT: Destruction of habitat, active persecution. Restriction and destruction of living spaces through the clearing of forests, urban and agricultural development. Destruction of many roosts as sanitary measures.

Centurio

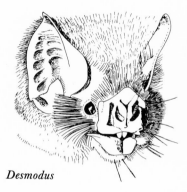

Desmodus

Diphylla

Anoura

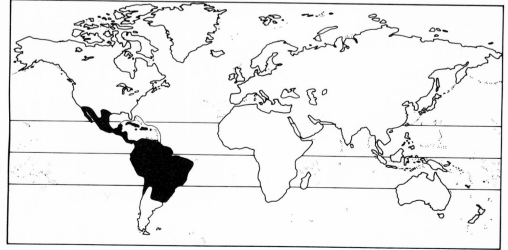

Funnel-eared bats, Longlegged bats

Family **Natalidae** with 1 genus and 4 species

Body size: HBL 35-55 mm; TL 30-60 mm; FL 27-41 mm; Wt 4-10 g.

Conspicuous characters: Skull vaulted behind the forehead, adult males with groups of sensory or secretory cells under the skin on the forehead ("natalid organs," function unknown). Muzzle long, without nose leaf. Funnel-shaped ears very large and far apart, very small tragus. Wings long and narrow. Short thumbs with their own wing membrane, robust claws. Fur long and thin,

Natalus

varying from gray or yellowish to reddish brown or chestnut brown. Echolocation call short, emitted through the mouth.

Reproduction: G unknown; Y1; BW unknown.

Life cycle: Unknown.
Diet: Insects.
Enemies: Unknown.

Habits and living space: Usually roost in caves, mines, and subterranean passages, there in the darker parts often together with other species of bats, occasionally in tree holes and under cliff ledges. Form small and large colonies. In tropical lowlands. Fluttering, mothlike flight. Hunt small insects.

Abundance/endangerment: Unknown.

Thumbless bats, Smoky bats

Family **Furipteridae** with 2 genera and 2 species

Body size: HBL 37-58 mm; TL 24-36 mm; FL 30-40 mm; Wt 3-5 g.

Conspicuous characters: Forehead region extremely high. Funnel-shaped ears separated, tragus present. Nostrils oval, pointing downward, no nose leaf present. Muzzle disk-shaped. Very small thumbs, enclosed by the wing membrane along with the claws. Wings proportionately long. Fairly long legs and short feet. Fur rather coarse, gray or grayish brown.

Reproduction: Unknown.

Life cycle: Unknown.

Diet: Insects.

Enemies: Unknown.

Habits and living space: Virtually nothing is known. One species (*Furipterus horrens*) was found in a cave in Panama; several individuals hung there in a large, high, well-lit chamber with other leaf-nosed bats. The second species (*Amorphochilus schnablii*) was

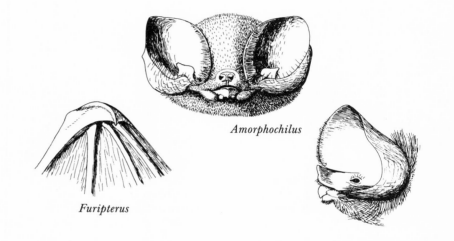

Amorphochilus

Furipterus

found in an abandoned sugar mill, a dark warehouse, and an irrigation tunnel. It is one of the few bat species that has been documented in the arid lowlands between the Andes and the western coast of South America.

Abundance/endangerment: Unknown.

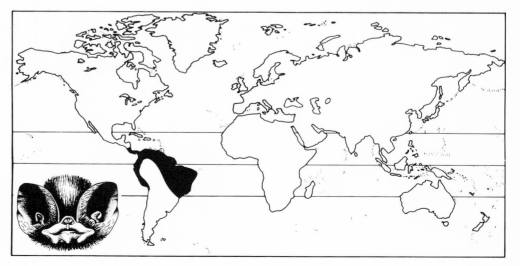

Disk-winged bats, New World sucker-footed bats

Family **Thyropteridae** with 1 genus and 2 species

BODY SIZE: HBL 34-52 mm; TL 25-33 mm; FL 27-38 mm; Wt 4-5 g.

CONSPICUOUS CHARACTERS: Muzzle long and narrow, with small warts above the nostrils; no nose leaf present. Cone-shaped ears separated, tragus present. Tip of the tail extends beyond the membrane. Thumbs have well-developed claws; fairly large suction discs on short stalks are located at the base of the thumb and the tarsus. The men mit gut ausgebildeten Krallen, an der

animals hang head-up and attach themselves to the substrate with the aid of the suction discs. Fur reddish brown or light brown. Underside whitish or brownish.

REPRODUCTION: G unknown; Y 1; BW unknown.

LIFE CYCLE: Unknown.

DIET: Insects.

ENEMIES: Unknown.

HABITS AND LIVING SPACE: In tropical rainforest. Daytime roosts in rolled-up leaves. Singly or in small groups.

ABUNDANCE/ENDANGERMENT: Unknown.

Thyroptera

Old World sucker-footed bats

Family **Myzopodidae** with 1 genus and 1 species

BODY SIZE: HBL 57 mm; TL 48 mm; FL 46 mm; Wt unknown.

CONSPICUOUS CHARACTERS: Very large, long ears with tragus. Upper lip overhangs the lower lip. Thumbs have vestigal claws; stalkless suction discs or pads are present at the base of the thumb and the tarsus. The tail extends beyond the membrane.

REPRODUCTION: Unknown.

LIFE CYCLE: Unknown.

DIET: Insects.

ENEMIES: Unknown.

HABITS AND LIVING SPACE: No details are known about the habits. Lives in palm forests. One animal was found in a rolled-up leaf, another in the leaf axis of a palm (*Ravenala*). Types of roosts probably similar to those of the disk-winged bats.

ABUNDANCE/ENDANGERMENT: Very rare. Probably endangered by destruction and reduction of its living space.

Myzopoda

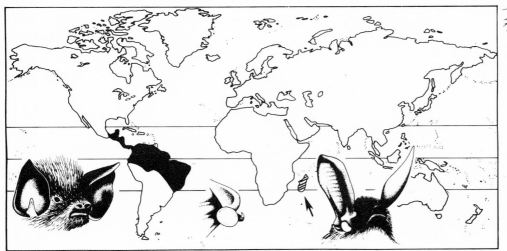

Common bats, Vesper bats, Evening bats

Family **Vespertilionidae** with approximately 40 genera and 300 species

BODY SIZE: HBL 32-105 mm; TL 25-75 mm; FL 22-75 mm; Wt 4-50 g.

CONSPICUOUS CHARACTERS: Massive skull, jaw shortened. Nose leaf never present. Large field of glands on the face; in several forms there are small, lobelike structures on the mouth. Ears usually separated, tragus present, in several species very large. Tail extends to edge of membrane or beyond. In a few genera small suction discs are present on the soles and joints. Fur color usually uniform brown, gray, or blackish brown;

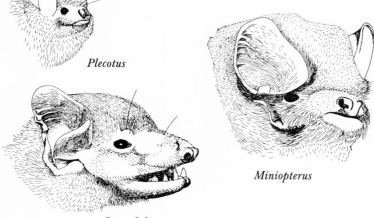

Plecotus

Scotophilus

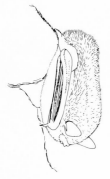

Miniopterus

tendency in all species to a lighter underside. A few species colorful (orange, orange-red, bright red, white spots, and the like), bright coloration usually present in species that roost in the open in trees during the day (camouflage function). Many forms of temperature regulation: in temperate zones hibernation, sometimes also daytime sleep lethargy. Echolocation calls short, usually emitted through the mouth.

REPRODUCTION: G 40-70, occasionally over 100 days; Y 1-2, in exceptional cases 4; BW up to 15 percent of the adult weight (known in only very few cases).

LIFE CYCLE: W at 1-2 months; SM at 1-3 years; LS 4-21 years.

DIET: Primarily insects; a few species prey on small fishes, scorpions, and other arthropods.

ENEMIES: Man, parasites, owls, diurnal birds of prey, snakes, martens, weasels.

HABITS AND LIVING SPACE: In caves, tunnels, subterranean passages, fissures in cliffs, rocky rubble, tree holes, foliage, bird's nests, buildings, and so on. From tropical rainforest to arid deserts, high altitudes, and isolated islands. Often form large colonies, but solitary species as well. Variable hunting strategies in prey capture.

ABUNDANCE/ENDANGERMENT: In all industrial countries seriously threatened by changes in habitat caused by destruction of living space, loss of food supply, toxic substances (through the food chain and contamination with impregnated building materials).

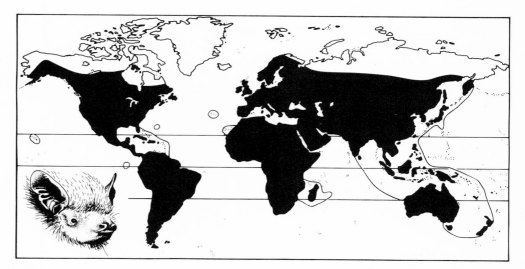

New Zealand short-tailed bats

Family **Mystacinidae** with 1 genus and 2 species

BODY SIZE: HBL approximately 60 mm; TL 18 mm; FL 43 mm; Wt 12-35 g.

CONSPICUOUS CHARACTERS: Snoutlike end of the muzzle. Small nasal disc with stiff hairs. Ears separated, large tragus. Claws on thumbs very long and with groove; toe claws also have grooves. Soles of feet soft and deeply furrowed. Wing membrane thick and in part leathery. Tail breaks through the top side of the membrane. Fur velvety grayish brown, brown, or blackish brown with slight gray suffusion.

REPRODUCTION: Unknown.

LIFE CYCLE: Unknown.

DIET: Insects, fruits, pollen, and nectar.

ENEMIES: Rats, nocturnal birds of prey, parasites.

HABITS AND LIVING SPACE: Daytime roosts in hollow tree trunks, in branches, or in caves in small groups (7-10 animals). For a bat, unusually well-adapted to life on the ground and very mobile there.

ABUNDANCE/ENDANGERMENT: One species extinct. Population of second species severely threatened, possibly by faunal contamination (rats).

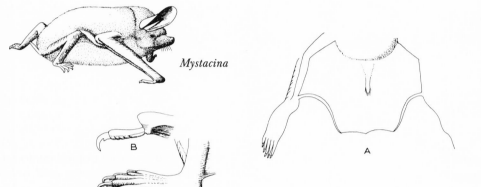

Mystacina

A. tail membrane, B. thumb claw, C. toe claws.

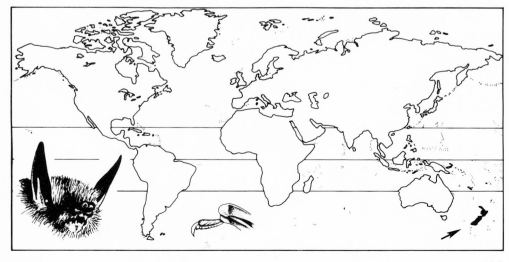

Free-tailed bats

Family **Molossidae** with 12 genera and 88 species

Body size: HBL 40-130 mm; TL 14-80 mm; FL 27-85 mm; Wt 8-170 g.

Conspicuous characters: Head usually thick and broad, lips furrowed, a number of stiff hairs with spoon-shaped tips on the face. Ears thickened and leathery, positioned forward and connected in the middle of the forehead, tragus present. Nostrils on the nasal protrusion, occasionally with horny processes (no nose leaf). Leathery wings long and narrow. Tail extends far beyond the short tail membrane. Short, sturdy legs with stiff hairs on the toes. Males often have glands on the throat and breast. Very short fur, two species completely bare except for individual scattered hairs. Fur velvety and brown or blackish brown. Echolocation calls short, emitted through the mouth.

Reproduction: G approximately 70-90 days; Y 1 (2); BW 3-4 g (up to 22 percent of the adult weight).

Life cycle: W at approximately 7-8 weeks; SM at 1-2 years; LS 8-20 years.

Diet: Insets.

Enemies: Man, nocturnal and diurnal birds of prey, parasites.

Habits and living space: In caves, tunnels, subterranean passages, buildings, foliage, fissures in cliffs (in part very narrow fissures), and so forth. Singly or in large colonies (containing thousands to millions of individuals). Caves are often used for long periods of time as daytime roosts (accumulation of large quantities of guano). Strong smell in roosts with large colonies. Insects captured primarily in flight. A few species tolerate or even prefer extremely high temperatures in the daytime roost.

Tadarida

Abundance/endangerment: Abundant in the tropics. The large colonies in the southern United States are in severe decline. Threatened by changes in habitat and use of pesticides.

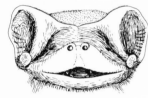

Molossus

Chiromeles

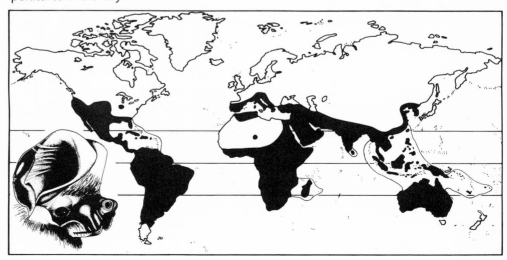

LITERATURE

ARLETTAZ, R.: Contribution à l'éco-éthologie du Molosse de Cestoni, *Tadarida teniotis* (Chiroptera), dans les Alpes valaisannes (sud-ouest de la Suisse). Z. Säugetierkunde **55**, 28–42, 1990

BECK, A.: Qualitative und quantitative Nahrungsanalysen an ausgewählten einheimischen Fledermausarten (Mammalia, Chiroptera). Diplomarbeit Universität Zürich, 1987

BEKIERZ, F. W. & H. BRASSELER: Bibliographie über Fledermaus-Bibliographien Chiroptera. Cour. Forsch.-Inst. Senckenberg **77**, 1–139, Frankfurt a. M., 1985

BERG, J.: Die Bedeutung der Fledermäuse in Religion, Mythos und Aberglaube und sich daraus ergebende Gefahren für das Leben der Fledertiere. Nyctalus (N.F.) **2**,2, 147–170, 1985

BLAB, J.: Grundlagen für ein Fledermaushilfsprogramm. Kilda-Verlag, Greven 1980

BRADBURY, J. W.: Social Organization and Communication. In: WIMMSATT, W. A.: Biology of Bats Vol. 3, Academic Press, New York, San Francisco, London 1977

BRAUN, M.: Rückstandsanalysen bei Fledermäusen. Z. Säugetierkunde **51**, 212–217, 1986

DAAN, S. & H. J. WICHERS: Habitat selection of bats hibernating in a limestone cave. Z. Säugetierkunde **33**, 267–287, 1968

DELPIETRO, H. A. & G. SIMON: Vampirfledermäuse, *Desmodus rotundus rotundus* (GEOFFREY), als Beute des Langohr-Scheinvampirs, *Chrotopterus auritus australis* (THOMAS). Nyctalus (N.F.) **2**, 3/4, 325–333, 1987

DOBAT, K. & T. PEIKERT-HOLLE: Blüten und Fledermäuse (Chiropterophilie). Verlag Waldemar Kramer, Frankfurt 1985

EHLERS, J.: Untersuchungen an Fledermäusen in einem Winterquartier in Deister unter besonderer Berücksichtigung der Flugaktivität in Abhängigkeit von exogenen Faktoren. Dissertation an der Tierärztlichen Hochschule Hannover, 1983

EISENTRAUT, M.: Aus dem Leben der Fledermäuse und Flughunde. VEB Gustav Fischer Verlag, Jena 1957

FELTEN, H. (ed.): Contributions to the knowledge of the bats of Thailand. Cour. Forsch.-Inst. Senckenberg **87**, 1–112, 1986

FENTON, M. B./RACEY, P. & J. M. V. RAYNER (eds.): Recent advances in the study of bats. Cambridge University Press, Cambridge 1987

FLEMING, T. H.: The Short-tailed Fruit Bat – A Study in Plant – Animal Interactions. The University of Chicago Press Chicago, London 1988

GABRISCH, K. & P. ZWART (eds.): Krankheiten der Wildtiere – Exotische und heimische Tiere in der Tierarztpraxis. Schlütersche Verlagsanstalt und Druckerei, Hannover 1988

GEBHARD, J.: Unsere Fledermäuse. Naturhist. Museum Basel 1985

GEBHARD, J.: Die Forschungsstation „Hofmatt" – Ein künstliches Fledermausquartier mit zahmen, in Gefangenschaft geborenen, freifliegenden und wilden, zugeflogenen Abendseglern *(Nyctalus noctula)*. Myotis **26**, 5–21, 1988

GEBHARD, J. & K. HIRSCHI: Analyse des Kotes aus einer Wochenstube von *Myotis myotis*. Mitteilungen der Naturforschenden Gesellschaft in Bern, N. F. 42. Band 1985

GÖRNER, M. & H. HACKETHAL: Säugetiere Europas. dtv, München 1988

GREENAWAY, F. & A. M. HUTSON: A Field Guide to British Bats. Bruce Coleman Books, Uxbridge, Middlesex 1990

GRIFFIN, D. R.: Listening in the Dark – The Acoustic Orientation of Bats and Men. Cornell University Press Ithaca, London 1986

GRIMMBERGER, E. & H. BORK: Untersuchungen und Populationsdynamik der Zwergfledermaus, *Pipistrellus p. pipistrellus* (SCHREBER 1774), in einer großen Population im Norden der DDR Teil 1. Nyctalus (N.F.) **1**, 1, 55–73 (1978)

GRIMMBERGER, E./HACKETHAL, H. & Z. URBANCZYK: Beitrag zum Paarungsverhalten der Wasserfledermaus, *Myotis daubentoni* (KUHL 1819), im Winterquartier. Z. Säugetierkunde **52**, 133–140, 1987

HAFFNER, M. & H.-P. B. STUTZ: Die Zwergfledermaus *(Pipistrellus pipistrellus)* klein, wendig und schnell. Fledermaus-Anzeiger **16**, 4, 1988

HAFFNER, M. & H.-P. B. STUTZ: Die Wasserfledermaus *(Myotis daubentoni)* Tiefflieger über stillen Wassern. Fledermaus-Anzeiger **16**, 6, 1988

HALL, L. S. & G. C. RICHARDS: Bats of Eastern Australia. Queensland Museum booklet No. 12, 1979

HANSBAUER, G.: Bestandssituation und Schutzmaßnahmen für in Felshöhlen und Stollen überwinternde Fledermausarten in den Bayerischen Alpen. Diplomarbeit FH Weihenstephan, 1987

HEIDECKE, D. & M. STUBBE: Populationsökologie von Fledermausarten Teil I + II. Martin-Luther-Universität Halle-Wittenberg, Wissenschaftliche Beiträge 1989/20 (P36), Halle (Saale) 1989

HEIDINGER, F.: Untersuchungen zum thermoregulativen Verhalten des Großen Mausohrs *(Myotis myotis)* in einem Sommerquartier. Diplomarbeit Ludwig-Maximilians-Universität München, 1988

HEINICKE, W. & A. KRAUSS: Zum Beutespektrum des Braunen Langohrs, *Plecotus auritus* L. Nyctalus (N.F.) **1**, 1, 49–52, 1978

HEISE, G.: Zu Vorkommen, Biologie und Ökologie der Rauhhautfledermaus *(Pipistrellus nathusii)* in der Umgebung von Prenzlau (Uckermark), Bezirk Neubrandenburg. Nyctalus (N.F.) **1**, 4/5, 281–300, 1982

HEISE, G.: Zur Fortpflanzungsbiologie der Rauhhautfledermaus *(Pipistrellus nathusii)*. Nyctalus (N.F.) **2**, 1, 1–15, 1984

HEISE, G.: Bemerkungen zur sozialen Körperpflege bei einheimischen Fledermäusen. Nyctalus (N.F.) **2**, 3/4, 258–260, 1987

HEISE, G.: Zum Transport von Fledermauswanzen (Cimicidae) durch ihre Wirte. Nyctalus (N.F.) **2**, 5, 469–473, 1988

HEISE, G. & A. SCHMIDT: Beiträge zur sozialen Organisation und Ökologie des Braunen Langohrs *(Plecotus auritus)*. Nyctalus (N.F.) **2**, 5, 445–465, 1988

HELMER, W. & H. J. G. A. LIMPENS: Echos in der Landschaft. Dendrocopos **18**, 3–8, 1991

HELVERSEN, O. v.: Bestimmungsschlüssel für die Europäischen Fledermäuse nach äußeren Merkmalen. Myotis **27**, 41–60, 1989

HELVERSEN, O. v.: New records of bats (Chiroptera) from Turkey. Zoology in the Middle East **3**, 5–18, 1989

HELVERSEN, O. v./ESCHE, M./KRETZSCHMAR, F. & M. BOSCHERT: Die Fledermäuse Südbadens. Mitt. bad. Landesver. Naturkd. u. Naturschutz (N.F.) **14**, 409–475, 1987

HELVERSEN, O. v. & R. WEID: Die Verbreitung einiger Fledermausarten in Griechenland. Bonn. zool. Beitr. 41, 1, 9–22, 1990

HIEBSCH, H.: Faunistische Kartierung der Fledermäuse in der DDR Teil 1. Nyctalus (N.F.) **1**, 6, 489–503, 1983

HIEBSCH, H. & D. HEIDECKE: Faunistische Kartierung der Fledermäuse in der DDR, Teil 2. Nyctalus (N.F.) **2**, 3/4, 213–246, 1987

HILL, J. E. & J. D. SMITH: Bats: A Natural History. British Museum (Natural History), Publication No. 887, London 1984

HORÁČEK, J.: Population Ecology of *Myotis myotis* in Central Bohemia (Mammalia; Chiroptera). Acta Universitas Carolinae – Biologica **1981**, 161–267, 1985

IUCN, 1990 IUCN Red List of Threatened Animals. IUCN, Gland, Switzerland and Cambridge, U. K. 1990

JÜDES, Ü. (O. J.): Fledermäuse und ihr Schutz. AG Fledermausschutz, Dorfstr. 15A, 2419 Kulpin.

JÜDES, U.: Zur Problematik eines Artenhilfsprogrammes „Fledermäuse". Natur und Landschaft **61**, 215–219, 1986

KALKO, E. K. V.: Jagd- und Echoortungsverhalten der Wasserfledermaus *Myotis daubentoni* (KUHL 1819) im Freiland. Diplomarbeit Universität Tübingen, 1987

KOCK, D.: Der spezifische Parasit *Phthiridium biarticulatum* (Diptera: Nycteribiidae) der Hufeisennasen (Rhinolophidae) in der DDR und Bemerkungen zur Nordgrenze des Vorkommens. Nyctalus (N.F.) **2**, 5, 368–388, 1988

KOEPCKE, J.: „Blattzelte" als Schlafplätze der Fledermaus *Ectophylla macconnelli* (THOMAS 1901) (Phyllostomidae) im tropischen Regenwald von Peru. Säugetierkundliche Mitteilungen **31**, 123–126, 1984

KRONWITTER, F.: Population Structure, Habitat Use and Activity Patterns of the Noctule Bat, *Nyctalus noctula* SCHREBER 1774 (Chiroptera: Vespertilionidae), revealed by Radio-tracking. Myotis **26**, 23–85, 1988

187

KRULL, D.: Untersuchungen zu Quartieransprüchen und Jagdverhalten von *Myotis emarginatus* (GEOFFROY 1806) im Rosenheimer Becken. Diplomarbeit Ludwig-Maximilians-Universität München, 1988

KRULL, D./SCHUMM, A./METZNER, W. & G. NEUWEILER: Foraging areas and foraging behavior in the notch-eared bat, *Myotis emarginatus* (Vespertilionidae)! Behav. Ecol. Sociobiol. **28**, 247–253, 1991

KULZER, E.: Winterschlaf. Stuttgarter Beiträge zur Naturkunde Serie C, Heft 14, 1981

KULZER, E.: Fledertiere. In: Grzimeks Enzyklopädie Säugetiere Bd. 1 (einschl. Unterkapitel von E. THENIUS, unter Mitarbeit von U. SCHMIDT), 532–631. Kindler Verlag, München 1988

KULZER, E./BASTIAN, H. V. & M. FIEDLER: Fledermäuse in Baden-Württemberg – Ergebnisse einer Kartierung in den Jahren 1980–1986 der Arbeitsgemeinschaft Fledermausschutz Baden-Württemberg. Beih. Veröff. Naturschutz Landschaftspflege Bad.-Württ. **50**, 1987

KUNZ, T. H. (ed.): Ecology of Bats. Plenum Press New York, London 1982

KUNZ, T. H. (ed.): Ecological and Behavioral Methods for the Study of Bats. Smithsonian Institution Press Washington, D. C., London 1988

LABES, R. & N. MESSAL: Fledermaus als Symbol eines militärischen Blutspendedienstes. Nyctalus (N.F.) **3**, 1, 59–60, 1989

MATTHEWS, L. H.: Das Leben der Säugetiere I. Die Enzyklopädie der Natur. Editions Rencontre, Lausanne 1972

MAYWALD, A. & B. POTT: Fledermäuse – Leben, Gefährdung, Schutz. Otto Maier, Ravensburg 1988

METZNER, W.: Ultraschallorientierung Fledermäuse. In: Naturmagazin draußen **41**, Deutsch-Luxemburgischer Naturpark, 48–59, HB Verlags- und Vertriebs GmbH 1985

MITCHELL-JONES, A. J. (ed.): The bat worker's manual. Nature Conservancy Council 1987

NABHITABHATA, J./SITTILERT, S./YENBUTRA, S. & H. FELTEN: Ein Zwerg unter den Säugetieren – Die Fledermaus *Craseonycteris thonglongyai* aus Thailand. Natur und Museum **112** (3), 81–84, 1982

NACHTIGALL, W. (ed.): Bat Flight – Fledermausflug. BIONA report 5, Gustav Fischer, Stuttgart, New York 1986

NAGEL, A. & J. DISSER: Rückstände von Chlorkohlenwasserstoff-Pestiziden in einer Wochenstube der Zwergfledermaus *(Pipistrellus pipistrellus)*. Z. Säugetierkunde **55**, 217–225, 1990

NEUWEILER, G.: Zum Sozialverhalten von Flughunden *(Pteropus g. giganteus)*. Lynx **10**, 61–64, 1969

NEUWEILER, G.: Die Ultraschall-Jäger. GEO **1**, 98–113, 1981

NEUWEILER, G.: Akustische Abbildungsprobleme bei Fledermäusen. Eröffnungsvortrag 6. Wiss. Tagung des Forschungsrates Rauchen und Gesundheit 26.–28. Feb. Titisee 1989

NEUWEILER, G.: Echoortende Fledermäuse – Jagdbiotope, Jagdstrategien und Anpassung des Echohörens. Biologie in unserer Zeit **3**, 169–176, 1990

NEUWEILER, G./METZNER, W./HEILMANN, U./RÜBSAMEN, R./ECKRICH, M. & H. H. COSTA: Foraging behaviour and echolocation in the rufous horseshoe bat of Sri Lanka. Behav. Ecol. Sociobiol. **20**, 53–67, 1987

OLDENBURG, W.: Winterschlaf vom Braunen Langohr, *Plecotus auritus* L., im Bodengeröll. Nyctalus (N.F.) **3**, 1, 1–4, 1989

PATZELT, E.: Fauna del Ecuador. Banco Central del Ecuador, Quito 1989

PERRIN, L. A.: Zur Biologie des Abendseglers *Nyctalus noctula* (SCHREBER 1774) in der Regio

Basiliensis. Inauguraldissertation Universität Basel, 1988

RACEY, P. A. & A. M. HUTSON: Chiroptera Specialist Group, Species. Newsletter of the Species Survival Commission IUCN – The World Conservation Union **15**, 50–51, 1990

RANSOME, R.: The Natural History of Hibernating Bats. Christopher Helm, London 1990

REARDON, T. B. & S. C. FLAVEL: A Guide to the Bats of South Australia. South Australian Museum, North Terrace, Adelaide 1987

RICHARDSON, P.: Bats. Whittet Books, London 1985

RICHARZ, K.: Bedrohung und Schutz der Gebäudefledermäuse. Schriftenreihe Bayer. Landesamt für Umweltschutz **73**, 15–35, 1986

RICHARZ, K.: Ein neuer Wochenstubennachweis der Mopsfledermaus *Barbastella barbastellus* (SCHREBER 1774) in Bayern mit Bemerkungen zu Wochenstubenfunden in der BRD und DDR sowie zu Wintervorkommen und Schutzmöglichkeiten. Myotis **27**, 71–80, 1989

RICHARZ, K.: Report of the successful transplantation of an nursery colony of the Lesser Horseshoe Bat *(Rhinolophus hipposideros)* and remarks about the actual status of this species in Bavaria. In: HANÁK, V./HORÁČEK, I. & J. GAISLER (eds.), European Bat Research 1987, Charles Univ. Press, Praha 659–670, 1989

RICHARZ, K.: Wir tun was für unsere Fledermäuse. Franckh-Kosmos, Stuttgart 1991

RICHARZ, K./LIMMBRUNNER, H. & F. KRONWITTER: Nachweise von Sommerkolonien der Zweifarbfledermaus *Vespertilio murinus* Linnaeus, 1758 in Oberbayern mit einer Übersicht aktueller Funde in Südbayern. Myotis **27**, 61–70, 1989

ROBERTSON, J.: The Complete Bat. Chatto & Windus, London 1990

ROER, H.: Gefährdung und Schutz mitteleuropäischer Wanderfledermäuse. In: Schutz wandernder Tierarten. Naturschutzaktuell Nr. 5, Kilda-Verlag, Greven 1981

ROER, H.: Zur Heimkehrfähigkeit der Zwergfledermaus *(Pipistrellus pipistrellus* SCHREBER 1774) (Mammalia: Chiroptera). Bonn. Zool. Beitr. **32**, 13–30, 1981

ROER, H. & W. EGSBAEK: Über die Balz der Wasserfledermaus *(Myotis daubentoni)* (Chiroptera) im Winterquartier. Lynx **10**, 85–91, 1969

SCHMIDT, U.: Vampirfledermäuse. Die Neue Brehm-Bücherei Nr. 515, A. Ziemsen Verlag, Wittenberg Lutherstadt 1978

SCHOBER, W.: Mit Echolot und Ultraschall. Herder, Freiburg 1983

SCHOBER, W. & E. GRIMMBERGER: Die Fledermäuse Europas. Franckh-Kosmos, Stuttgart 1987

SCHUMM, A.: Echoortungsoptimierung bei *Myotis emarginatus*: Die Anpassung der Ultraschallaute an verschiedene Jagdhabitate und -strategien. Eine Feldstudie an Wimperfledermäusen in Oberbayern. Diplomarbeit Ludwig-Maximilians Universität, München 1988

STEBBINGS, R. E. & F. GRIFFITH: Distribution and Status of Bats in Europe. Inst. of Terrestrial Ecology Monks Wood Experimental Station, Abbots Ripton Huntington 1986

STEBBINGS, R. E.: Conservation of European Bats. Christopher Helm, London 1988

STRATMANN, B.: Faunistisch-ökologische Beobachtungen an einer Population von *Nyctalus noctula* im Revier Ecktannen des StFB Waren (Müritz). Nyctalus (N.F.) **1**, 1, 2–22, 1978

STRAHAN, R. (ed.): The Australian Museum Complete Book of Australian Mammals. Angus & Robertson Publishers London, Sydney, Melbourne 1983

STUTZ, H.-P. B.: Der Große Abendsegler *(Nyctalus noctula)* rasanter Riese am freien Himmel. Fledermaus-Anzeiger **16**, 3, 1988

STUTZ, H.-P. B.: Die Rauhhautfledermaus *(Pipistrellus nathusii),* bedächtiger und strukturgebundener Patrouillenjäger. Fledermaus-Anzeiger **16**, 5, 1988

STUTZ, H.-P. B. & M. HAFFNER: Aktiver Fledermausschutz Band 2, Richtlinien für die Erhaltung und Neuschaffung von Fledermausquartieren in und an Bäumen, in Höhlen und Stollen. FEBEX Haffner & Stutz, Zürich 1986

TUPINIER, D.: La Chauve – souris et l'homme. L'Harmattan, Paris 1989

TURNER, D. C.: The Vampire Bat – A Field Study in Behavior and Ecology. The John Hopkins University Press Baltimore, London 1975

TUTTLE, M. D.: America's Neighborhood Bats. University of Texas Press, Austin 1988

VOGEL, S.: Etho-ökologische Untersuchungen an zwei Mausohrkolonien *(Myotis myotis)* im Rosenheimer Becken. Diplomarbeit Universität Gießen 1988

VOUTE, A. M. & C. SMEENK: Vleermuizen. Waanders Uitgervers, Zwolle 1991

WIRTH, R. & M. RIFFEL: Bedrohte Flughunde. Zoologische Gesellschaft für Arten- und Populationsschutz e.V. – Mitgliederinformation 11–15, 1989

WOLZ, J.: Wochenstuben-Quartierwechsel bei der Bechsteinfledermaus. Z. Säugetierkunde **51**, 65–74, 1986

YALDEN, B. W. & P. A. MORRIS: The lives of bats. David & Charles, London 1975

Wichtige Beiträge zum Fledermausschutz in den Heften **73** (1980), **81** (1988) und **92** (1989) der Schriftenreihe des Bayerischen Landesamtes für Umweltschutz, Rosenkavalierplatz 3, 8000 München 81.

ADDRESSES

Bezugsquellen

Fledermausziegel
Arbeitsgemeinschaft Ziegel-
dach e.V.
Schaumburg-Lippe-Str. 4
D-5300 Bonn

Heißluftverfahren
RUHO-Bautenschutz GmbH
Holtfeld 101–111
D-4807 Borgholzhausen

Fledermauskästen
(Holzbeton)
Natur- und Vogelschutzbedarf
Gerhard Strobel
Tulpenstr. 10
7031 Weil 3/Breitenstein

Karl Grund Vogelschutzgeräte
8425 Neustadt/Donau

PURUS – Dr. Reichle
Postfach 31
6800 Mannheim

SCHWEGLER-Vogelschutz-
geräte GmbH
Heinkelstr. 35
7060 Schorndorf

Fledermaus-Detektoren
Jüdes-Ultraschall
Dorfstr. 15a
2419 Kulpin

Experten:

Baden-Württemberg

Landesanstalt für Umwelt-
schutz
(LFU) Institut für Ökologie
und Naturschutz
Bannwaldallee 32
7500 Karlsruhe 21
Tel. 0721/84061

Prof. Dr. Erwin Kulzer
Institut für Biologie III
Auf der Morgenstelle 28
7400 Tübingen
Tel. 07071/292623

Monika Braun
Koordinationsstelle für Fle-
dermausschutz Nordbaden
Staatl. Museum für
Naturkunde Karlsruhe
Erbprinzenstr. 13
7500 Karlsruhe 1
Tel. 0721/175165

Arbeitsgemeinschaft Fleder-
mausschutz
Institut für Biologie I
Universität Freiburg
Albertstr. 21a
7800 Freiburg i. Br.
Tel. 0761/700508

Bayern

Landesamt für Umweltschutz
Rosenkavalierplatz 3
8000 München 81
Tel. 089/92141

Fledermauskoordinationsstelle
Südbayern: Alois Liegl,
Alfred Schumm
Regierung von Oberbayern
Höhere Naturschutzbehörde
Maximilianstr. 39
8000 München 22
Tel. 089/2176302

Fledermauskoordinationsstelle
Nordbayern:
Prof. Dr. Otto v. Helversen
Zoologisches Institut II
Universität Erlangen
Staudtstr. 5
8520 Erlangen
Tel. 09131/858051

Berlin

Senator für Stadtentwicklung
und Landschaftspflege
Lindenstr. 20–25
1000 Berlin 61

Jürgen Klawitter
Marschnerstr. 22
1000 Berlin 45
Tel. 030/8345860

Bremen

Der Senator für Umwelt und
Gesundheit
Birkenweg 34
2800 Bremen 1

Hamburg

Naturschutzamt Hamburg
Steinsdamm 22
2000 Hamburg 1
Tel. 040/248251

Rainald Hoffmann
c/o DBV-Geschäftsstelle
Habichtstr. 125
2000 Hamburg 60
Tel. 040/616664

Hessen

Dr. Klaus Richarz
(Geschäftsführer AGFH)
Staatliche Vogelschutzwarte
für Hessen, Rheinland-Pfalz
und Saarland –
Institut für angewandte Vogel-
kunde
Steinauer Str. 44
6000 Frankfurt/M. 60
Tel. 069/411532 und 418348

Dr. Dieter Kock
Senckenberginstitut
Senckenberganlage 25
6000 Frankfurt/M.
Tel. 069/7542-343/333

Niedersachsen

Niedersächsisches
Landesverwaltungsamt
Fachbehörde für Naturschutz
Scharnhorststr. 1
3000 Hannover 1

Alfred Benk
Peperfeld 10
3000 Hannover 91
Tel. 0511/468347

Friedel Knolle
Thilingstr. 38
3380 Goslar
Tel. 05321/85101

Nordrhein-Westfalen

Landesanstalt für Ökologie,
Landschaftsentwicklung und
Forstplanung (LÖLF)
Leipnitzstr. 10
4350 Recklinghausen
Tel. 02361/3051

AK Fledertierschutz
c/o Matthias Vetten
Schloßstr. 78
4000 Düsseldorf
Tel. 0211/487334

Dr. Henning Vierhaus
Teichstr. 13
4772 Bad Sassendorf-Lohne
Tel. 02921/55623

Rheinland-Pfalz

Landesamt für Umweltschutz
Rheinland-Pfalz
Amtsgerichtsplatz 1
6504 Oppenheim

Michael Veith
Universität Mainz
Institut für Zoologie
Saarstr. 21
6500 Mainz
Tel. 06131/392718

Manfred Weishaar
Im Hainbruch 3
5501 Gusterath
Tel. 06588/515

' **Saarland**

Landesamt für Umweltschutz
Don-Bosco-Str. 1
6600 Saarbrücken 6

Christine Harbusch
Am Schwalbacher Berg 155
6631 Emsdorf
Tel. 06831/59886

Schleswig-Holstein

Landesamt für Naturschutz
und Landschaftspflege
Schleswig-Holstein
Hansaring 1
2300 Kiel 1

AG Fledermausschutz
c/o Dr. Ulrich Jüdes
Dorfstr. 15A
2419 Kulpin
Tel. 04541/3781

Neue Länder

Die Adressen der in den neuen
Ländern zuständigen An-
sprechpartner können über
Dr. Joachim Haensel
Naturschutzbund Deutsch-
land e.V., Büro Berlin
Eichwalder Str. 100
O-1251 Gosen
erfragt werden.

Schweiz

Jürgen Gebhard
Naturhistorisches Museum
Augustinergasse 2
CH-4001 Basel

Dr. Marianne Haffner
Dr. Hans-Peter Stutz
Benedikt-Fontana-Weg 15
CH-8049 Zürich

Österreich

Dr. Kurt Bauer
Dr. Friederike Spitzenberger
Säugetiersammlung des
Naturhistorischen Museums
in Wien
Postfach 417
A-1014 Wien

Niederlande

Peter Lina
E. De Boer
Van Rijk Straat 13
2331 H H Leiden

**Fledermausschutz
international**

Bat Conservation
International
P.O. Box 162603
Austin,
Texas 78716
USA

Index of Scientific Names

Index of Common Names

Acknowledgement

The author of the text thanks all the Bat scientists and Bat protectors who are mentioned in this book. Without their work and efforts a collection like this would not have been possible. The recent friendly relationships established with many colleagues are the result of our common interest and have been very helpful in the creation of this book. Especially helpful were the contacts with MONIKA BRAUN (Karlsruhe), JÜRGEN GEBHARD (Basel), Dr. MARIANNE HAFFNER (Zurich), Prof. Dr. OTTO VON HELVERSEN (Erlangen), Dr. JOHN EDWARDS HILL (Edenbridge), Prof. Dr. ERWIN KULZER (Tübingen), Dr. WALTER METZNER (San Diego), Prof. Dr. GERHARD NEUWEILER (Munich), Dr. HUBERT ROER (Bonn), Dr. WILFRIED SCHOBER (Leipzig), and Dr. HANS-PETER STUTZ (Zurich). For the competent advice about the update of the world map of Bat populations, I want to thank Dr. DIETER KOCK (Frankfurt), for the population maps of Europe, JÜRGEN GEBHARD (Basel), Prof. Dr. OTTO VON HELVERSEN (Erlangen), Dr. DIETER KOCK (Frankfurt), Dr. HUBERT ROER (Bonn), and Dr. FRIEDERIKE SPITZENBERGER (Vienna). Much from the works of the "Auer-Fledermausgruppe" which I look after, influenced this book. The electrifying enthusiasm of the lecturer BÄRBEL OFTRING (Stuttgart), in combination with the sympathetic and creative nature of the artist MARIANNE GOLTE-BECHTLE (Stuttgart) helped me to get through some tedious periods in the last stages of the book project. I owe my family deepest gratitude for their tremendous understanding and their sacrifice of many hours we would have enjoyed together.

A very special acknowledgement from the authors of the pictures and the text applies to Dr. BRIGITTE and Dr. WILLI ISSEL (Augsburg). The friendly and always helpful nature of this great Bat-scientist couple taught both of us friends the flutter!

Photo Credits

151 color prints: Ph. Coffey (1, 126 t.); S. Dalton/NHPA (1, p. 4/5); G.&H. Denzau (6, p. 62, 66 b., 67 t., 110, 111 t.); K.H. Gleixner (1, p. 143 t.l.); E. Haupt, Senckenberg Museum (1, p. 18 b.); D. Krull (2, p. 47); E. Kulzer (1, p. 49 b.); H. Limbrunner (11, p. 39, 106, 107, 117, 125 t., 139 m.l., 139 m.r., 139 b.l., 143 m.r.); E. Patzelt (2, p. 23 b., 60); K. Richarz (9, p. 78 t., 131, 134, 135 t); A. Steinhauser (1, p. 111 b.); M. Tuttle (23, p. 6, 7, 8, 12, 14/15, 49 t., 51, 52, 53, 54, 55, 59, 63, 82 t., 83, 113, 127, 128); A. Limbrunner (all others) and 3 b/w-pictures courtesy of Deutsches Museum München (1, p. 108) and of K. Richarz (1, p. 100 b.) and A. Triller (1, p. 100 t.).

9 Colorgraphics from M. Golte-Bechtle (7, p. 19 t., 47, 56, 57); H.Seehausen (1,p. 126) and B. Zwickel-Noelle (1, p. 119) as well as 116 b/w graphics from the archive (19, p. 36, 65, 80, 81); M. Golte-Bechtle (66, p. 12, 18, 20, 21, 24, 25, 28/29, 32, 33, 37, 40, 41, 43, 44, 45, 46, 48 l., 59, 61, 62, 63, 68, 69, 73, 77, 84, 85, 88, 89 t.r., 92, 93, 97, 124, 129, 133, 136, 137, 138 r., 140 r., 141 r., 144 r., 145 r., 147 l., 153 r., 157 r., 179 l., 179 r.), O. v. Helversen (27; p. 141 l., 142 t., 145 l., 146 r., 148 r., 149 l., 150 r., 151 l., 152 r., 154 r., 155 r., 156 r., 157 l., 158 r., 159 l., 159 r., 160 r., 161 t., 162 r., 163 l., 164 r., 165 t., 166 r., 167 l., 168 r., 169 l., 169 r.); J.-C. Rost (3, p 89 t. l., 89 b., 167 r.); and T. Schneehagen (1, p. 163 r.). All of the population maps of the European species from B. Zwickel-Noelle according to originals from K. Richarz.

The Publisher acknowledges all of the following for their permission to use copyright protected material: Carl Hanser Verlag München Wien (1979), Günter Kunert, Die Schreie der Fledermäuse. Geschichten, Gedichte, Aufsätze (p. 9); Kindler Verlag (1988), Erwin Kulzer, Heutige Fledertiere, Grzimeks Enzyklopädie Säugetiere vol. 1 (p. 50, 94, 95); Verlag Paul Parey (1987), E. Grimmberger, H. Hackethal, Z. Urbanczyk in Zeitschrift für Säugetierkunde 52 (p. 68); HB Verlags und Vertriebs GmbH Walter Metzner, Ultraschall, Naturmagazin draußen 41 (p. 22/23); Badischen Landesverein für Naturkunde und Naturschutz e. V., O. v. Helversen et. al., Die Fledermäuse Südbadens, Mitt. bad. Landesverband Naturkunde und Naturschutz 14, 2, 1987 (p. 69/70); Ná Rondí Muzeum-Praha, Gerhard Neuweiler, Lynx 10, 1969 (p. 68/69, 73); Verlag Dr. Waldemar Kramer for pictures from K. Dobat and T. Peikert-Holle, Blüten und Fledermäuse (3, p. 57 b., 58, 105); Gustav Fischer Verlag for pictures from W. Nachtigall, Bat Flight, Biona Report 5 (2, p. 109); Forschungsinstitut Senckenberg for drawings from E. Junqueira (2, p. 174 t. l.) from "Natur und Museum" vol. 112, No. 3; John E. Hill and James D. Smith (1984) for pictures from their book "Bats" (19, p. 48 r., 72, 101, 171 b., 172 b., 173 b., 174 b., 175 b., 176 b., 177 b., 178 b., 179 b., 180 b., 181 b., 182 b., 183 b. l., 184 b., 185 b., 186 b.- maps slightly altered); David & Charles Publishers (1975) for pictures from D. W. Yalden and P. A. Morris, "The Lives of Bats" (50, p. 19 b., 171 t., 172 t., 173 t., 174 b. l., 175 t., 176 t., 177 t., 178 t., 180 l., 180 t., 181 t., 182 t., 183 r., 184 t., 185 t., 186 t.); W. Schober and E. Grimmberger for the Sonargram einheimische Fledermäuse from their book "Die Fledermäuse Europas" (20, p. 140, 141, 142, 146, 147, 149, 151, 152, 153, 155, 158, 159, 160, 161, 162, 165, 167, 169).

ENDPAPERS:

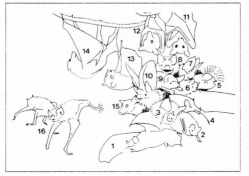

Who is who?

1. Serotine (Eptesicus serotinus), 2. Particolored Bat (Vespertilio murinus), 3. Horseshoe bat (Rhinolophus), 4. Mexican Long-nosed Bat (Choeronycteris mexicana), 5. Free-tailed bat (Tadarida chapini), 6. White bat (Ectophylla macconnelli), 7. Sword-nosed Bat (Lonchorhina aurita), 8. Lattice-winged Bat (Centurio senex), 9. Egyptian Free-tailed Bat (Tadarida aegyptiaca), 10. Common Long-eared Bat (Plecotus auritus), 11. Aftican Rousette Fruit Bat (Rousettus aegyptiacus), 12. Flying fox (Synconycteris australis), 13. Tubnosed fruit bat (Nyctimene), 14. Bismarck Flying Fox (Pteropus neohibernicus), 15. Flying fox, 16. Common Vampire (Desmodus rotundus).